Where'd He Get That?

A Biblical Cross-Reference to Ernest Holmes' *The Science of Mind*

By Rev. Margo Ruark

The Peace Center, Berwyn, IL
www.thepeacecenter.info

Where'd He Get That? A Biblical Cross-Reference To Ernest Holmes' The Science of Mind

Where'd He Get That? A Biblical Cross-Reference to Ernest Holmes' The Science of Mind
© Margo Ruark, 2008, 2010, 2013 revised edition.

ISBN 10: 0615742629
ISBN 13: 978-0-615-74262-5

Cover design by Margo Ruark

All rights reserved. No part of this publication may be reproduced in any form without written permission from the publisher.

Published by:
The Peace Center
P O Box 98
Berwyn, IL 60402-0098
USA
www.thepeacecenter.info

Contents

FOREWORD BY REV. DR. JANE CLAYPOOL	4
PREFACE	6
CHANGES TO THIS EDITION	7
INTRODUCTION	8
A Most Common Question	8
Christian Roots of New Thought	8
Dr. Holmes Relationship to the Christian Faith	11
Ernest Holmes Discovers Emerson	12
New Thought as the New Christianity	13
Dr. Holmes' Relationship to Jesus	14
The Bible in Light of Religious Science	16
Dr. Holmes Assumes We Know Our Bibles…AND A LOT MORE!	16
Which Bible Did Dr. Holmes Use?	16
How Dr. Holmes Integrates the Bible	17
The Top Ten Bible Verses Referred to in the Text	18
References to Thinkers Outside the Bible	19
All Other Thinkers in Order of Frequency Mentioned in the Text	20
TABLE I: BIBLE VERSES CITED IN *THE SCIENCE OF MIND* BY BOOK OF THE BIBLE FROM GENESIS TO REVELATIONS	21
TABLE II: BIBLE VERSES CITED IN *THE SCIENCE OF MIND* BY ORDER OF APPEARANCE	80
TABLE III: OTHER THINKERS CITED IN *THE SCIENCE OF MIND* ORGANIZED BY ORDER OF APPEARANCE	137
APPENDIX A: NEW THOUGHT FAMILY TREE	203
APPENDIX B: FULL BIBLIOGRAPHY FROM THE 1926 EDITION OF *THE SCIENCE OF MIND*	206
APPENDIX C: CHRONOLOGICAL HISTORY OF REFERENCES TO "THE LAW OF ATTRACTION" IN RELIGIOUS AND METAPHYSICAL LITERATURE	209

FOREWORD BY REV. DR. JANE CLAYPOOL

Dr. Jane Claypool is Founder and Spiritual Leader, Carlsbad Center for Spiritual Living, Carlsbad, CA. She is a Former Member, Board of Directors, International Centers for Spiritual Living and Former Chair, Department of Education.

Margo Ruark, Director of the Peace Center in Berwyn, IL, is an educated woman in the style of that famous Transcendentalist, Margaret Fuller. She has three Master's degrees including one in Philosophy/Esthetics from the University of Uppsala, Sweden.

Ruark has served with Global Services of the Centers for Spiritual Living for several years and is currently chair of the Translations Department. She devised the original idea of creating a chart to help translators discover the origins of Holmes quotes. That original idea has flowered into a useful gem that is now accessible to all New Thought ministers.

Where'd He Get That? A Biblical Cross-Reference to Ernest Holmes' The Science of Mind is a monumental achievement. The book is destined to become an invaluable tool that sits right beside the computer of every Sunday speech writer. Any New Thought minister or teacher who cares about Holmes's ideas and their origins will be able to use it in talks and in classes. I think every minister in the field will want to have and use a copy right now.

We call the founder of Religious Science, Ernest Holmes, "The Great Synthesizer" and this reference book, which traces the ideas found in *The Science of Mind* textbook to their original source will certainly prove that the name is well deserved. Not only is the book easy to use but it is fascinating to peruse. One wonders how Ernest Holmes found the time to read as widely as he did. While the Bible is his main source for quotes, the other sources range far and wide, proving Holmes's wide interest and understanding of other religious traditions and ancient philosophy plus modern psychology.

Ruark has done us all a great service. I am thrilled that someone with the academic skills to research the material and to give us accurate facts, citing sources, pointing out mistakes, and misquotes took on the job. From the beginning of my ministerial studies, 25 years ago, I have been frustrated by the lack of Biblical scholarship that prevails, not because anyone was lazy or deliberately withholds information, but because it isn't easy to map the mind of a great thinker and writer such as Ernest Holmes. The problem is compounded by the lack of chapter and verse or other attribution.

Using the power of internet search engines, her philosophy background, New Thought theology, and her brilliant mind, Ruark has covered a lot of material in this practical volume. *Where'd He Get That?* is easy to use since nearly all of it is in chart form and you simply start by finding the page number of *The Science of Mind* textbook, and read across the page. If you can read a bus timetable, you can use this book

Ruark points out inaccuracies that Holmes made and sometimes adds notes to clarify an idea. Most of the time the little inaccuracies don't matter and they certainly don't keep people from using Science of Mind Principle to improve their lives. However, I have had more than one student who was very familiar with the Bible question the textbook. Those of us gifted with students who know their Bible get tired of saying, "I don't know" and we truly will treasure Ruark's research.

One of my early memories of the ministry was teaching my first Bible class. Since I did not grow up reading the Bible, I was amazed to find that nearly everyone in my class knew more about it than I did. Most of the students were older women who could quote chapter and verse and sing the songs (in harmony) that went with it. I immediately began a crash course in Bible history. One of the first things I learned was that Bible history and scholarship is an extremely complicated subject. There are scholars who devote their whole lives to the Old Testament or to the New Testament. I also learned that the opinions of the scholars had to be taken in context of their religious beliefs.

I have learned a great deal about the Bible in the last quarter of a century. Rev. Ruark's book taught me a great deal more. Her book is very valuable and will continue to be so, even though fewer of our current students have a great familiarity with Bible chapter and verse.

According to Rev. Ruark's research, 30 years ago 70% of the general population were in church on Sunday and today it is 40%. My own experience is that the majority of young people who come to our Center have not been church goers and do not know much about the Bible. We might be tempted to skip it but as Ruark says, Dr. Holmes assumes that his average reader has read the King James Bible and that they know most of the stories. She says, "If we really want to more fully appreciate the principles taught by *The Science of Mind*, we need to understand where they came from and how Dr. Holmes developed them."

I agree with her although I know not all New Thought ministers think it is important. They seem to teach Principle as though we have no need for an understanding of source. History and lineage are not important to all teachers but I could not go forward without knowing where the material came from. There are many students who feel the same way. There are also many newcomers who need to know about our relationship to the Bible before they can continue studying.

The question of whether or not we are a Christian religion comes up all the time. Ministers hold very different views about the answer to that question. Some say yes, others say no and quite a few say maybe yes and maybe no. The section that covers this question in Ruark's book is lucid and helpful but you will still have to make up own mind.

I didn't change my stand although I was very interested in what Ruark said. When people ask me if I am a Christian, I usually avoid answering and when I am pushed, I say no. When people ask me if Religious Science is a Christian teaching, my answer leans more toward yes. Holmes clearly loved the Bible even though he honored all religious teachings. I did not grow up reading the Bible and I'll never be a Bible thumper. I seldom read anything except a few psalms and I certainly don't believe in the inerrancy of the Bible.

I'm especially grateful to Rev. Ruark for clarifying the other quotes in the Textbook and demonstrating their sources. She added so much information that put the Bible and *The Science of Mind* textbook into new perspective for me. The last section of the book, (perhaps 25%) is a chart tracing ideas presented in *The Science of Mind* textbook that came from non-Biblical sources. A great many are credited to Emerson and Troward but Annie Besant, an early leader of Theosophy is in there and so is Plotinus.

After reading Ruark's book, I felt even more in awe of Holmes. The Bible is a wonderful book and so were all the other wonderful sources that Holmes used to create a brilliant new book – *The Science of Mind* textbook. Ernest Holmes was truly the great synthesizer and Margo Ruark had proved it beyond any reasonable doubt.

PREFACE

Originally conceived as a tool for translators, this compendium evolved to become an equally rich resource for ministers and teachers of *The Science of Mind*. It serves as a comprehensive reference for writing and researching talks, as well as a helpful adjunct to the various Bible courses in *The Science of Mind* curriculum. For individuals in self-study, this book is a valuable companion to the concordance of the Bible and *The Science of Mind* textbook. You won't become an overnight Bible scholar with this text, but you will be able to discuss Holmes from this viewpoint with those who are.

My heartfelt thanks extend to Dr. Jane Claypool, (Author, Founder and Co-Spiritual Leader of the Center for Spiritual Living in Carlsbad, CA) and Rev. Mike Gerdes (my former Co-Director at The Peace Center in Berwyn, IL) for their valuable suggestions for improving the work. Many thanks also go to Mr. Bertil von Knorring, Gothenburg, Sweden, whose brilliant translation of *The Science of Mind* in Swedish sparked this project in consciousness, and whose willingness to "get it right" fuelled its fruition. May you find happiness in all you do!

Where'd He Get That? not only provides the bibliographic sources we have been missing for generations, but also presents an intellectual history of the thinker Ernest Holmes and his flagship work, *The Science of Mind.* I have been stimulated to delve into the source books and the Bible as never before, and it is my heartfelt desire that you do too.

--Rev. Margo Ruark, 2013

To read more about Ernest Holmes' background, his understanding of God, and the evolution of his Christianity:

Holmes, Fenwicke, *Ernest Holmes, His Life and Times*. New York: Dodd, Mead & Company, 1970.
Vahle, Neal, *Open At the Top, The Life of Ernest Holmes*, Mill Valley, CA: Open View Press, 1993.
Armor, Reginald, *That Was Ernest,* Marina del Ray, CA: DeVorss Publications, 1999.

CHANGES TO THIS EDITION

This edition of *Where'd He Get That?* has a few changes to accommodate a larger distribution (a good thing!). First, the landscape layout was traded for a conventional portrait design, allowing for fewer pages and some economies of scale. The content has been completely revised and expanded from the original 2008 edition. The introduction contains several new sections that expound on the Christian roots of New Thought and Dr. Holmes' relationship to the Christian faith from boyhood into his ministry.

I have also included a table of citations from "everybody else" Ernest Holmes quoted or referred to. It must be said that without current Internet search technology, creating this new section would not have been possible. It was almost a detective's thrill to locate the original full text source documents for many of his unreferenced quotations. Likewise, however, the Internet is a double-edged sword. Just as useful information gets propagated at an exponential rate, so do fallacies and folklore. There are many quotations credited to Ralph Waldo Emerson, for example, that do not appear in any of the primary source writings. In instances where Ernest Holmes misquotes one of his sources, these erroneous citations now appear in hundreds of places on the Internet.

Oftentimes, Ernest Holmes prefaces a quote with verbiage such as "it has been said that…" or "the ancients wrote…" Some exact sources of these came up right away on a simple Google search. However, some quotations rendered "no hits." Knowing they had to come from somewhere, and knowing how Dr. Holmes liked to paraphrase, I took the liberty of suggesting his source, using my best-informed guess. On a few occasions, Dr. Holmes mistakenly credits authors with ideas they didn't originate. These items are shaded and my best-informed guess is offered. "Exact source unknown" notations are italicized in the table and are presented as food for thought. Readers may not agree and I would greatly appreciate your comments and suggestions.

It is also worthy of mention that Ernest Holmes wrote original poetry as a hobby. He used it in his talks and recited his works in private salons at his home.[1] Therefore, readers will find several passages of Dr. Holmes' poetry inserted into *The Science of Mind.*

This new edition also contains three appendices. Appendix A contains the New Thought family tree prepared by Rev. Celeste Terkel of the Fremont Center for Spiritual Living, California. It illustrates my point in the introduction, Greek philosophers notwithstanding, that the roots of New Thought are Christian.

Appendix B contains a fully documented list of the footnoted suggested readings at the end of some chapters in the 1926 edition of *The Science of Mind.* Using the citations as they appeared made finding these sources next to impossible, as they are mostly incomplete, or in some cases incorrect.

Appendix C is a table of historical references to the Law of Attraction. Because Dr. Holmes' could have used any or all of these sources, the sheer volume of them required its own section. The Law of Attraction is a key component of the teaching and its meaning changes slightly depending on the source.

---

[1] Bendall, George, *The Holmes Papers*, Volume 1, Torrance, CA: The Martin Press, 1989, p 232

INTRODUCTION

A Most Common Question

One of the most common questions from newcomers to *The Science of Mind* is, "Is *The Science of Mind* a Christian teaching based on the Bible?" For years I answered that question by saying, "more than some, less than others." I would qualify my answer by explaining that we are a Christian teaching insofar as we teach the teachings of Jesus. And while we use the Bible as a source of inspiration, we do not base our religious authority on it, as does mainstream Christianity. Nor do we defer to it as the complete inerrant word of God. Other times, I answered with what is presented on page 67-68 of *The Science of Mind*: "In many respects, the Christian Bible is the greatest book ever written, and does truly point a way to eternal values. But it is only ONE explanation and cannot be considered the ONLY light on religion, for there are many others whose combined teachings weave the story of Truth into a complete and unified pattern."

Through my work with verifying the Swedish translation of *The Science of Mind*[2], I subsequently came to the conclusion that *The Science of Mind* is a Christian teaching more than it is non-denominational or anything else. I say that because the basis of our teaching, *The Science of Mind* textbook, is almost exclusively based on Ernest Holmes' comprehension of Biblical principles.

It is a widely held misconception that *The Science of Mind* is a synthesis of truths from all world religions. While that is a nice sound byte, it is not supported in the textbook. While there are a handful of passing references to scriptures from other religions, their combined numbers are less than one percent of the total Bible references found. Dr. Holmes' manner of speaking and writing relied heavily on the Bible. Quoting the Bible and using its language was part and parcel of how he expressed himself and how he communicated the teaching.

In *The Science of Mind*, there are about 720 references to 377 unique verses of the Bible. On an average, there is *at least one* reference to the Bible found on every page of the textbook! By no means did Dr. Holmes elucidate the entire Bible: indeed, he only incorporated a tiny fraction of its 31,000 verses. Yet, we cannot deny that what Scripture is present, comes from the Christian Bible. So prevalent are the passages, and so numerous the implicit and explicit references to the Bible that we may conclude that *The Science of Mind* is a Christian teaching.

Christian Roots Of New Thought

Even before Ernest Holmes made his mark on New Thought, Christian ideology was already well entrenched in the movement. Major New Thought forebears such as Emanuel Swedenborg, Immanuel Kant, Phineas Parkhurst Quimby, Mary Baker Eddy, Ralph Waldo Emerson, Judge Thomas Troward, and Emma Curtis Hopkins were all confessed Christians, although the orthodoxy may not have accepted them as such. I have chosen to present these writers because they are at the top of the "family tree" of New Thought (see Appendix A) and because many of their ideas appear repackaged as *The Science of Mind*.

---

[2] *Vetenskapen om Medvetandet*, 2010. Translation by Bertil von Knorring. Translated with permission, Science of Mind Publishing.

The writings of scientist and Swedish Nobleman Emmanuel Swedenborg (1688-1772) were a major influence of early New Thought. Swedenborg devoted the last decades of his life to studying Scripture and published eighteen theological titles that drew on the Bible, reasoning, and his own spiritual experiences. These works presented a Christian theology that New Thought embraced, namely a new perspective on the nature of God, the reality of Spirit, and the oneness of creation with the Creator.[3] Swedenborg himself did not endeavor to start a church, but 15 years after his death, his followers founded the Swedenborgian faith in England, and it was soon established in the United States. It is not surprising that a Swedenborgian minister, Warren Felt Evans, would join the ranks of New Thought providing the bridge between the two schools of thought. In *The Science of Mind*, Ernest Holmes cites Emmanuel Swedenborg twice and Warren Felt Evans three times.

Immanuel Kant (1724-1804) influenced New Thought by his writings such as *Religion within the Boundaries of Pure Reason* by introducing Jesus as the example of what all humans could aspire to become, rather than a figure of substitutional atonement.[4] He also wrote about how the concept of God impacted the life and actions of humans and world order, which landed him as one of the great metaphysicians of the Enlightenment period. Kant confessed the human mind, limited by its dependence on space and time, could never come up with an airtight argument for God's existence outside of time and space. He therefore became one of the proponents of the notion of an *"a priori"* knowledge of God, that is, an inborn knowledge we all share that does not depend on experience or intellectual learning. Ernest Holmes quotes Kant twice in *The Science of Mind.*

Phineas Parkhurst Quimby (1802-1866), often called the "Father of New Thought," wrote, in his essay, *Comparison Between Christians 1800 Years Ago & Now*[5], "This difference was the same in Paul's day and he says, 'Show me your religion without works, and I will show you mine by my works.' To be a disciple of Jesus is to put his wisdom into practice." Quimby wrote many essays and lectured on the science of Christianity, and metaphysical interpretations of various Bible passages. Through his popular healing practice Quimby was able to prove that God was a Principle anyone could use to be healed. He was convinced that all disease, in the last analysis, had its roots in the mind, and that healing therefore must be effected through mental influence.

One of Quimby's most famous patients was Mary Baker Eddy (1821-1910), the founder of the Christian Science Church. While she agreed with Quimby that all disease was a result of error in the mind, it was her earnest Puritan faith in Christ Jesus that separated her from Quimby from the beginning. Eddy carried on the allegorical Bible interpretation technique of Quimby, which was later taught by her student Emma Curtis Hopkins, the "teacher of teachers" to Ernest Holmes and his contemporaries. The complete lineage appears in Appendix A.

"Christian Science is based on the Bible, as Mary Baker Eddy found Jesus' teachings to be fundamental to her theology. It is true that she also experimented with hydropathy, homeopathy, as well as other healing methods—practiced by Phineas Quimby and others—during the mid-1800s. However, Christian Science is a complete departure from these earlier systems, both in its treatment of disease and in its Christianity."[6]

Ralph Waldo Emerson, (1803-1882) was the son of a Unitarian minister and his family lineage contained a long line of ministers. He too, wanted to be a minister and after intermittently attending Harvard Divinity School, he became an ordained Unitarian minister at the Second Church of

---

[3] Robert H. Kirven and George F. Dole, *Scientist Explores Spirit* Swedenborg Foundation, 1996.

[4] Stanford Encyclopedia of Philosophy, "Kant's Philosophy of Religion" http://plato.stanford.edu/entries/kant-religion/

5 *The Complete Collected Works of Dr. Phineas Parkhurst Quimby*, Phineas Parkhurst Quimby Philosophical Society of New England, Manchester, CT: Seed of Life Publishing, 2008.

[6] "Frequently Asked Questions about Mary Baker Eddy" – www.christianscience.com

Boston. Due to his losses of many loved ones, he began questioning his Christian beliefs and resigned his position as minister. He would devote most of the remainder of his life to travel, making an exhaustive inquiry of Christian thought, writing, exploring western classic and eastern philosophy, and lecturing. His "Divinity School Address"[7] got him labeled as an atheist by the orthodoxy. However, as time went on, other writers of the Transcendentalist movement incorporated Emerson's metaphysical themes of the Divine appearing as Nature everywhere, even in man. Before long, the criticism about his religious persuasion subsided. Outside of the Bible, Emerson is the source Ernest Holmes references the most, 27 times.

The metaphysical and esoteric writings of Judge Thomas Troward (1847-1916), British Divisional Judge of the North Indian Punjab, also had a profound effect on Ernest Holmes. Troward's collected writings, including *Bible Mystery and Bible Meaning, The Creative Process in the Individual, The Law and the Word, The Edinburgh Lectures on Mental Science and the Doré Lectures on Mental Science,* constituted the main body of Troward's monumental contribution to what he called "Mental Science". Troward was raised in the Church of England and had read the Bible daily from boyhood. Therefore, his books, have a clear Christian bent. His philosophical system, which appealed to Ernest Holmes, removed the intellectual, theological and emotional obstacles to understanding the relationship between the individual human being and the Eternal Principle of the Universe. In addition to influencing the New Thought Movement in the United States, he is also credited to contributing the more liberal ideas of the Church of England. After Emerson, Judge Troward was the next most utilized source outside of the Bible with 18 citations in *The Science of Mind*.

Emma Curtis Hopkins (1853-1925) was the teacher of many New Thought leaders and the author of several books on Christian mysticism: *High Mysticism, Scientific Christian Mental Practice, The Gospel Series in Spiritual Science,* and *Bible Interpretations.* Her writings are insights into the practical application of metaphysical science as exemplified most particularly by Jesus Christ. Ms. Hopkins's Christian roots are particularly solidified in what many consider her masterpiece work, *Scientific Christian Mental Practice.* Mrs. Hopkins refers to it as "the method of Jesus Christ" with "the absolute meanings of the words of Jesus Christ" elucidated.

She further states: "As we understand Jesus Christ, we have His Mind. When we have His Mind wholly, we have an understanding of the apostle's injunction, 'Let this mind be in you which was also in Christ Jesus.'. . .In this healing practice we have had many a thinker touching on the enchanting borders of the Science, but only Jesus who could wholly prove his words . . .. His words would heal the instant He sent them.[8]

Hopkins was a student of Mary Baker Eddy and Christian Science, and later departed to start her own seminary in Chicago. Among her students were many who later became prominent teachers and leaders within the New Thought movement, including:

- Malinda Cramer, Nona L. Brooks, Fannie Brooks co-founders of Divine Science;
- Charles Fillmore and Myrtle Fillmore, co-founders of the Unity who were ordained by Hopkins in 1891;
- Harriet Emilie Cady, author of Lessons in Truth;
- Annie Rix Militz, founder of The Home of Truth;
- Ella Wheeler Wilcox, New Thought poetess,
- William Walker Atkinson, prolific New Thought author.
- and considerably later Ernest Holmes, founder of the Church of Religious Science.

---

[7] *Delivered before the Senior Class in Divinity College, Cambridge, Sunday Evening, July 15, 1838.*

[8] Hopkins, Emma Curtis. *Scientific Christian Mental Practice*, (1888) p.147

Ernest Holmes references Emma Curtis Hopkins twice in the text.

While the New Thought Family Tree[9] contains many more founders too numerous to mention here, we cannot ignore the fact that the overwhelming majority came from a White Anglo-Saxon Protestant Christian background.

Dr. Holmes' Relationship to the Christian Faith

Ernest Shurtleff Holmes was brought up in a Christian household where daily Bible reading and prayers were part of everyday life. His middle name was taken from a popular young preacher who had a poetic temperament, wrote hymns and was a friend of the Holmes family. As a boy, his family had three books in the house that were read ardently: *The King James Bible*, *The Illustrated Story of the Bible* and a book of verse. Ernest's love for the Bible had developed because of its use in family prayers throughout his boyhood

Ernest's mother, Anna, was a woman of great faith and she enjoyed her conversations with Rev. Shurtleff on all topics related to the nature of God, man, the meaning of life and other inspirational subjects. Throughout his childhood, Ernest attended the Congregationalist church with his parents and the boys knew more about the Bible than other children of their own age. Anna impressed upon her sons the immediate presence of God and raised them without religious fear of the Devil, or of going to Hell. For a woman of her day, she was well educated, and taught school for a time. She valued independence of thought and originality.

Ernest Holmes mentioned often that spirituality as presented by his mother was serene, safe, and gave the family assurance that God would take care of them. Ernest's father, William, saw it as his role to protect the boys from fear-based dualism. Dualism was a popular theme of the day in the local churches. It was conveyed by many preachers in gory detail of how the path to Hell was paved with the bodies of unbaptized infants.

In his book Ernest *Holmes, His Life and Times,* brother Fenwicke Holmes reports what his father said after hearing one such sermon in a new town: "On the way home, Father stopped the horse and let him nibble grass by the roadside while he turned an spoke to us. "Don't be scared, boys, about the worms of the dust. Reverend Ernest Shurtleff wouldn't say you are worms. You are not worms, and it's a big lie. Jesus said, 'Ye are gods,' and you are like God if you keep that way. Man was made by God. Any other story is a lie."[10]

Anna enjoyed talking to local ministers, even after Rev. Shurtleff had traveled on. They often incorporated Anna's liberal views into their sermons and she warned the boys never to tell anyone. Eventually, young Ernest began asking questions about the ministers who came to call on the family and who preached in the local church. "How does he know?" "Did God talk to him?" "How come God requires so much information on current events and people's private lives?"

As a pre-teen, Ernest had his first internal wrestling match with Christian piety. It was a beautiful spring Sunday and he was planning to pick flowers in the woods after church. His Sunday school teacher was defiantly against any pleasure on the Sabbath and made him promise he wouldn't go. After making this promise, he remembered what Jesus said to the Pharisees when they admonished him for healing the sick on the Sabbath, "Which of you shall have an ass or an ox fallen into a pit, and will not straightway pull him out on the Sabbath day?" (Luke 14:5) After careful consideration, he decided that if it was acceptable to pull one ass out a ditch or pit on the Sabbath, you might as well go into the woods and look for more that might need rescuing. Ernest

---
[9] New Thought History, TriCity Church of Religious Science, Fremont, CA 2005. See Appendix A.

[10] Holmes, Fenwicke, *Ernest Holmes His Life and Times*. New York: Dodd, Mead & Company, 1970, p.37.

later reported he regretted the whole episode, not because he broke his word, but because he gave it in the first place, for an idea he didn't believe in.

As a teen, Ernest spent a year in Boston with his aunt, attending a Baptist church, an experience that added more questions to his metaphysical and philosophical inquiries. His questions were often met with Baptist theology rather than with philosophical discourse and deeper reasoning. This lack of an authentic thoughtful response disappointed him and was a major contributor why he developed an independent philosophy of life on his own. From this point forward, he analyzed every religious proposition with logic and reason. If the argument unraveled, he would dismiss it and move on with his inquiry. From an early age, he held a great respect for logical thinking especially pertaining to religious ideas.

While in his early teens, one of his teachers taught him how to 'listen to trees' in nature. At school, he would skip class to listen to trees, read poetry of Wordsworth and the Psalms, and find answers to his own questions on God, the Devil, the literal interpretation of the Bible and others. He would reflect on answering the abstract questions of "Who Am I?" "Why Am I Here?", "Who is God?" It was while playing hooky that he developed his skills in original thinking and using logic to resolve answers to his questions within himself. He grew confident in the truths he discovered because they passed the rigor of his reasoning process.

By age 18 he had attracted into his life many original thinkers on spiritual matters who encouraged him to think for himself. He decided he could not develop this skill in conventional education and he made a decision to conduct his learning about God and life in the world of the living.

Two of his brothers became protestant ministers, one became a missionary overseas and one did mission work in the United States. His brother Fenwicke said his conventional training as a Congregationalist minister had an "unquestioned bearing . . . upon both Ernest and myself in our very near as well as our distant future."[11]

At age 18, Ernest moved back to Boston and again attended the Baptist church with his aunt. He liked spending time at the church but took issue with the prevailing dualism there. "If Hell is in the Bible, then somebody made a mistake. Something inside me knows it isn't true," he told one Baptist theologian.

Nonetheless, he was baptized as a Baptist but was disappointed it didn't do something to him. He didn't feel different at all. His attraction to the Baptists dwindled over the following months as he reached for the next phase of his understanding of Christianity.

Ernest Holmes Discovers Emerson

The time around the turn of the 20th century was the hotbed of expanding ideas of Christianity in which Ernest Holmes found himself as a fish in water. Many new American religions were taking root, most of them based on Christianity: Mormonism, Theosophy, Browning Societies, Spiritualism, Swedenborgianism, Christian Science, hands-on faith healing, and the hypnosis techniques practices by the Christian healer Phineas P. Quimby.

When he was 20, Ernest Holmes discovered Emerson's *Essays* lying on his brother's living room table, which drew him into contemplating a Christianity without a devil or *a redeemer*. He began to embrace the idea that God was something on the inside, not something on the outside of himself. He became so familiar with Emerson he could quote entire sections of the essays verbatim.

---

[11] Ibid. Holmes, Fenwicke. P. 114.

Discovering Emerson only intensified his study of the Bible as he read it in a completely new light. Emerson was a new kind of Christian, certainly a theist, a poet and an agitator of Christian orthodoxy. Ernest Holmes said, "Having had some light from the Bible, I began a more thorough study and got a lot of help from it and often found confirmation of my new ideas. This was itself a worthwhile pursuit and I followed the practice throughout life."[12]

While in Boston, he was invited to attend the Mother Church of the Christian Scientists. He bought Mary Baker Eddy's book *Science and Health with Key to the Scriptures* and quoted frequently from it. He began comparing her writings to those of Emerson finding many points in common. Most of all, Christian Science brought the new concept of prayer to Ernest's life. Universal or Divine Principle, as Mrs. Eddy called it, could be called upon for healing, independent of Christian faith or any particular religious faith. While he never joined the Christian Science church, he accepted its major principles as true and held great respect for Mrs. Eddy and her organization. It was only after he discovered the larger body of New Thought writings, of among others Christian Larson, that he abandoned Christian Science altogether.

At age 25, Ernest traveled to California to visit Fenwicke who was now leading a church in Venice, California. Ernest decided to stay on and help him with his church in Venice. He got a job as a playground director with the public schools and also built a successful youth program at Fenwicke's church, the first of its kind. Ernest's first ministry was with youth and he was a kid-magnet!

While in Venice, he read voraciously and got the idea of creating a fusion of metaphysics, psychology, philosophy, Christianity and the best of Eastern thought, and the best of the poets like Whitman, Wordsworth and Browning. He read Troward, and all the current metaphysical writers. Ernest Holmes had no real knowledge of any religions beyond Christianity when he got the idea of creating this fusion, but he felt that religion should represent the highest and best thoughts of man throughout history. After infusing his mind with what he thought was the highest and best thinking of the ages, he began to write. He started a magazine on metaphysical healing and attended every lecture he could on metaphysics. One such visit to Seattle resulted in his ordination as a Divine Science minister in 1916.

New Thought as the New Christianity

Ernest began his own career as a metaphysical lecturer and "Christian clergyman" which was his full time job. Ernest Holmes did not experience a "call" to the ministry. He did not have a vision or hear a voice directing him in the path of spiritual leader. He always insisted that his rise to enlightenment was a natural growth using the same law and same power indwelling in everyone.

Eventually, Fenwicke resigned his post as a Congregationalist minister to assist Ernest at his metaphysical enterprise. Ernest and Fenwicke enjoyed a successful lecture career and the main themes of the talks were healing and reinterpretation of the scriptures. Fenwicke wrote, "We had instantaneous overwhelming success and were exultant to be alive in such an age."[13] In the early days of the movement, people were drawn in droves to New Thought due to a desperate need for physical healing and for the abundant life promised by Jesus. Clearly, they had their work cut out for them.

In 1927, the Holmes brothers released the first issue of *Science of Mind Magazine* as "A Magazine of Christian Philosophy" and early issues contained articles such as "Finding the Christ," and "Knowing your Bible Intelligently".

---

[12] Ibid. Holmes, Fenwicke. P. 80

[13] Ibid. Holmes, Fenwicke, p. 167.

One of Ernest's favorite sayings, reports his close friend and biographer Reginald Armor, was "Some day we are going to really try out the teaching of Jesus Christ and practice Christianity."[14] "We are Christian and more," emphasized Ernest Holmes. "It [Religious Science] is not just a Christian philosophy, although it is a Christian denomination."[15]

In *The Science of Mind* textbook, reissued in 1938, Ernest Holmes devoted 56 pages of the text to the teachings of Jesus and placed "The Healing Christ", or the Divine Presence inside every man. He wrote: "The man Jesus became the Christ through a complete realization of the Unity of Spirit and the Absoluteness of His word."[16] He also included a chapter called "Finding the Christ"[17] in which he explains his idea of Christ as a Universal Principle of Sonship and how every person can partake of the Christ consciousness by recognizing their Sonship, the Living Presence of the Divine within.

In one of his last sermons, Dr Holmes discussed the future of the church, not about strategy and material growth, but about how to preserve and expand the fundamental principles already known. A professor of Philosophy at the University of Southern California remarked afterwards "We [Religious Science] are conducting the greatest spiritual experiment since the dawn of Christianity."[18]

Dr. Holmes Relationship to Jesus

To say that *The Science of Mind* is not Christian defies the evidence as well as the way Ernest Holmes lived his life. Another Holmes biographer, Neal Valhe added to this perception in his book, *Open at the Top*. Valhe writes, "Holmes did not believe in the Trinitarian God of Christian teaching, which asserted the existence of three persons in one God—Father, Son, and Holy Spirit. "God", said Holmes, "is not a person. God is a Presence . . . .God is Universal Principle. Therefore it is appropriate to think of God, not only as a principle, forever pushing forward into expression, but as Infinite Person."[19]

Throughout his book, Neal Valhe describes how Dr. Holmes spoke of Jesus in exalted terms. He called Jesus, "the most glorious soul who ever trod our planet," "the most tremendous example of the possibility of man," "a way shower of truth and life," "the most profound philosopher who ever lived," a consciously cosmic soul." Jesus stood alone, Holmes said, "as a man who knew himself and realized his relationship to the perfect Whole." The birth of Jesus, Holmes said "was undoubtedly the greatest historical even in the history of the human race."

While he clearly believed there was an historical Jesus, who did admirable deeds, we should not make the mistake of deifying Jesus the person and forgetting we are dealing with a Christ principle[20]. Holmes made a clear distinction between "Jesus" and "Christ." "Jesus is the man; Christ is the realization of a conscious union of God and Man." Christ represented the "universal

---

[14] Armor, Reginald C. *That Was Ernest*. Marina del Ray, CA: DeVorss Publications, 1999. p.141

[15] Bendall, George P., *The Holmes Papers: The Philosophy of Ernest Holmes*, Torrance, CA: The Martin Press, 1989. p. 3.

[16] Holmes, Ernest. *The Science Of Mind,* New York: Dodd, Mead & Company, 1938, p. 337.

[17] Ibid. Holmes, Ernest. pp. 357-370.

[18] Op. cit. Holmes, Fenwicke. p. 286.

[19] Valhe, Neal, *Open at the Top. The Life of Ernest Holmes,* Mill Valley, CA: Open View Press, 1993. p. 7.

[20] Op Cit. Holmes, Ernest. p. 359-360.

possibility" for all men. "Every man is a potential Christ from the least to the greatest; the same life runs throughout us all, threading itself into the patterns of our individuality."[21]

Holmes asserted that mainstream Christianity had misinterpreted the teachings of Jesus and tried to make him the great exception instead of the great example. Holmes did not criticize Christianity for lack of sincerity in its desire to follow its great teacher. "The great mistake," he said was in "a misconception of his message." Holmes thought the problem lay in Christianity's literal interpretation of the Biblical message. "If the life and message and work of Jesus was to be taken with absolute literal meaning, then in a way, the unique form of Jesus would become God, and unfortunately would lose for us the perspective of the most tremendous example of the possibility of man." Jesus never tried to set himself apart from other men. What he was trying to do was reveal to the people of his day that they too were sharers of the Divine Nature.[22]

Dr. Holmes stated in an article in *Science of Mind Magazine* that "No doubt if we penetrated completely into the meaning of Jesus' teachings, we would have a perfect explanation for our own philosophy."[23] In his last years, Ernest was working on a Bible recording, a tape of the highlights of Isaiah, which he called the *Song of Isaiah*, and an edited version of the Psalms and Proverbs. In this recording, he eliminated the negative and accentuated the positive attitudes in those scriptures and called it the *Wisdom of Solomon*.[24]

The Bible was with Ernest Holmes until the very end. Passages from the Bible were read at Ernest Holmes' funeral as well as some excerpts from his key teachings.

Despite this preponderance of history, many people still find it difficult to accept *The Science of Mind* as a Christian teaching. Many still easily confuse it with Scientology or Christian Science. Those who are looking for alternatives to mainstream Protestantism, evangelical moralizing or charismatic elitism will find *The Science of Mind* a liberating breath of fresh air in that the teachings of Jesus are emphasized rather than dogma about salvation and forgiveness of sin. However, those looking for crosses, statues, and involved rituals of absolution will doubt that *The Science of Mind* is Christian. One elderly visitor remarked, "What's wrong with you people? You don't have no crosses or statues or hymnals or nothin'! I could hardly tell I was in a church!"

Many Jewish people enjoy the positive thinking aspects of our teaching, but are turned off by the discussions and celebrations of "The Christ within" especially during the holidays. "Are you Christian? You must be!" remarked one Jewish visitor. "'I am the way the truth and the life: no one cometh unto the Father but by me.' You have no idea how hard it is to listen to that!" This Jewish man explained that according to his faith, Jesus Christ did not embody the personal qualifications of the Messiah. So what is the spiritual benefit of cultivating, honoring, or celebrating the Christ within? The point is some people cannot hear or embrace the part about Christ being a Principle, not a person.

So *The Science of Mind* teaching has sat in a pinch of being not Christian enough for some and way too Christian for others. Since its establishment as a form of organized religion, Religious Science has had to defend, explain, and justify its theological presence in the spiritual landscape of the country, and now the world. Ernest Holmes would answer his critics with this simple phrase, "Just try out the teaching!"

---

[21] Ibid. Vahle, pp 48-49.

[22] Ibid. Vahle, p. 49.

[23] Ibid. Vahle. p. 51.

[24] Op. cit. Bendall, p. 19.

The Bible in Light of Religious Science

Dr. Raymond Charles Barker is reported to have refused to sell Dr. Holmes' book, *The Bible in Light of Religious Science* at the First Church of Religious Science in New York because it embarrassed him with its errors and misquotations of scripture. Therefore, it may appear that Holmes was not a Bible scholar. Bible scholarship, however, was never his intention. Holmes' strength was his ability to take profound principles from the Bible, expand them and synthesize them into something practical, timely and of deep spiritual meaning for today.

Dr. Holmes Assumes We Know Our Bibles…and a LOT MORE!

Dr. Holmes assumes the average reader of *The Science of Mind* has read the Bible, more specifically, the King James Version and that we are familiar with Biblical characters. He presumes we know who Adam, Eve, David, Solomon, the anti-Christ, and the Samaritans were. He also surmises we know the disciples by name. He also assumes the average reader is familiar with the philosophers he mentions: Plato, Socrates, Plotinus, Spinoza, Swedenborg, Kant, and the neo-Platonics—also Emerson and Thomas Troward. He expects readers to have a familiarity with spiritual concepts such as kismet, nirvana, and karma. Likewise Dr. Holmes expects us to have an appreciation of the poetry of Robert Browning, Tennyson, Wadsworth, and Whitman.

As I have worked with translators, I have recognized that some people of other cultures shared this knowledge and some did not. As I taught *The Science of Mind*, I recognized many Americans did not know Biblical context when they read it, let alone poets and philosophers. As new generations of people enter the New Thought movement, we see a departure from prior generations who were avid church goers, Bible readers, and students of the classics. Thirty years ago, 70% of the general population were in church on Sunday. Today about 40% are, according to a recent poll by the Gallup News Service.[25] In some countries, Sweden, Finland, Iceland and Japan for example, that number dips to 4% or less.[26] Fifty years ago, most graduated from high school with a knowledge of literature and philosophy. In today's society, even with the best liberal arts education, most students will be lacking in at least one of these areas of Bible knowledge, literature, or philosophy. So how are we to really grasp what Holmes is saying in *The Science of Mind* when we are missing some of the basic know-how?

If we really want to more fully appreciate the principles taught by *The Science of Mind*, we need to understand where they came from and how Dr. Holmes developed them. We need to better understand our Bibles. Sooner or later, we are going to have to read them. To understand and then be able to teach *The Science of Mind* in all its fullness is possible when we know where the references came from and the various appearances they take on in Dr. Holmes' writing style, phraseology, and linguistic cadence.

Which Bible Did Dr. Holmes Use?

The Biblical references Dr. Holmes used are quoted from the King James Bible. Oddly enough in the title page to Part Five, "Teachings From The New Testament", there is a reference to the *Scofield Reference Edition* of the Bible. The *Scofield Reference Edition* is the King James Version with commentary by a self proclaimed Bible scholar named Cyrus Ingerson Scofield (1843 – 1921). *The Scofield Reference Edition* was first published in 1909. Scofield was a controversial public figure, claiming to have been ordained and possessing a Doctorate degree, neither of which

---

[25] Frank Newport, "Just Why Do Americans Attend Church?" *Gallup News Service,* April 6, 2007.

[26] University of Michigan, Institute for Social Research, *World Values Survey,* Dec. 10, 1997.

he could verify. Despite his moral and legal problems which were grist for the tabloids of his day, he wrote a Bible correspondence course that is still in use today by the Moody Bible Institute. Scofield is credited as being the one who invented the concepts of "the rapture" and "substitutionary atonement" (Jesus died a wicked bloody death to atone for your sins) and founded the fundamentalist Christian movement of Premillenialism. He included them in his commentary, which people began to take as part of the gospel itself. Believe what we may about Scofield, his commentary was in wide circulation in the early 1900's when Dr. Holmes was doing his most prolific writing. With the exception of one reference to a "resurrection body, then, will not be snatched from some Cosmic Shelf" (p.376-2), Holmes left out Scofield's editorial comments when he wrote *The Science of Mind*.

How Dr. Holmes Integrates the Bible

Some observations should be noted about Dr. Holmes' use of the Bible throughout *The Science of Mind*:

- **He paraphrases freely** from the given Biblical text, such as his continued use of the phrase "fallen short of" versus what the King James Bible says is "come short of" the glory of God. *"For all have sinned, and come short of the glory of God;"* (Romans 3:23).
- **He peppers his language with archaic words from the Bible.** For example, The eternal is forever "begetting" (SOM p. 357-2); life "beguiles" us (SOM p. 473-6) or an activity of consciousness where the spirit "quickens" the body (SOM p.414-4).
- **Some verses are neatly referenced, most are not.** If you don't know them, you won't know to look for them, or recognize them. That's where this compendium becomes an important resource.
- **With liberal use of quotation marks, he often combines a section from one verse with a section of another** to appear as if it's all the same verse from the Bible. For example on p. 304-3 and again on p. 405-2, he writes, "They could not enter in because of their unbelief, and because they limited the Holy One of Israel." This phrase is a combination of either Hebrews 4:6 *"Seeing therefore it remaineth that some must enter therein, and they to whom it was first preached entered not in because of unbelief "* or Hebrews 3:19 *"So we see that they could not enter in because of unbelief "* and a section of Psalms 78:41, *"Yea, they turned back and tempted God, and limited the Holy One of Israel."* Another example is on p. 311-1, when he writes as one passage: "God is not a God of the dead but of the living, for in His sight are all alive," he combines part of Matthew 22:32 *"I am the God of Abraham, and the God of Isaac, and the God of Jacob? God is not the God of the dead, but of the living."* with part of Luke 20:38 *"For he is not a God of the dead, but of the living: for all live unto him."* Or on p. 313-4 he writes, "except the branch abide in the vine, it shall not bear fruit." Here the idea of the vine and branches is from John 15:5 *"I am the vine, ye are the branches: He that abideth in me, and I in him, the same bringeth forth much fruit: for without me ye can do nothing."* and the idea of bearing fruit from John 15:8 *"Herein is my Father glorified, that ye bear much fruit; so shall ye be my disciples."*
- **He condenses longer verses**, often leaving out the middle section, joining beginning and end into what appeared to be an intact verse. On p. 484 he writes, "There is no condemnation to them...who walk...after the Spirit." The entire verse this is based on, Romans 8:1, reads: *"There is therefore now no condemnation to them which are in Christ Jesus, who walk not after the flesh, but after the Spirit."* He also does this action with the expression "knock and we shall find" on p. 435, when the Bible verse this is based on, Matthew 7:7 reads, *"Seek and ye shall find; knock and it shall be opened unto you."*
- **He makes up words and coins his own phrases** based on King James English. For example, he made up the phrase "to pray aright" (158-1, 436-1) which is not used in the

Bible. What are used are the words "to pray amiss" (James 4:3), or to have one's "heart aright"(Psalms 78:8).

- **He makes a couple misquotations.** For example, the concept of "the Holy Comforter" (p. 480-5) described as the One to make things known to us is correctly found in John 14:26, not John 14:16 as he cites. Dr. Holmes says he's quoting Mark 11:24 on page 290-1 when he writes, "When ye pray, believe that ye have and ye shall receive." The verse in the Bible actually reads, *"Therefore I say unto you, What things soever ye desire, when ye pray, believe that ye receive them, and ye shall have them."* Dr. Holmes reversed the words "have" and "receive".

- **Some verses he uses are found in multiple places in the Bible,** such as the phrase "a house divided" appears in three different places in the Bible. The phrase "comes in the name of the Lord" is found eight different places and he could have gotten these passages from any or all these sources.

- **He uses Biblical cadence to make up his own material.** For example what appears to be a "real" verse on p. 231-3 "I will lift mine eyes unto God from whom comes my perfect sight," is really a derivation of Psalms 121:1 "I will lift mine eyes unto the hills from whence cometh my help."

- **Quotations around a word or phrase don't mean he's quoting any source in particular.** Some phrases which sound like they ought to be from the Bible because of their context with other Bible verses are not from the Bible at all. For example, on p. 307 are several Bible passages which have quotation marks around them and right in the middle are two passages: "Onlook thou the Deity and the Deity will onlook thee." And: "Act as though I am and I will be"-- an idea which is used several times in the text. Or "His lines have gone out into all places." (p. 330) or "Behold, thou, my face forevermore" (p 131-1, 185-3). These passages are not in the Bible, or in any other known scriptures. In the third table of "other thinkers," I have postulated my best guess as to where the inspiration may have come from.

- **Perhaps his greatest and most profound liberty** was in Chapter 22 he deliberately rewrites John 3:18 (and the Nicene Creed for that matter!) *"He that believeth on him is not condemned: but he that believeth not is condemned already, because he hath not believed in the name of the only begotten Son of God."* In Chapter 22, he changes the placing of the word "only" (p 357-1) to read "The Son, begotten of the *only* Father – *not* 'the only begotten Son of God.'" This deliberate switch came to be a major tenet of *The Science of Mind,* that anyone can be a Christ when they consciously recognize and embody their Divine Sonship.

Dr. Holmes was a lover of the Bible, but not a Bible scholar. He clearly found great inspiration from it. In 1928, he wrote in the Foreword to *The Bible in Light of Religious Science,* "The Bible was written by human beings whose thought was reaching toward ultimate Reality, and, if it is to be understood, it must be read with the same motive." By use and example, Dr. Holmes demonstrates that we can embrace the Bible, and other scripture for that matter, taking the good we can find in it and making it our own.

The Top Ten Bible Verses Referred to in the Text

Here is a list of the top ten most frequently quoted passages in *The Science of Mind*. At the top of the list with 22 references is Exodus 3:14, where Moses meets the "I AM" at the burning bush from the Old Testament. At the metaphysical level those two words, the phrase "I Am," are the most powerful in *The Science of Mind.* First, the I Am represents the Universal expressing in the and through the individual and second, in it is the womb of Universal Creation since whatever you put after those two words, is created.

At a close second is another Old Testament verse, Isaiah 55:11 where the prophet tells us his word shall not return to him void, but fulfilled and prospered. This reference appears 17 times in *The Science of Mind*.

In this edition, I chose not to combine the three verses that support the idea of Jesus' statement "it is done unto you as you believe." Two of the three made the top ten on their own, that is Matthew 8:13 and John 15:7 with 10 occurrences each. The third verse, Matthew 9:27-29, regarding the two blind men, had five occurrences. Combined, these verses supporting the same concept would have totaled 25 occurrences, taking first place on the list.

Rank	Verse	Text	Count
1.	Exodus 3:14	And God said unto Moses, I AM THAT I AM: and he said, Thus shalt thou say unto the children of Israel, I AM hath sent me unto you.	22
2.	Isaiah 55:11	So shall my word be that goeth forth out of my mouth: it shall not return unto me void, but it shall accomplish that which I please, and it shall prosper in the thing whereto I sent it.	17
3.	John 7:24	Judge not according to the appearance, but judge righteous judgment.	13
4.	Luke 17:21	Neither shall they say, Lo here! or, lo there! for, behold, the kingdom of God is within you.	12
5.	Matthew 8:13	And Jesus said unto the centurion, Go thy way; and as thou hast believed, so be it done unto thee. And his servant was healed in the selfsame hour.	10
6.	Hebrews 11:3	Through faith we understand that the worlds were framed by the word of God, so that things which are seen were not made of things which do appear.	10
7.	John 15:7	If ye abide in me, and my words abide in you, ye shall ask what ye will, and it shall be done unto you.	10
8.	John 8:32	And ye shall know the truth, and the truth shall make you free.	10
9.	Acts 17:28	For in him we live, and move, and have our being; as certain also of your own poets have said, For we are also his offspring.	8
10.	John 14:10	Believest thou not that I am in the Father, and the Father in me? the words that I speak unto you I speak not of myself: but the Father that dwelleth in me, he doeth the works.	8

References to Thinkers Outside the Bible

In 237 references to the writings of others outside the Bible, Ernest Holmes cited 35 other thinkers or sources that could be verified. The table on the following page lists all these other sources in order of frequency. The top three verified sources referenced are (after Plotinus, the remainder of sources are quoted four times or less):

Rank	Author cited or referenced:	Count
1.	Ralph Waldo Emerson	27
2.	Judge Thomas Troward	18
3.	Plotinus and Plotinus scholar Dean William Ralph Inge	11

All Other Thinkers in Order of Frequency Mentioned in the Text

1	Ralph Waldo Emerson	19	Dictionaries
2	Thomas Troward	20	Aristotle
3	Plotinus/Inge	21	St. Thomas Aquinas
4	Plato	22	John Milton
5	Robert Browning	23	William Wordsworth
6	Benedict Spinoza	24	Lewis Carroll
7	Sir Oliver Lodge	25	Demosthenes
8	James Russell Lowell	26	Rudyard Kipling
9	Dr. Richard Maurice Bucke	27	Horace Walpole
10	Warren Felt Evans	28	Emmet Fox
11	Bhagavad-Gita	29	Rabindrath Tagore
12	Walt Whitman	30	Meister Eckhart
13	Alfred Lord Tennyson	31	Thomson Jay Hudson
14	William Shakespeare	32	Emma Curtis Hopkins
15	Anne Besant	33	Fenwicke Holmes
16	Buddha	34	Ralph Waldo Trine
17	Immanuel Kant	35	Samuel Taylor Coleridge
18	Emanuel Swedenborg		

There were a total of 100 quotations where the exact source could not be determined. In these cases, an educated guess was made based on the context. As previously mentioned, these are shaded in the table. Of these, 21 were miscitations such as "Emerson wrote" or "when Browning wrote" when they did not. These instances appear in italics in the table. Again in these instances, an informed guess was made as to the true source of the quotation.

TABLE I: BIBLE VERSES CITED IN *THE SCIENCE OF MIND* ORGANIZED BY BOOK OF THE BIBLE FROM GENESIS TO REVELATIONS

Unique Verse Nr.	Bible Verse	Citation	Ernest Holmes reference	Page in SOM text
		OLD TESTAMENT		
1	Genesis 1:1	In the beginning God created the heaven and the earth.	In the beginning God!	063-2
	Genesis 1:1	In the beginning God created the heaven and the earth.	In the beginning God created the heavens and the earth	067-2
2	Genesis 1:1-31	In the beginning God created the heaven and the earth. And the earth was without form, and void; and darkness was upon the face of the deep. And the Spirit of God moved upon the face of the waters. And God said, Let there be light: and there was light. And God saw the light, that it was good: and God divided the light from the darkness. And God called the light Day, and the darkness he called Night. And the evening and the morning were the first day. . . . And God blessed them, and God said unto them, Be fruitful, and multiply, and replenish the earth, and subdue it: and have dominion over the fish of the sea, and over the fowl of the air, and over every living thing that moveth upon the earth. . . . And God saw every thing that he had made, and, behold, it was very good. And the evening and the morning were the sixth day.	Without repeating the well-known account (rather accounts, for there are two) of Creation, as given in the Bible	064-3
3	Genesis 1:2	And the earth was without form, and void; and darkness was upon the face of the deep. And the Spirit of God moved upon the face of the waters.	the Spirit, had not yet moved upon the waters	063-2
	Genesis 1:2	And the earth was without form, and void; and darkness was upon the face of the deep.	In the theoretical beginning of creation, the world was "without form and void."	117-1
4	Genesis 1:3	And God said, Let there be light: and there was light.	Light: "Let there be light and there was light."	607

Where'd He Get That? A Biblical Cross-Reference To Ernest Holmes' The Science of Mind

Unique Verse Nr.	Bible Verse	Citation	Ernest Holmes reference	Page in SOM text
5	Genesis 1:26	And God said, Let us make man in our image, after our likeness: and let them have dominion over the fish of the sea, and over the fowl of the air, and over the cattle, and over all the earth, and over every creeping thing that creepeth upon the earth.	So God gave man dominion over all earthly things.	065-6
	Genesis 1:26	And God said, Let us make man in our image, after our likeness: and let them have dominion over the fish of the sea, and over the fowl of the air, and over the cattle, and over all the earth, and over every creeping thing that creepeth upon the earth.	He must make him in His own image and likeness	065-3
	Genesis 1:26	And God said, Let us make man in our image, after our likeness: and let them have dominion over the fish of the sea, and over the fowl of the air, and over the cattle, and over all the earth, and over every creeping thing that creepeth upon the earth.	incredible possibilities of dominion	138-1
	Genesis 1:26	And God said, Let us make man in our image, after our likeness: and let them have dominion over the fish of the sea, and over the fowl of the air, and over the cattle, and over all the earth, and over every creeping thing that creepeth upon the earth.	Claim our power and dominion	250-6
	Genesis 1:26	And God said, Let us make man in our image, after our likeness: and let them have dominion over the fish of the sea, and over the fowl of the air, and over the cattle, and over all the earth, and over every creeping thing that creepeth upon the earth.	We should claim our dominion and power in Spirit.	252-5
	Genesis 1:26	And God said, Let us make man in our image, after our likeness: and let them have dominion over the fish of the sea, and over the fowl of the air, and over the cattle, and over all the earth, and over every creeping thing that creepeth upon the earth.	Adam was permitted to name all creation and man was supposed to exercise an authority over all that is below him	410-3

Unique Verse Nr.	Bible Verse	Citation	Ernest Holmes reference	Page in SOM text
6	Genesis 1:28	And God blessed them, and God said unto them, Be fruitful, and multiply, and replenish the earth, and subdue it: and have dominion over the fish of the sea, and over the fowl of the air, and over every living thing that moveth upon the earth.	he was given the power to have dominion	065-6
7	Genesis 1:31	And God saw every thing that he had made, and, behold, it was very good. And the evening and the morning were the sixth day.	And God viewing all that He had created saw that it was it was good, "very good."	065-7
8	Genesis: 2:6-25	And the LORD God formed man of the dust of the ground, and breathed into his nostrils the breath of life; and man became a living soul. And the LORD God planted a garden eastward in Eden; and there he put the man whom he had formed And out of the ground made the LORD God to grow every tree that is pleasant to the sight, and good for food; the tree of life also in the midst of the garden, and the tree of knowledge of good and evil... And the LORD God caused a deep sleep to fall upon Adam, and he slept: and he took one of his ribs, and closed up the flesh instead thereof; And the rib, which the LORD God had taken from man, made he a woman, and brought her unto the man. And Adam said, This is now bone of my bones, and flesh of my flesh: she shall be called Woman, because she was taken out of Man. Therefore shall a man leave his father and his mother, and shall cleave unto his wife: and they shall be one flesh. And they were both naked, the man and his wife, and were not ashamed	Without repeating the well-known account (rather accounts, for there are two) of Creation, as given in the Bible	064-3

Where'd He Get That? A Biblical Cross-Reference To Ernest Holmes' The Science of Mind

Unique Verse Nr.	Bible Verse	Citation	Ernest Holmes reference	Page in SOM text
9	Genesis 2:19-20	And out of the ground the LORD God formed every beast of the field, and every fowl of the air; and brought them unto Adam to see what he would call them: and whatsoever Adam called every living creature, that was the name thereof. And Adam gave names to all cattle, and to the fowl of the air, and to every beast of the field;	I will let him name everything I have created	065-5
	Genesis 2:19-20	And out of the ground the LORD God formed every beast of the field, and every fowl of the air; and brought them unto Adam to see what he would call them: and whatsoever Adam called every living creature, that was the name thereof. And Adam gave names to all cattle, and to the fowl of the air, and to every beast of the field;	Adam was permitted to name all creation and man was supposed to exercise an authority over all that is below him	410-3
10	Genesis 2:22	And the rib, which the LORD God had taken from man, made he a woman, and brought her unto the man.	Eve, the woman in the case, was made from a rib of Adam.	473-5
11	Genesis 3:1-5	Now the serpent was more subtil than any beast of the field which the LORD God had made. And he said unto the woman, Yea, hath God said, Ye shall not eat of every tree of the garden? And the woman said unto the serpent, We may eat of the fruit of the trees of the garden: But of the fruit of the tree which is in the midst of the garden, God hath said, Ye shall not eat of it, neither shall ye touch it, lest ye die. And the serpent said unto the woman, Ye shall not surely die: For God doth know that in the day ye eat thereof, then your eyes shall be opened, and ye shall be as gods, knowing good and evil.	should he listen to this "tale of the serpent"	055-3
12	Genesis 3:8	And they heard the voice of the LORD God walking in the garden in the cool of the day: and Adam and his wife hid themselves from the presence of the LORD God amongst the trees of the garden.	The Voice of God, "walking in the garden in the cool of the day," means the introspective and meditative part of us	474-3
13	Genesis 3:22	And the LORD God said, Behold, the man is become as one of us, to know good and evil: and now, lest he put forth his hand, and take also of the tree of life, and eat, and live for ever:	He shall become as one of us and live forever	474-1
	Genesis 3:22	And the LORD God said, Behold, the man is become as one of us, to know good and evil: and now, lest he put forth his hand, and take also of the tree of life, and eat, and live for ever:	Fall: This is the meaning of God saying, "he shall become as one of us and live forever."	592

Where'd He Get That? A Biblical Cross-Reference To Ernest Holmes' The Science of Mind

Unique Verse Nr.	Bible Verse	Citation	Ernest Holmes reference	Page in SOM text
	Genesis 3:23-24	Therefore the LORD God sent him forth from the garden of Eden, to till the ground from whence he was taken. So he drove out the man; and he placed at the east of the garden of Eden Cherubims, and a flaming sword which turned every way, to keep the way of the tree of life.	We are reminded here of another symbol, one used in the Old Testament, that of the serpent which cast Adam and Eve out of the Garden of Eden. *NOTE: The serpent did not cast out Adam and Eve, God did. God cursed the serpent and made him eat dust all the days of his life.*	473-2
14	Genesis 7:17-24	And the flood was forty days upon the earth; and the waters increased, and bare up the ark, and it was lift up above the earth. And the waters prevailed, and were increased greatly upon the earth; and the ark went upon the face of the waters. And the waters prevailed exceedingly upon the earth; and all the high hills, that were under the whole heaven, were covered. Fifteen cubits upward did the waters prevail; and the mountains were covered. And all flesh died that moved upon the earth, both of fowl, and of cattle, and of beast, and of every creeping thing that creepeth upon the earth, and every man: All in whose nostrils was the breath of life, of all that was in the dry land, died. And every living substance was destroyed which was upon the face of the ground, both man, and cattle, and the creeping things, and the fowl of the heaven; and they were destroyed from the earth: and Noah only remained alive, and they that were with him in the ark. And the waters prevailed upon the earth an hundred and fifty days.	The meaning of the Flood or Deluge (which is recorded in every sacred scripture we have ever heard of or read)	120-3
15	Exodus 3:14	And God said unto Moses, I AM THAT I AM: and he said, Thus shalt thou say unto the children of Israel, I AM hath sent me unto you.	I AM - I AM-ness -The I AM	069-3
	Exodus 3:14	And God said unto Moses, I AM THAT I AM: and he said, Thus shalt thou say unto the children of Israel, I AM hath sent me unto you.	the day when he first said "I am"	072-3
	Exodus 3:14	And God said unto Moses, I AM THAT I AM: and he said, Thus shalt thou say unto the children of Israel, I AM hath sent me unto you.	It only knows "I AM."	157-4
	Exodus 3:14	And God said unto Moses, I AM THAT I AM: and he said, Thus shalt thou say unto the children of Israel, I AM hath sent me unto you.	God creates by contemplating His own I-AM-NESS	196-4

Where'd He Get That? A Biblical Cross-Reference To Ernest Holmes' The Science of Mind

Unique Verse Nr.	Bible Verse	Citation	Ernest Holmes reference	Page in SOM text
	Exodus 3:14	And God said unto Moses, I AM THAT I AM: and he said, Thus shalt thou say unto the children of Israel, I AM hath sent me unto you.	an incarnation of the Universal "I Am."	217-1
	Exodus 3:14	And God said unto Moses, I AM THAT I AM: and he said, Thus shalt thou say unto the children of Israel, I AM hath sent me unto you.	the soul recognizes its own I-Am-ness	220-3
	Exodus 3:14	And God said unto Moses, I AM THAT I AM: and he said, Thus shalt thou say unto the children of Israel, I AM hath sent me unto you.	every time man says "I am"	323-3
	Exodus 3:14	And God said unto Moses, I AM THAT I AM: and he said, Thus shalt thou say unto the children of Israel, I AM hath sent me unto you.	when a man says "I am"	336-2
	Exodus 3:14	And God said unto Moses, I AM THAT I AM: and he said, Thus shalt thou say unto the children of Israel, I AM hath sent me unto you.	recognizing the I-Am-ness	336-3
	Exodus 3:14	And God said unto Moses, I AM THAT I AM: and he said, Thus shalt thou say unto the children of Israel, I AM hath sent me unto you.	The greater a man's consciousness of this Indwelling I AM	344-2
	Exodus 3:14	And God said unto Moses, I AM THAT I AM: and he said, Thus shalt thou say unto the children of Israel, I AM hath sent me unto you.	To the illumined, has ever come self-realization and I-AM-NESS	367-5
	Exodus 3:14	And God said unto Moses, I AM THAT I AM: and he said, Thus shalt thou say unto the children of Israel, I AM hath sent me unto you.	"I am that I am."	372-3
	Exodus 3:14	And God said unto Moses, I AM THAT I AM: and he said, Thus shalt thou say unto the children of Israel, I AM hath sent me unto you.	this I Am appears no longer to be	374-2
	Exodus 3:14	And God said unto Moses, I AM THAT I AM: and he said, Thus shalt thou say unto the children of Israel, I AM hath sent me unto you.	The "I AM" is both individual and universal	413-1
	Exodus 3:14	And God said unto Moses, I AM THAT I AM: and he said, Thus shalt thou say unto the children of Israel, I AM hath sent me unto you.	The individual "I" is a complement to the universal "I AM."	417-3
	Exodus 3:14	And God said unto Moses, I AM THAT I AM: and he said, Thus shalt thou say unto the children of Israel, I AM hath sent me unto you.	I am that which thou art; thou art that which I am	423-3
	Exodus 3:14	And God said unto Moses, I AM THAT I AM: and he said, Thus shalt thou say unto the children of Israel, I AM hath sent me unto you.	"I Am" has a dual meaning	477-6
	Exodus 3:14	And God said unto Moses, I AM THAT I AM: and he said, Thus shalt thou say unto the children of Israel, I AM hath sent me unto you.	God was revealed to Moses as the great "I AM"	477-6
	Exodus 3:14	And God said unto Moses, I AM THAT I AM: and he said, Thus shalt thou say unto the children of Israel, I AM hath sent me unto you.	Moses taught that "I AM" is the First Principle of all life	477-6

Unique Verse Nr.	Bible Verse	Citation	Ernest Holmes reference	Page in SOM text
	Exodus 3:14	And God said unto Moses, I AM THAT I AM: and he said, Thus shalt thou say unto the children of Israel, I AM hath sent me unto you.	unto the perfect "I AM"	478-1
	Exodus 3:14	And God said unto Moses, I AM THAT I AM: and he said, Thus shalt thou say unto the children of Israel, I AM hath sent me unto you.	the individual "I" the son of the eternal "I AM."	479-5
	Exodus 3:14	And God said unto Moses, I AM THAT I AM: and he said, Thus shalt thou say unto the children of Israel, I AM hath sent me unto you.	Great Discovery:....The ability to affirm, to say "I AM," to be conscious of one's relationship to the Universe	596
16	Exodus 14:13	And Moses said unto the people, Fear ye not, stand still, and see the salvation of the LORD, which he will shew to you to day: for the Egyptians whom ye have seen to day, ye shall see them again no more for ever.	Stand still and watch the sure salvation of the Lord	217-1
	Exodus 14:13	And Moses said unto the people, Fear ye not, stand still, and see the salvation of the LORD, which he will shew to you to day: for the Egyptians whom ye have seen to day, ye shall see them again no more for ever.	Humility: "Stand still and watch the sure salvation of the Lord."	598
17	Exodus 34:29-30	And it came to pass, when Moses came down from mount Sinai with the two tables of testimony in Moses' hand, when he came down from the mount, that Moses wist not that the skin of his face shone while he talked with him. And when Aaron and all the children of Israel saw Moses, behold, the skin of his face shone; and they were afraid to come nigh him.	All mystics have seen this Cosmic Light. This is why it is said there were illumined. They have all had the same experience, whether it was Moses coming down from the mountain, . . .- where suddenly he became conscious of this light.	344-3
18	Numbers 21:8-9	And the LORD said unto Moses, Make thee a fiery serpent, and set it upon a pole: and it shall come to pass, that every one that is bitten, when he looketh upon it, shall live. And Moses made a serpent of brass, and put it upon a pole, and it came to pass, that if a serpent had bitten any man, when he beheld the serpent of brass, he lived.	When Moses lifted up the serpent, those who looked upon it were healed.	472-6
19	Deut. 6:4	Hear, O Israel: The LORD our God is one LORD:	Hear O Israel, the Lord our God is One Lord	330-2
	Deut. 6:4	Hear, O Israel: The LORD our God is one LORD:	Remember the teachings of Moses, the "god is One."	453-6
	Deut. 6:4	Hear, O Israel: The LORD our God, the LORD is one!	Unity: "The Lord our God is One God…"	640
	Deut. 6:4	Hear, O Israel: The LORD our God is one LORD: (Old Testament)	The fundamental premise upon which the philosophy of the Bible is develop is that Spirit is One.	082-3

Where'd He Get That? A Biblical Cross-Reference To Ernest Holmes' The Science of Mind

Unique Verse Nr.	Bible Verse	Citation	Ernest Holmes reference	Page in SOM text
20	Deut. 11:25-27	There shall no man be able to stand before you: for the LORD your God shall lay the fear of you and the dread of you upon all the land that ye shall tread upon, as he hath said unto you. Behold, I set before you this day a blessing and a curse; A blessing, if ye obey the commandments of the LORD your God, which I command you this day:	Moses referred to the same thing when he said that he had set a blessing and a curse before the Children of Israel	461-2
21	Joshua 24:15	And if it seem evil unto you to serve the LORD, choose you this day whom ye will serve;	they must choose whom they would serve.	461-2
22	I Samuel 3:9	Therefore Eli said unto Samuel, Go, lie down: and it shall be, if he call thee, that thou shalt say, Speak, LORD; for thy servant heareth. So Samuel went and lay down in his place.	Speak Lord for thy servant heareth	258-1
23	I Kings 19:12	And after the earthquake a fire; but the LORD was not in the fire: and after the fire a still small voice.	Little attention has been given to that still, small voice	072-4
24	II Kings 4:1-4	Now there cried a certain woman of the wives of the sons of the prophets unto Elisha, saying, Thy servant my husband is dead; and thou knowest that thy servant did fear the LORD: and the creditor is come to take unto him my two sons to be bondmen. And Elisha said unto her, What shall I do for thee? tell me, what hast thou in the house? And she said, Thine handmaid hath not any thing in the house, save a pot of oil. Then he said, Go, borrow thee vessels abroad of all thy neighbours, even empty vessels; borrow not a few. And when thou art come in, thou shalt shut the door upon thee and upon thy sons, and shalt pour out into all those vessels, and thou shalt set aside that which is full.	I bring all "the empty vessels" knowing they will be filled	557-3
25	Ezra 9:5	And at the evening sacrifice I arose up from my heaviness; and having rent my garment and my mantle, I fell upon my knees, and spread out my hands unto the LORD my God,	Jesus tears the mantle of unreality from the shoulders of hypocrisy	435-2
26	Job 14:14	If a man die, shall he live again? all the days of my appointed time will I wait, till my change come.	something rises from within and says with Job: "Though I die, yet shall I live."	108-2
27	Job 19:26	And though after my skin worms destroy this body, yet in my flesh shall I see God:	In my flesh shall I see God	330-4
	Job 19:26	And though after my skin worms destroy this body, yet in my flesh shall I see God:	"In my flesh I shall see God."	510-3
28	Job 22:28	Thou shalt also decree a thing, and it shall be established unto thee: and the light shall shine upon thy ways.	Logos: Thou shalt also decree a thing, and it shall be established unto thee."	608
29	Job 38:33	Knowest thou the ordinances of heaven? canst thou set the dominion thereof in the earth?	Love alone overcomes all and justifies the eternity of her dominion	460-3

Where'd He Get That? A Biblical Cross-Reference To Ernest Holmes' The Science of Mind

Unique Verse Nr.	Bible Verse	Citation	Ernest Holmes reference	Page in SOM text
30	Psalms 17:5	Uphold my steps in Your paths, That my footsteps may not slip.	My feet shall not falter, for they are kept upon the path of Life through the Power of the Eternal Spirit.	528-4
31	Psalms 18:26	With the pure thou wilt shew thyself pure; and with the froward thou wilt shew thyself froward.	To the pure thou wilt show thyself pure: to the froward thou wilt show thyself froward	402-3
32	Psalms 19:4	Their line is gone out through all the earth, and their words to the end of the world. In them hath he set a tabernacle for the sun,	"His lines have gone out into all places."	330-3
	Psalms 19:4	Their line is gone out through all the earth, and their words to the end of the world. In them hath he set a tabernacle for the sun,	For his lines have gone out into all places	546-2
33	Psalms 19:7	The law of the LORD is perfect, converting the soul: the testimony of the LORD is sure, making wise the simple.	The law of the Lord is perfect	054-1
	Psalms 19:7	The law of the LORD is perfect, converting the soul: the testimony of the LORD is sure, making wise the simple.	"The Law of the Lord is perfect."	522-1
34	Psalms 23:3	He restoreth my soul: he leadeth me in the paths of righteousness for his name's sake.	Do ultimately compel experience into the path of true righteousness	270-1
35	Psalms 23:4	Yea, though I walk through the valley of the shadow of death, I will fear no evil: for thou art with me; thy rod and thy staff they comfort me.	"I will fear no evil, for Thou art with me."	529-4
	Psalms 23:4	Yea, though I walk through the valley of the shadow of death, I will fear no evil: for thou art with me; thy rod and thy staff they comfort me.	"I will fear no evil, for Thou art with me."	533-2
36	Psalms 23:6	Surely goodness and mercy shall follow me all the days of my life: and I will dwell in the house of the LORD for ever.	Only good and loving-kindness shall "follow me all the days of my life."	039-4
	Psalms 23:6	Surely goodness and mercy shall follow me all the days of my life: and I will dwell in the house of the LORD for ever.	And joy shall accompany us through the ages yet to come.	514-3
37	Psalms 31:3	For You are my rock and my fortress; Therefore, for Your name's sake, Lead me and guide me.	Command my soul to turn to Thee for guidance and light	537-2
38	Psalms 33:9	For he spake, and it was done; he commanded, and it stood fast.	He spake and it was done	068-5
	Psalms 33:9	For he spake, and it was done; he commanded, and it stood fast.	GOD SPEAKS AND IT IS DONE!	069-3
39	Psalms 42:7	Deep calls unto deep at the noise of Your waterfalls; All Your waves and billows have gone over me.	As deep cries unto deep, so my thought cries unto Thee and Thou dost answer	550-1
40	Psalms 46:10	Be still, and know that I am God: I will be exalted among the heathen, I will be exalted in the earth.	Be still and know that I am God.	264-4
	Psalms 46:10	Be still, and know that I am God: I will be exalted among the heathen, I will be exalted in the earth.	to be still and know that the inner light shines	369-1
	Psalms 46:10	Be still, and know that I am God: I will be exalted among the heathen, I will be exalted in the earth.	"Be still and know that I am god."	514-2

Where'd He Get That? A Biblical Cross-Reference To Ernest Holmes' The Science of Mind

Unique Verse Nr.	Bible Verse	Citation	Ernest Holmes reference	Page in SOM text
41	Psalms 51:1	Have mercy upon me, O God, according to thy lovingkindness: according unto the multitude of thy tender mercies blot out my transgressions.	"I will blot out their transgressions and remember them no longer against them	412-2
42	Psalms 51:6	Behold, You desire truth in the inward parts, And in the hidden part You will make me to know wisdom.	Compel me to follow the course of Truth and Wisdom	537-2
43	Psalms 66:18	If I regard iniquity in my heart, the Lord will not hear me:	The entire world is suffering from one big fear...the fear that God will not answer our prayers	156-3
44	Psalms 73:24	You will guide me with Your counsel, And afterward receive me to glory.	Compel me to follow Thee and let me not pursue the paths of my own counsel.	550-1
45	Psalms 78:8	And might not be as their fathers, a stubborn and rebellious generation; a generation that set not their heart aright, and whose spirit was not stedfast with God.	Prays aright	158-1
	Psalms 78:8	And might not be as their fathers, a stubborn and rebellious generation; a generation that set not their heart aright, and whose spirit was not stedfast with God.	To pray aright	281-2
	Psalms 78:8	And might not be as their fathers, a stubborn and rebellious generation; a generation that set not their heart aright, and whose spirit was not stedfast with God.	We do not "pray aright" when we are in opposition	436-1
46	Psalms 78:41 and Hebrews 4:6	Heb 4:6 Seeing therefore it remaineth that some must enter therein, and they to whom it was first preached entered not in because of unbelief: Ps 78:41 Yea, they turned back and tempted God, and limited the Holy One of Israel.	"They could not enter because of their unbelief, and because they limited the Holy One of Israel."	128-1
	Psalms 78:41 and Hebrews 4:6	Heb 4:6 Seeing therefore it remaineth that some must enter therein, and they to whom it was first preached entered not in because of unbelief: Ps 78:41 Yea, they turned back and tempted God, and limited the Holy One of Israel.	"They could not enter because of their unbelief," and because they "limited the Holy One of Israel."	304-3
	Psalms 78:41 and Hebrews 4:6	Heb 4:6 Seeing therefore it remaineth that some must enter therein, and they to whom it was first preached entered not in because of unbelief: Ps 78:41 Yea, they turned back and tempted God, and limited the Holy One of Israel.	They could not enter because of their unbelief, and because they limited the Holy One of Israel	405-2
47	Psalms 82:6	I have said, Ye are gods; and all of you are children of the most High.	I have said, Ye are Gods and all of you are the children of the most high	333-5
	Psalms 82:6	I have said, Ye are gods; and all of you are children of the most High.	I have said, Ye are Gods and all of you are the children of the most high	364-2
48	Psalms 85:13	Righteousness will go before Him, And shall make His footsteps our pathway.	I will follow Thy footsteps and learn of Thee all the wondrous secrets of Life	537-4
49	Psalms 91:1	He that dwelleth in the secret place of the most High shall abide under the shadow of the Almighty.	The secret place of the Most High	169-3

Where'd He Get That? A Biblical Cross-Reference To Ernest Holmes' The Science of Mind

Unique Verse Nr.	Bible Verse	Citation	Ernest Holmes reference	Page in SOM text
	Psalms 91:1	He that dwelleth in the secret place of the most High shall abide under the shadow of the Almighty.	"Heavenly Consciousness" which is the "secret place of the Most High" in man	218-1
	Psalms 91:1	He that dwelleth in the secret place of the most High shall abide under the shadow of the Almighty.	Shall we not learn to enter the "secret place of the Most High"	431-5
	Psalms 91:1	He that dwelleth in the secret place of the most High shall abide under the shadow of the Almighty.	I have found that the Secret Place of God is within my own Soul	516-2
	Psalms 91:1	He that dwelleth in the secret place of the most High shall abide under the shadow of the Almighty.	And I enter into "The Secret Place of The Most High."	527-1
	Psalms 91:1	He that dwelleth in the secret place of the most High shall abide under the shadow of the Almighty.	Joy awaits upon me in the "Secret Place of the Most High."	536-3
50	Psalms 102:7	I watch, and am as a sparrow alone upon the house top	"His eye is on the sparrow and I know He watches me."	515-2
51	Psalms 103:1	Bless the LORD, O my soul; And all that is within me, bless His holy name!	"Bless the Lord, O my Soul, and all that is within me, bless His holy Name."	534-2
52	Psalms 121:1	I will lift up mine eyes unto the hills, from whence cometh my help.	I will lift up my eyes unto God from whom comes my perfect sight	231-3
53	Psalms 121:4	Behold, He who keeps Israel Shall neither slumber nor sleep.	"He who neither slumbers or sleeps"	538-2
54	Psalms 145:16	Thou openest thine hand, and satisfiest the desire of every living thing.	"He openeth his hand and satisfieth the desire of every living thing."	157-3
55	Proverbs 2:9	Then you will understand righteousness and justice, Equity and every good path.	Guide Thou my feet; compel my way; direct my paths and me in Thy Presence.	529-1
56	Proverbs 3:17	Her ways are ways of pleasantness, and all her paths are peace.	With Solomon are we happy when we find Wisdom, for "Her ways are ways of pleasantness and all her paths are peace."	495-2
57	Proverbs 4:23	Keep thy heart with all diligence; for out of it are the issues of life.	Keep thy heart with all diligence; for out of it are the issues of life.	238-4
58	Proverbs 11:17	The merciful man doeth good to his own soul: but he that is cruel troubleth his own flesh.	He that is cruel troubleth his own flesh	232-3
59	Proverbs 23:7	For as he thinketh in his heart, so is he: Eat and drink, saith he to thee; but his heart is not with thee.	As a man thinketh in his heart, so is he.	137-1
60	Eccl. 7:29	Lo, this only have I found, that God hath made man upright; but they have sought out many inventions.	The Scriptures say: "God hath made man upright; but they have sought out many inventions."	196-1
	Eccl. 7:29	Lo, this only have I found, that God hath made man upright; but they have sought out many inventions.	God hath made man upright; but they have sought out many inventions.	310-4
	Eccl. 7:29	Lo, this only have I found, that God hath made man upright; but they have sought out many inventions.	Inventions of the human mind	310-4
	Eccl. 7:29	Lo, this only have I found, that God hath made man upright; but they have sought out many inventions.	In the beginning God made man perfect, but he has sought out many inventions.	310-4
61	Isaiah 7:9	If ye be not firm in faith, ye shall surely not be made firm. [The Bible, English Standard Version]	"Be firm and ye shall be made firm"	307-3

Where'd He Get That? A Biblical Cross-Reference To Ernest Holmes' The Science of Mind

Unique Verse Nr.	Bible Verse	Citation	Ernest Holmes reference	Page in SOM text
62	Isaiah 40:31	But those who wait on the LORD Shall renew their strength; They shall mount up with wings like eagles, They shall run and not be weary, They shall walk and not faint	In thy Strength do I daily walk and live;	542-2
63	Isaiah 42:16	And I will bring the blind by a way that they knew not; I will lead them in paths that they have not known: I will make darkness light before them, and crooked things straight. These things will I do unto them, and not forsake them.	Therefore, the road is made straight before me	559-3
64	Isaiah 45.5-7	The Old Testament establishes God as First Cause: I am the LORD, and there is none else, there is no God beside me: I girded thee, though thou hast not known me: That they may know from the rising of the sun, and from the west, that there is none beside me. I am the LORD, and there is none else. form the light, and create darkness: I make peace, and create evil: I the LORD do all these things. NOTE: Jesus did not say anything about First Cause.	Therefore, we may read Buddha, Jesus, Plato, Socrates, Aristotle, Swedenborg, Emerson, Whitman, Browning or any of the other great mystics, no matter in what age they have lived, and we shall find the same Ultimate [First Cause].	342-1
65	Isaiah 45:22	Look unto me, and be ye saved, all the ends of the earth: for I am God, and there is none else.	Look unto me and be ye saved, all the ends of the earth.	185-3
66	Isaiah 50:5	The Lord GOD hath opened mine ear, and I was not rebellious, neither turned away back.	The Lord Jehovah hath opened thine ear	257-6
67	Isaiah 55:11	So shall my word be that goeth forth out of my mouth: it shall not return unto me void, but it shall accomplish that which I please, and it shall prosper in the thing whereto I sent it.	That, unto where it was sent	057-1
	Isaiah 55:11	So shall my word be that goeth forth out of my mouth: it shall not return unto me void, but it shall accomplish that which I please, and it shall prosper in the thing whereto I sent it.	So shall my word that goeth forth not return unto me void.	146-3
	Isaiah 55:11	So shall my word be that goeth forth out of my mouth: it shall not return unto me void, but it shall accomplish that which I please, and it shall prosper in the thing whereto I sent it.	that his word is the law of that whereunto it was spoken	169-3
	Isaiah 55:11	So shall my word be that goeth forth out of my mouth: it shall not return unto me void, but it shall accomplish that which I please, and it shall prosper in the thing whereto I sent it.	that our word has accomplished "that, whereunto it was sent."	176-1
	Isaiah 55:11	So shall my word be that goeth forth out of my mouth: it shall not return unto me void, but it shall accomplish that which I please, and it shall prosper in the thing whereto I sent it.	This word is the law unto the thing whereunto it is spoken	184-3

Where'd He Get That? A Biblical Cross-Reference To Ernest Holmes' The Science of Mind

Unique Verse Nr.	Bible Verse	Citation	Ernest Holmes reference	Page in SOM text
	Isaiah 55:11	So shall my word be that goeth forth out of my mouth: it shall not return unto me void, but it shall accomplish that which I please, and it shall prosper in the thing whereto I sent it.	The Law unto the thing whereto they are spoken	188-2
	Isaiah 55:11	So shall my word be that goeth forth out of my mouth: it shall not return unto me void, but it shall accomplish that which I please, and it shall prosper in the thing whereto I sent it.	Your word is the law unto the thing unto which it is spoken	203-3
	Isaiah 55:11	So shall my word be that goeth forth out of my mouth: it shall not return unto me void, but it shall accomplish that which I please, and it shall prosper in the thing whereto I sent it.	So shall my word be that goeth forth out of my mouth: it shall not return unto me void	212-2
	Isaiah 55:11	So shall my word be that goeth forth out of my mouth: it shall not return unto me void, but it shall accomplish that which I please, and it shall prosper in the thing whereto I sent it.	This word is the law unto the thing whereunto it is spoken	216-2
	Isaiah 55:11	So shall my word be that goeth forth out of my mouth: it shall not return unto me void, but it shall accomplish that which I please, and it shall prosper in the thing whereto I sent it.	the words he uses are the Law unto the thing whereto they are spoken	262-2
	Isaiah 55:11	So shall my word be that goeth forth out of my mouth: it shall not return unto me void, but it shall accomplish that which I please, and it shall prosper in the thing whereto I sent it.	it is the law unto that thing where unto it is spoken	263-4
	Isaiah 55:11	So shall my word be that goeth forth out of my mouth: it shall not return unto me void, but it shall accomplish that which I please, and it shall prosper in the thing whereto I sent it.	Our word becomes a law unto the thing for which it is spoken	304-1
	Isaiah 55:11	So shall my word be that goeth forth out of my mouth: it shall not return unto me void, but it shall accomplish that which I please, and it shall prosper in the thing whereto I sent it.	"So shall my word be that goeth forth out of my mouth--it shall prosper."	307-3
	Isaiah 55:11	So shall my word be that goeth forth out of my mouth: it shall not return unto me void, but it shall accomplish that which I please, and it shall prosper in the thing whereto I sent it.	My word comes back to me laden with the fruits of its own speech	543-3
	Isaiah 55:11	So shall my word be that goeth forth out of my mouth: it shall not return unto me void, but it shall accomplish that which I please, and it shall prosper in the thing whereto I sent it.	The Word of my mouth shall bear fruit. It shall accomplish and prosper, and shall not return unto me void.	544-2
	Isaiah 55:11	So shall my word be that goeth forth out of my mouth: it shall not return unto me void, but it shall accomplish that which I please, and it shall prosper in the thing whereto I sent it.	My Word is the law unto the thing whereunto it is sent, and it cannot come back empty-handed	544-2
	Isaiah 55:11	So shall my word be that goeth forth out of my mouth: it shall not return unto me void, but it shall accomplish that which I please, and it shall prosper in the thing whereto I sent it.	My Word is the law unto the thing whereunto it is spoken	544-2

Where'd He Get That? A Biblical Cross-Reference To Ernest Holmes' The Science of Mind

Unique Verse Nr.	Bible Verse	Citation	Ernest Holmes reference	Page in SOM text
	Isaiah 58:11	And the LORD shall guide thee continually, and satisfy thy soul in drought, and make fat thy bones: and thou shalt be like a watered garden, and like a spring of water, whose waters fail not.	Lord: "And the Lord shall guide thee continually"	608
68	Isaiah 65:24	And it shall come to pass, that before they call, I will answer; and while they are yet speaking, I will hear.	Before they call, I will answer	153-2
	Isaiah 65:24	And it shall come to pass, that before they call, I will answer; and while they are yet speaking, I will hear.	Before they call, I will answer is the divine promise	174-2
	Isaiah 65:24	And it shall come to pass, that before they call, I will answer; and while they are yet speaking, I will hear.	Before they call, I will answer	289-4
	Isaiah 65:24	And it shall come to pass, that before they call, I will answer; and while they are yet speaking, I will hear.	Desire: "Before they call, will I answer."	584
	Isaiah 65:24	And it shall come to pass, that before they call, I will answer; and while they are yet speaking, I will hear.	Thanksgiving: "before they ask will I answer"	637
69	Jeremiah 23:24	Can any hide himself in secret places that I shall not see him? saith the LORD. Do not I fill heaven and earth? saith the LORD.	There is no place where God is not.	330-3
70	Jeremiah 31:34	And they shall teach no more every man his neighbour, and every man his brother, saying, Know the LORD: for they shall all know me, from the least of them unto the greatest of them, saith the LORD: for I will forgive their iniquity, and I will remember their sin no more.	We should learn to let go of our mistakes and remember them no longer against ourselves.	502-2
71	Jeremiah 33:2-3	Thus saith the LORD the maker thereof, the LORD that formed it, to establish it; the LORD is his name; Call unto me, and I will answer thee, and shew thee great and mighty things, which thou knowest not.	In that day they call upon me, I will answer	148-4
72	Ezekiel 3:10	Moreover he said unto me, Son of man, all my words that I shall speak unto thee receive in thine heart, and hear with thine ears.	Illumination: "Speak to Him, thou, for He hears."	599
73	Zechariah 2:10	Sing and rejoice, O daughter of Zion: for, lo, I come, and I will dwell in the midst of thee, saith the LORD.	"I Am is in the midst of thee"	413-3
74	Malachi 1:9	9And now, I pray you, beseech God that he will be gracious unto us: this hath been by your means:	The Seal of Approval is upon me	526-4
75	Malachi 3:8	Will a man rob God? Yet ye have robbed me. But ye say, Wherein have we robbed thee? In tithes and offerings.	Robbing God	036-1
76	Malachi 3:10	Bring ye all the tithes into the storehouse, that there may be meat in mine house, and prove me now herewith, saith the LORD of hosts, if I will not open you the windows of heaven, and pour you out a blessing, that there shall not be room enough to receive it.	Prove me now herewith, saith the Lord of Hosts, if I will not open you the windows of heaven, and pour you out a blessing, that there shall not be room to receive it.	307-3

Unique Verse Nr.	Bible Verse	Citation	Ernest Holmes reference	Page in SOM text
		NEW TESTAMENT		
77	Matthew 1:23	Behold, a virgin shall be with child, and shall bring forth a son, and they shall call his name Emmanuel, which being interpreted is, God with us.	Emmanuel or God with us	113-1
78	Matthew 3:2	And saying, Repent ye: for the kingdom of heaven is at hand.	Behold! The Kingdom of Heaven is at hand.	217-2
	Matthew 3:2	And saying, Repent ye: for the kingdom of heaven is at hand.	Look out and see Thy good. It is not afar off, but is at hand	512-3
	Matthew 3:2	And saying, Repent ye: for the kingdom of heaven is at hand.	I shall not doubt nor fear, for my salvation is from On High, and the day of its appearing is now at hand.	521-3
79	Matthew 3:17	And lo a voice from heaven, saying, This is my beloved Son, in whom I am well pleased.	there is a voice ever proclaiming: "This is my Beloved Son."	367-1
80	Matthew 4:4	But he answered and said, It is written, Man shall not live by bread alone, but by every word that proceedeth out of the mouth of God.	It is written that man shall not live by bread alone, but by every word that proceedeth out of the mouth of God.	427-3
81	Matthew 4:17	From that time Jesus began to preach, and to say, Repent: for the kingdom of heaven is at hand.	Behold! The Kingdom of Heaven is at hand.	217-2
82	Matthew 5:5	Blessed are the meek: for they shall inherit the earth.	The meek shall inherit the earth	427-5
83	Matthew 5:6	Blessed are they which do hunger and thirst after righteousness: for they shall be filled.	Blessed are they who hunger and thirst after righteousness (right living) for they shall be filled	223-2
	Matthew 5:6	Blessed are they which do hunger and thirst after righteousness: for they shall be filled.	They who hunger and thirst after righteousness shall be filled.	428-4
84	Matthew 5:7	Blessed are the merciful: for they shall obtain mercy.	Blessed are the merciful; for they shall obtain mercy	429-1
85	Matthew 5:8	Blessed are the pure in heart: for they shall see God.	Blessed are the pure in heart: for they shall see God.	240-2
	Matthew 5:8	Blessed are the pure in heart: for they shall see God.	The pure in heart shall see God	429-4
86	Matthew 5:9	Blessed are the peacemakers: for they shall be called the children of God.	The peacemakers are called the children of God	429-5
87	Matthew 5:14	Ye are the light of the world. A city that is set on an hill cannot be hid.	Ye are the light of the world	362-4
	Matthew 5:14	Ye are the light of the world. A city that is set on an hill cannot be hid.	Ye are the light of the world	430-2
88	Matthew 5:23-24	Therefore if thou bring thy gift to the altar, and there rememberest that thy brother hath ought against thee; Leave there thy gift before the altar, and go thy way; first be reconciled to thy brother, and then come and offer thy gift.	Therefore if thou bring thy gift to the altar, and there rememberest that thy brother hath ought against thee; leave there thy gift before the altar, and go thy way; first be reconciled to thy brother, and then come and offer thy gift.	285-4
89	Matthew 5:26	Verily I say unto thee, Thou shalt by no means come out thence, till thou hast paid the uttermost farthing.	There is a Law in the Universe which exacts the uttermost farthing	032-3
	Matthew 5:26	Verily I say unto thee, Thou shalt by no means come out thence, till thou hast paid the uttermost farthing.	BUT THE LAST FARTHING IS PAID WHEN WE LET GO AND TRUST IN THE LAW OF GOOD.	502-3

Where'd He Get That? A Biblical Cross-Reference To Ernest Holmes' The Science of Mind

Unique Verse Nr.	Bible Verse	Citation	Ernest Holmes reference	Page in SOM text
90	Matthew 5:39	But I say unto you, That ye resist not evil: but whosoever shall smite thee on thy right cheek, turn to him the other also.	When Jesus said: "Resist not"	303-2
	Matthew 5:39	But I say unto you, That ye resist not evil: but whosoever shall smite thee on thy right cheek, turn to him the other also.	Jesus tells us to resist not evil	430-5
91	Matthew 5:44	But I say unto you, Love your enemies, bless them that curse you, do good to them that hate you, and pray for them which despitefully use you, and persecute you;	Jesus tells us...to love our enemies	430-5
92	Matthew 5:45	That ye may be the children of your Father which is in heaven: for he maketh his sun to rise on the evil and on the good, and sendeth rain on the just and on the unjust.	God "maketh His sun to rise on the evil and on the good, and sendeth rain on the just and on the unjust."	028-1
	Matthew 5:45	That ye may be the children of your Father which is in heaven: for he maketh his sun to rise on the evil and on the good, and sendeth rain on the just and on the unjust.	Judgment: "He sendeth rain on the just and on the unjust."	603
93	Matthew 5:48	Be ye therefore perfect, even as your Father which is in heaven is perfect.	Be ye therefore perfect, even as your Father...	053-5
	Matthew 5:48	Be ye therefore perfect, even as your Father which is in heaven is perfect.	Be ye therefore perfect, even as your Father...	185-2
	Matthew 5:48	Be ye therefore perfect, even as your Father which is in heaven is perfect.	Today my body responds to the Divine Behest: "Be perfect."	549-1
94	Matthew 6:4	so that your giving may be in secret. Then your Father, who sees what is done in secret, will reward you.	The Father who seeth in secret	430-6
95	Matthew 6:6	But thou, when thou prayest, enter into thy closet, and when thou hast shut thy door, pray to thy Father which is in secret; and thy Father which seeth in secret shall reward thee openly.	Pray to Father who is in secret	217-2
	Matthew 6:6	But thou, when thou prayest, enter into thy closet, and when thou hast shut thy door, pray to thy Father which is in secret; and thy Father which seeth in secret shall reward thee openly.	And this Father who seeth in secret	431-1
	Matthew 6:6	But thou, when thou prayest, enter into thy closet, and when thou hast shut thy door, pray to thy Father which is in secret; and thy Father which seeth in secret shall reward thee openly.	Our prayers are to be made to God in the secret place of our own being.	431-1
	Matthew 6:6	But thou, when thou prayest, enter into thy closet, and when thou hast shut thy door, pray to thy Father which is in secret; and thy Father which seeth in secret shall reward thee openly.	Silence: We enter the inner chamber of our mind and close the door on all discord and confusion	633
96	Matthew 6:9	After this manner therefore pray ye: Our Father which art in heaven, Hallowed be thy name.	Our Father which art in heaven	343-4
	Matthew 6:9	After this manner therefore pray ye: Our Father which art in heaven, Hallowed be thy name.	Our Father which art in heaven	365-2

Where'd He Get That? A Biblical Cross-Reference To Ernest Holmes' The Science of Mind

Unique Verse Nr.	Bible Verse	Citation	Ernest Holmes reference	Page in SOM text
	Matthew 6:9	After this manner therefore pray ye: Our Father which art in heaven, Hallowed be thy name.	We cannot come unto the "Father Which Art in Heaven"	422-3
97	Matthew 6:10	Thy kingdom come, Thy will be done in earth, as it is in heaven.	Thy will be done	268-4
	Matthew 6:10	Thy kingdom come, Thy will be done in earth, as it is in heaven.	Compel my will to do thy bidding	536-4
	Matthew 6:10	Thy kingdom come, Thy will be done in earth, as it is in heaven.	O Spirit of Life, control my every action and thought	537-4
98	Matthew 6:11	Give us this day our daily bread.	Jesus said, "Give us this day our daily bread'"	286-1
99	Matthew 6:14-15	For if ye forgive men their trespasses, your heavenly Father will also forgive you: But if ye forgive not men their trespasses, neither will your Father forgive your trespasses.	We are told God will forgive us after we have forgiven others.	431-4
100	Matthew 6:20	But lay up for yourselves treasures in heaven, where neither moth nor rust doth corrupt, and where thieves do not break through nor steal:	Our treasure is already in heaven	432-1
101	Matthew 6:22-23	The light of the body is the eye: if therefore thine eye be single, thy whole body shall be full of light. But if thine eye be evil, thy whole body shall be full of darkness. If therefore the light that is in thee be darkness, how great is that darkness!	The Single Eye –	xv
	Matthew 6:22-23	The light of the body is the eye: if therefore thine eye be single, thy whole body shall be full of light. But if thine eye be evil, thy whole body shall be full of darkness. If therefore the light that is in thee be darkness, how great is that darkness!	The mind and body must be kept pure – must be kept "single"	229-5
	Matthew 6:22-23	The light of the body is the eye: if therefore thine eye be single, thy whole body shall be full of light. But if thine eye be evil, thy whole body shall be full of darkness. If therefore the light that is in thee be darkness, how great is that darkness!	"If our eye is single, we shall be filled with light."	432-2
	Matthew 6:22-23	The light of the body is the eye: if therefore thine eye be single, thy whole body shall be full of light. But if thine eye be evil, thy whole body shall be full of darkness. If therefore the light that is in thee be darkness, how great is that darkness!	Duality: "If the eye is "single" to the good, if the vision remains steadfast, we become one with it.	587
102	Matthew 6:26	Behold the fowls of the air: for they sow not, neither do they reap, nor gather into barns; yet your heavenly Father feedeth them. Are ye not much better than they?	birds, who do not gather into barns	432-2
103	Matthew 6:27	Which of you by taking thought can add one cubit unto his stature?	Who by taking thought can add one cubit to his stature?	194-3
	Matthew 6:27	Which of you by taking thought can add one cubit unto his stature?	By taking thought, you do not add one cubit to Reality	489-3
104	Matthew 6:28	And why take ye thought for raiment? Consider the lilies of the field, how they grow; they toil not, neither do they spin:	They toil not nor do they spin.	432-2

Where'd He Get That? A Biblical Cross-Reference To Ernest Holmes' The Science of Mind

Unique Verse Nr.	Bible Verse	Citation	Ernest Holmes reference	Page in SOM text
105	Matthew 6:28-29	And why take ye thought for raiment? Consider the lilies of the field, how they grow; they toil not, neither do they spin: And yet I say unto you, That even Solomon in all his glory was not arrayed like one of these.	"Consider the lilies of the field, they toil not neither do they spin, yet…Solomon in all his glory was not arrayed as one of these."	556-6
106	Matthew 6:33	But seek ye first the kingdom of God, and his righteousness; and all these things shall be added unto you.	But we are to seek the kingdom first	432-3
	Matthew 6:33	But seek ye first the kingdom of God, and his righteousness; and all these things shall be added unto you.	And Jesus tells us to seek the Kingdom of God first and that all else will be added unto us.	490-1
107	Matthew 7:1,2	Judge not, that ye be not judged. For with what judgment ye judge, ye shall be judged: and with what measure ye mete, it shall be measured to you again.	It must be measured out to us according to our own measuring.	280-2
	Matthew 7:1,2	Judge not, that ye be not judged. For with what judgment ye judge, ye shall be judged: and with what measure ye mete, it shall be measured to you again.	Judge not that ye be not judged, for with what judgment ye judge ye shall be judged, and with what measure ye mete, it shall be measured to you again.	433-2
	Matthew 7:1,2	Judge not, that ye be not judged. For with what judgment ye judge, ye shall be judged: and with what measure ye mete, it shall be measured to you again.	Judgment: "Judge not that ye be not judged, for with what judgment ye judge, ye shall be judged."	603
108	Matthew 7:7	Ask, and it shall be given you; seek, and ye shall find; knock, and it shall be opened unto you:	And I say unto you, ask and it shall be given unto you.	157-3
	Matthew 7:7	Ask, and it shall be given you; seek, and ye shall find; knock, and it shall be opened unto you:	It shall be opened to us when we knock	435-3
109	Matthew 7:9	Or what man is there of you, whom if his son ask bread, will he give him a stone?	They have not received a stone when they asked for bread	428-5
110	Matthew 7:17,18	Even so every good tree bringeth forth good fruit; but a corrupt tree bringeth forth evil fruit. A good tree cannot bring forth evil fruit, neither can a corrupt tree bring forth good fruit.	Good thoughts and a good harvest	448-5
111	Matthew 7:21	Not every one that saith unto me, Lord, Lord, shall enter into the kingdom of heaven; but he that doeth the will of my Father which is in heaven.	It is not everyone who says "Lord, Lord," who enters the kingdom of harmony;	436-3
	Matthew 7:21	Not every one that saith unto me, Lord, Lord, shall enter into the kingdom of heaven; but he that doeth the will of my Father which is in heaven.	Not everyone who says Lord, Lord, but those who do the will of Truth, enter in.	499-5
112	Matthew 7:24	Therefore whosoever heareth these sayings of mine, and doeth them, I will liken him unto a wise man, which built his house upon a rock:	The wise man builds his house on the solid rock of Truth	436-5
113	Matthew 8:8	The centurion answered and said, Lord, I am not worthy that thou shouldest come under my roof: but speak the word only, and my servant shall be healed.	The Centurion would not allow Jesus to come to his house, but asked him to speak the word only.	437-2

Unique Verse Nr.	Bible Verse	Citation	Ernest Holmes reference	Page in SOM text
	Matthew 8:8	The centurion answered and said, Lord, I am not worthy that thou shouldest come under my roof: but speak the word only, and my servant shall be healed.	"Speak the word only, and my servant shall be healed."	437-3
114	Matthew 8:10	When Jesus heard it, he marveled, and said to them that followed, Verily I say unto you, I have not found so great faith, no, not in Israel.	Jesus said, "I have not found so great faith, no, not in all Israel."	161-1
	Matthew 8:10	When Jesus heard it, he marveled, and said to them that followed, Verily I say unto you, I have not found so great faith, no, not in Israel.	no wonder Jesus marveled at his faith	437-3
115	Matthew 8:13	And Jesus said unto the centurion, Go thy way; and as thou hast believed, so be it done unto thee. And his servant was healed in the selfsame hour.	It Is Done Unto Us	x
	Matthew 8:13	And Jesus said unto the centurion, Go thy way; and as thou hast believed, so be it done unto thee. And his servant was healed in the selfsame hour.	It is done unto you as you believe	037-1
	Matthew 8:13	And Jesus said unto the centurion, Go thy way; and as thou hast believed, so be it done unto thee. And his servant was healed in the selfsame hour.	AS MUCH AS WE CAN BELIEVE will be done unto us	038-1
	Matthew 8:13	And Jesus said unto the centurion, Go thy way; and as thou hast believed, so be it done unto thee. And his servant was healed in the selfsame hour.	It is done unto you AS you believe.	140-2
	Matthew 8:13	And Jesus said unto the centurion, Go thy way; and as thou hast believed, so be it done unto thee. And his servant was healed in the selfsame hour.	It is done unto you as you believe.	157-4
	Matthew 8:13	And Jesus said unto the centurion, Go thy way; and as thou hast believed, so be it done unto thee. And his servant was healed in the selfsame hour.	Go thy way; and as thou hast believed, so be it done unto thee.	161-1
	Matthew 8:13	And Jesus said unto the centurion, Go thy way; and as thou hast believed, so be it done unto thee. And his servant was healed in the selfsame hour.	"It is done unto you as you believe."	301-2
	Matthew 8:13	And Jesus said unto the centurion, Go thy way; and as thou hast believed, so be it done unto thee. And his servant was healed in the selfsame hour.	As thou hast believed, so be it done.	307-3
	Matthew 8:13	And Jesus said unto the centurion, Go thy way; and as thou hast believed, so be it done unto thee. And his servant was healed in the selfsame hour.	Go thy way; and as thou hast believed, so be it done unto thee.	437-3
	Matthew 8:13	And Jesus said unto the centurion, Go thy way; and as thou hast believed, so be it done unto thee. And his servant was healed in the selfsame hour.	"It is done unto us as we believe."	466-3
	Matthew 8:13	And Jesus said unto the centurion, Go thy way; and as thou hast believed, so be it done unto thee. And his servant was healed in the selfsame hour.	Knowledge: "It is done unto us as we believe."	604

Where'd He Get That? A Biblical Cross-Reference To Ernest Holmes' The Science of Mind

Unique Verse Nr.	Bible Verse	Citation	Ernest Holmes reference	Page in SOM text
116	Matthew 9:2	And, behold, they brought to him a man sick of the palsy, lying on a bed: and Jesus seeing their faith said unto the sick of the palsy; Son, be of good cheer; thy sins be forgiven thee.	This explains why Jesus said: "Thy sins be forgiven thee."	237-2
117	Matthew 9:5,6	For whether is easier, to say, Thy sins be forgiven thee; or to say, Arise, and walk? But that ye may know that the Son of man hath power on earth to forgive sins, (then saith he to the sick of the palsy,) Arise, take up thy bed, and go unto thine house.	Why is it that Jesus could say to the paralyzed man, "Take up thy bed and walk"?	281-3
	Matthew 9:5,6	For whether is easier, to say, Thy sins be forgiven thee; or to say, Arise, and walk? But that ye may know that the Son of man hath power on earth to forgive sins, (then saith he to the sick of the palsy,) Arise, take up thy bed, and go unto thine house.	Jesus Forgives a Man and Heals Him	437-5
	Matthew 9:5,6	For whether is easier, to say, Thy sins be forgiven thee; or to say, Arise, and walk? But that ye may know that the Son of man hath power on earth to forgive sins, (then saith he to the sick of the palsy,) Arise, take up thy bed, and go unto thine house.	For whether is easier, to say, Thy sins be forgiven thee; or to say, Arise, take up thy bed, and go unto thine house.	438-1
118	Matthew 9:16,17	No man putteth a piece of new cloth unto an old garment, for that which is put in to fill it up taketh from the garment, and the rent is made worse. Neither do men put new wine into old bottles: else the bottles break, and the wine runneth out, and the bottles perish: but they put new wine into new bottles, and both are preserved.	No man puts a piece of new cloth on an old garment or new wine into old bottles	439-2
119	Matthew 9:20	And, behold, a woman, which was diseased with an issue of blood twelve years, came behind him, and touched the hem of his garment:	And, behold, a woman, which was diseased with an issue of blood twelve years, came behind him, and touched the hem of his garment:	439-4
120	Matthew 9:21	For she said within herself, If I may but touch his garment, I shall be whole.	For she said within herself, If I may but touch his garment, I shall be whole.	439-4
121	Matthew 9:22	But Jesus turned him about, and when he saw her, he said, Daughter, be of good comfort; thy faith hath made thee whole. And the woman was made whole from that hour.	And the woman was made whole from that hour	439-4
122	Matthew 9:27-29	And when Jesus departed thence, two blind men followed him, crying, and saying, Thou Son of David, have mercy on us. And when he was come into the house, the blind men came to him: and Jesus saith unto them, Believe ye that I am able to do this? They said unto him, Yea, Lord. Then touched he their eyes, saying, According to your faith be it unto you.	According to our beliefs and faith	032-1

Unique Verse Nr.	Bible Verse	Citation	Ernest Holmes reference	Page in SOM text
	Matthew 9:27-29	And when Jesus departed thence, two blind men followed him, crying, and saying, Thou Son of David, have mercy on us. And when he was come into the house, the blind men came to him: and Jesus saith unto them, Believe ye that I am able to do this? They said unto him, Yea, Lord. Then touched he their eyes, saying, According to your faith be it unto you.	Jesus said: "As thou has believed, so be it done unto thee"	127-1
	Matthew 9:27-29	And when Jesus departed thence, two blind men followed him, crying, and saying, Thou Son of David, have mercy on us. And when he was come into the house, the blind men came to him: and Jesus saith unto them, Believe ye that I am able to do this? They said unto him, Yea, Lord. Then touched he their eyes, saying, According to your faith be it unto you.	It is done unto us	280-1
	Matthew 9:27-29	And when Jesus departed thence, two blind men followed him, crying, and saying, Thou Son of David, have mercy on us. And when he was come into the house, the blind men came to him: and Jesus saith unto them, Believe ye that I am able to do this? They said unto him, Yea, Lord. Then touched he their eyes, saying, According to your faith be it unto you.	According to your faith	280-2
	Matthew 9:27-29	And when Jesus departed thence, two blind men followed him, crying, and saying, Thou Son of David, have mercy on us. And when he was come into the house, the blind men came to him: and Jesus saith unto them, Believe ye that I am able to do this? They said unto him, Yea, Lord. Then touched he their eyes, saying, According to your faith be it unto you.	"According to your faith be it unto you."	439-6
123	Matthew 10:8	Heal the sick, cleanse the lepers, raise the dead, cast out devils: freely ye have received, freely give.	Freely ye have received, freely give.	440-2
124	Matthew 10:12,13	And when ye come into an house, salute it. And if the house be worthy, let your peace come upon it: but if it be not worthy, let your peace return to you.	And when ye come into an house, salute it. And if the house be worthy, let your peace come upon it: but if it be not worthy, let your peace return to you.	440-5
125	Matthew 10:20	For it is not ye that speak, but the Spirit of your Father which speaketh in you.	For it is not ye that speak, but the Spirit of your Father which speaketh in you	441-1
126	Matthew 10:36	And a man's foes shall be they of his own household.	And a man's foes shall be they of his own household	441-3
127	Matthew 10:39	He that findeth his life shall lose it: and he that loseth his life for my sake shall find it.	"he that findeth his life shall lose it; and he that loseth his life, shall find it."	440-3

Where'd He Get That? A Biblical Cross-Reference To Ernest Holmes' The Science of Mind

Unique Verse Nr.	Bible Verse	Citation	Ernest Holmes reference	Page in SOM text
128	Matthew 10:41	He that receiveth a prophet in the name of a prophet shall receive a prophet's reward; and he that receiveth a righteous man in the name of a righteous man shall receive a righteous man's reward.	He that receiveth a prophet in the name of a prophet shall receive a prophet's reward; and he that receiveth a righteous man in the name of a righteous man shall receive a righteous man's reward.	442-1
129	Matthew 11:18,19	For John came neither eating nor drinking, and they say, He hath a devil.: The Son of man came eating and drinking, and they say, Behold a man gluttonous, and a winebibber, a friend of publicans and sinners. But wisdom is justified of her children.	"For John came neither eating nor drinking, and they say, He hath a devil.: The Son of man came eating and drinking, and they say, Behold a man gluttonous, and a winebibber, a friend of publicans and sinners. But wisdom is justified of her children.	442-2
	Matthew 11:19	The Son of man came eating and drinking, and they say, Behold a man gluttonous, and a winebibber, a friend of publicans and sinners. But wisdom is justified of her children	Wisdom is justified of her children."	442-3
130	Matthew 11:27	All things are delivered unto me of my Father: and no man knoweth the Son, but the Father; neither knoweth any man the Father, save the Son, and he to whomsoever the Son will reveal him.	And no man knoweth the Son, but the Father; neither knoweth any many the Father, save the Son, and he to whomsoever the Son will reveal him.	443-2
131	Matthew 11:28	Come unto me, all ye that labour and are heavy laden, and I will give you rest.	Come unto me all ye that labor and are heavy laden and I will give ye rest.	335-4
	Matthew 11:28	Come unto me, all ye that labour and are heavy laden, and I will give you rest.	Come unto me all ye that labor and are heavy laden and I will give you rest.	444-1
132	Matthew 12:13	Then saith he to the man, Stretch forth thine hand. And he stretched it forth; and it was restored whole, like as the other.	When Jesus said to the man, "Stretch forth thine hand,"	212-3
133	Matthew 12:25	And Jesus knew their thoughts, and said unto them, Every kingdom divided against itself is brought to desolation; and every city or house divided against itself shall not stand:	We should be careful not to divide our mental house against itself	161-4
	Matthew 12:25	And Jesus knew their thoughts, and said unto them, Every kingdom divided against itself is brought to desolation; and every city or house divided against itself shall not stand:	Such a house can not stand.	383-1
	Matthew 12:25	And Jesus knew their thoughts, and said unto them, Every kingdom divided against itself is brought to desolation; and every city or house divided against itself shall not stand:	And Jesus knew their thoughts	448-2
	Matthew 12:25	And Jesus knew their thoughts, and said unto them, Every kingdom divided against itself is brought to desolation; and every city or house divided against itself shall not stand:	Jesus understanding what was in their minds, told them that a house divided against itself cannot stand;	448-3
134	Matthew 12:28	But if I cast out devils by the Spirit of God, then the kingdom of God is come unto you.	If I cast out devils by the spirit of God, then the Kingdom of God has come unto you	448-3

Where'd He Get That? A Biblical Cross-Reference To Ernest Holmes' The Science of Mind

Unique Verse Nr.	Bible Verse	Citation	Ernest Holmes reference	Page in SOM text
135	Matthew 12:47,48	Then one said unto him, Behold, thy mother and thy brethren stand without, desiring to speak with thee. But he answered and said unto him that told him, Who is my mother? and who are my brethren?	But he answering said unto him that told him, Who is my mother? And who are my brethren?	449-4
136	Matthew 13:12	For whosoever hath, to him shall be given, and he shall have more abundance: but whosoever hath not, from him shall be taken away even that he hath.	Whosoever hath, to him shall be given, and he shall have more abundance; but whosoever hath not, from him shall be taken away even that he hath	449-6
137	Matthew 13:16	But blessed are your eyes, for they see: and your ears, for they hear.	Blessed are your eyes, for they see; and your ears, for they hear	451-2
138	Matthew 13:31-32	Another parable put he forth unto them, saying, The kingdom of heaven is like to a grain of mustard seed, which a man took, and sowed in his field: Which indeed is the least of all seeds: but when it is grown, it is the greatest among herbs, and becometh a tree, so that the birds of the air come and lodge in the branches thereof.	The kingdom of heaven is like a grain of mustard seed	451-4
139	Matthew 13:33	Another parable spake he unto them; The kingdom of heaven is like unto leaven, which a woman took, and hid in three measures of meal, till the whole was leavened.	The kingdom of heaven is like leaven.	451-5
	Matthew 13:33	Another parable spake he unto them; The kingdom of heaven is like unto leaven, which a woman took, and hid in three measures of meal, till the whole was leavened.	"Leaven the whole lump of subjectivity"	451-5
140	Matthew 13:45-46	Again, the kingdom of heaven is like unto a merchant man, seeking goodly pearls: Who, when he had found one pearl of great price, went and sold all that he had, and bought it.	The kingdom of heaven is likened unto a pearl of great price, for which a man will sell all that he has, that he may possess it.	452-2
141	Matthew 14:25	And in the fourth watch of the night Jesus went unto them, walking on the sea.	Since we can not walk on water we take a boat.	219-2
142	Matthew 14:29-31	And he said, Come. And when Peter was come down out of the ship, he walked on the water, to go to Jesus. But when he saw the wind boisterous, he was afraid; and beginning to sink, he cried, saying, Lord, save me. And immediately Jesus stretched forth his hand, and caught him, and said unto him, O thou of little faith, wherefore didst thou doubt?	Christ places His hand in the outstretched hand of the Universe, and walks unafraid through life.	370-1
143	Matthew 15:13	But he answered and said, Every plant, which my heavenly Father hath not planted, shall be rooted up.	Declare: "every plant which my Heavenly Father hath not planted, shall be rooted up."	234-5
	Matthew 15:13	But he answered and said, Every plant, which my heavenly Father hath not planted, shall be rooted up.	"Every plant which my Heavenly Father hath not planted, shall be rooted up."	506-4
144	Matthew 15:14	Let them alone: they be blind leaders of the blind. And if the blind lead the blind, both shall fall into the ditch.	The blind leading the blind	055-4

Unique Verse Nr.	Bible Verse	Citation	Ernest Holmes reference	Page in SOM text
	Matthew 15:14	Let them alone: they be blind leaders of the blind. And if the blind lead the blind, both shall fall into the ditch.	he would be truly "the blind leading the blind.".	228-1
	Matthew 15:14	Let them alone: they be blind leaders of the blind. And if the blind lead the blind, both shall fall into the ditch.	But the blind cannot lead the blind.	415-2
	Matthew 15:14	Let them alone: they be blind leaders of the blind. And if the blind lead the blind, both shall fall into the ditch.	If the blind lead the blind, both shall fall into the ditch.	453-5
145	Matthew 15:18-20	But those things which proceed out of the mouth come forth from the heart; and they defile the man. For out of the heart proceed evil thoughts, murders, adulteries, fornications, thefts, false witness, blasphemies: These are the things which defile a man: but to eat with unwashen hands defileth not a man.	Not what we eat or drink, but what we think, defiles.	453-1
146	Matthew 16:24-27	Then said Jesus unto his disciples, If any man will come after me, let him deny himself, and take up his cross, and follow me. For whosoever will save his life shall lose it: and whosoever will lose his life for my sake shall find it. For what is a man profited, if he shall gain the whole world, and lose his own soul? or what shall a man give in exchange for his soul? For the Son of man shall come in the glory of his Father with his angels; and then he shall reward every man according to his works.	Who would save his life would lose it	454-2
147	Matthew 17:1-2	And after six days Jesus taketh Peter, James, and John his brother, and bringeth them up into an high mountain apart, And was transfigured before them: and his face did shine as the sun, and his raiment was white as the light.	Jesus was the greatest of all the mystics and, once at least, after a period of illumination, his face was so bright that his followers could not look upon it.	344-3
148	Matthew 17:15	Lord, have mercy on my son: for he is lunatick, and sore vexed: for ofttimes he falleth into the fire, and oft into the water.	Healing the Lunatic	456-1
149	Matthew 17:17	Then Jesus answered and said, O faithless and perverse generation, how long shall I be with you? how long shall I suffer you? bring him hither to me.	Bring him hither to me.	456-1
150	Matthew 17:18	And Jesus rebuked the devil; and he departed out of him: and the child was cured from that very hour.	And Jesus rebuked the devil; and he departed out of him.	456-1
151	Matthew 17:19-20	Then came the disciples to Jesus apart, and said, Why could not we cast him out? And Jesus said unto them, Because of your unbelief: for verily I say unto you, If ye have faith as a grain of mustard seed, ye shall say unto this mountain, Remove hence to yonder place; and it shall remove; and nothing shall be impossible unto you.	When Jesus explained to his disciples that they had failed to heal because of lack of faith, they protested that they did have faith in God. Jesus explained to them that this was insufficient; they must have the faith of God.	317-3

Unique Verse Nr.	Bible Verse	Citation	Ernest Holmes reference	Page in SOM text
152	Matthew 17:20	And Jesus said unto them, Because of your unbelief: for verily I say unto you, If ye have faith as a grain of mustard seed, ye shall say unto this mountain, Remove hence to yonder place; and it shall remove; and nothing shall be impossible unto you.	If ye have faith as a grain of mustard seed	162-2
153	Matthew 17:21	Howbeit this kind goeth not out but by prayer and fasting.	Fasting and prayer	455-3
154	Matthew 18:3	And said, Verily I say unto you, Except ye be converted, and become as little children, ye shall not enter into the kingdom of heaven.	The child-like faith	443-1
	Matthew 18:3	And said, Verily I say unto you, Except ye be converted, and become as little children, ye shall not enter into the kingdom of heaven.	We must become as little children	456-3
155	Matthew 18:10	Take heed that ye despise not one of these little ones; for I say unto you, That in heaven their angels do always behold the face of my Father which is in heaven.	"Behold thou my face forevermore"	185-3
156	Matthew 18:18	Verily I say unto you, Whatsoever ye shall bind on earth shall be bound in heaven: and whatsoever ye shall loose on earth shall be loosed in heaven.	Whatsoever ye shall bind on earth shall be bound in heaven; and whatsoever ye shall loose on earth shall be loosed in heaven.	457-1
157	Matthew 18:21-22	Then came Peter to him, and said, Lord, how oft shall my brother sin against me, and I forgive him? till seven times? Jesus saith unto him, I say not unto thee, Until seven times: but, Until seventy times seven.	He says we should forgive until seventy times seven.	457-4
158	Matthew 19:26	But Jesus beheld them, and said unto them, With men this is impossible; but with God all things are possible.	With God all things are possible	169-3
159	Matthew 21:9	And the multitudes that went before, and that followed, cried, saying, Hosanna to the son of David: Blessed is he that cometh in the name of the Lord; Hosanna in the highest.	The student of Truth will receive all that comes in the name of the Lord*	459-6
160	Matthew 21:21-22	Jesus answered and said unto them, Verily I say unto you, If ye have faith, and doubt not, ye shall not only do this which is done to the fig tree, but also if ye shall say unto this mountain, Be thou removed, and be thou cast into the sea; it shall be done. And all things, whatsoever ye shall ask in prayer, believing, ye shall receive.	The things we need we are to ask for—and we are to believe that we receive them!	458-2
161	Matthew 22:32	I am the God of Abraham, and the God of Isaac, and the God of Jacob? God is not the God of the dead, but of the living.	God is not a God of the dead but of the living for in His sight all are alive.	311-1
	Matthew 22:32	I am the God of Abraham, and the God of Isaac, and the God of Jacob? God is not the God of the dead, but of the living.	God is not a God of the dead but of the living: for all live unto Him.	313-3

Where'd He Get That? A Biblical Cross-Reference To Ernest Holmes' The Science of Mind

Unique Verse Nr.	Bible Verse	Citation	Ernest Holmes reference	Page in SOM text
162	Matthew 22:36-40	Jesus said unto him, Thou shalt love the Lord thy God with all thy heart, and with all thy soul, and with all thy mind. This is the first and great commandment. And the second is like unto it, Thou shalt love thy neighbour as thyself. On these two commandments hang all the law and the prophets.	The two great commandments are to love God and our brother man.	459-3
163	Matthew 24:35	Heaven and earth shall pass away, but my words shall not pass away.	Heaven and earth shall pass away	054-1
164	Matthew 24:35	Heaven and earth shall pass away, but my words shall not pass away.	And Jesus said, "Heaven and earth shall pass away, but my words shall not pass away."	173-4
	Matthew 24:35	Heaven and earth shall pass away, but my words shall not pass away.	Jesus said: "Heaven and earth shall pass away, but my words shall not pass away."	212-2
165	Matthew 25:31	When the Son of man shall come in his glory, and all the holy angels with him, then shall he sit upon the throne of his glory:	an arbitrary God, sending some to heaven and some to hell, all "for His glory."	365-3
166	Matthew 26:39	And he went a little farther, and fell on his face, and prayed, saying, O my Father, if it be possible, let this cup pass from me: nevertheless not as I will, but as thou wilt.	Let this cup pass from me	277-2
167	Matthew 26:52	Then said Jesus unto him, Put up again thy sword into his place: for all they that take the sword shall perish with the sword.	All that take the sword shall die by the sword	127-3
	Matthew 26:52	Then said Jesus unto him, Put up again thy sword into his place: for all they that take the sword shall perish with the sword.	"...for all they that take the sword shall perish with the sword."	460-1
168	Matthew 28:2	And, behold, there was a great earthquake: for the angel of the Lord descended from heaven, and came and rolled back the stone from the door, and sat upon it.	Roll away the stone	217-2
169	Matthew 28:20	lo, I am with you always, even to the end of the age." Amen	I shall walk no more alone	543-1
170	Mark 1:22	And they were astonished at his doctrine: for he taught them as one that had authority, and not as the scribes.	For He taught them as one having authority, and not as the scribes	203-3
171	Mark 2:5	When Jesus saw their faith, he said unto the sick of the palsy, Son, thy sins be forgiven thee.	This explains why Jesus said: "Thy sins be forgiven thee."	237-2
172	Mark 3:25	And if a house be divided against itself, that house cannot stand.	The Spiritual Universe should no longer be divided against Itself.	286-1
	Mark 3:25	And if a house be divided against itself, that house cannot stand.	The Universe is not divided against Itself.	499-3
173	Mark 4:39	And he arose, and rebuked the wind, and said unto the sea, Peace, be still. And the wind ceased, and there was a great calm.	Be still O soul and know	369-2

Unique Verse Nr.	Bible Verse	Citation	Ernest Holmes reference	Page in SOM text
174	Mark 8:23-25	And he took the blind man by the hand, and led him out of the town; and when he had spit on his eyes, and put his hands upon him, he asked him if he saw ought. And he looked up, and said, I see men as trees, walking. After that he put his hands again upon his eyes, and made him look up: and he was restored, and saw every man clearly.	how else could Jesus have told the blind man to look up--He said up and not down.	2603
175	Mark 11:24	Therefore I say unto you, What things soever ye desire, when ye pray, believe that ye receive them, and ye shall have them.	When ye pray, believe that ye have and ye shall receive	290-1
	Mark 11:24	Therefore I say unto you, What things soever ye desire, when ye pray, believe that ye receive them, and ye shall have them.	"Whatsoever things we desire" when we pray we should "Believe that we have them."	398-3
176	Mark 12:17	And Jesus answering said unto them, Render to Caesar the things that are Caesar's, and to God the things that are God's. And they marveled at him.	Render therefore, unto Caesar the things which are Caesar's; and unto God the things that are God's.	276-3
177	Mark 12:29	And Jesus answered him, The first of all the commandments is, Hear, O Israel; The Lord our God is one Lord: (New Testament)	The fundamental premise upon which the philosophy of the Bible is develop is that Spirit is One.	082-3
178	Mark 12:32	And the scribe said unto him, Well, Master, thou hast said the truth: for there is one God; and there is none other but he:	which is God, "beside which there is none other."	216-1
179	Luke 1:19	And the angel answering said unto him, I am Gabriel, that stand in the presence of God; and am sent to speak unto thee, and to shew thee these glad tidings.	[This is what the mystics call] "The Angel of God's Presence."	306-4
180	Luke 2:12-14	And suddenly there was with the angel a multitude of the heavenly host praising God, and saying, Glory to God in the highest, and on earth peace, good will toward men.	The farmer has seen the Heavenly Host in his fields.	041-3
	Luke 2:12-14	And suddenly there was with the angel a multitude of the heavenly host praising God, and saying, Glory to God in the highest, and on earth peace, good will toward men.	Thoughts of peace and good will…will produce harmony	232-3
181	Luke 6:27	But I say unto you which hear, Love your enemies, do good to them which hate you,	Jesus tells us to resist not evil, to love our enemies	430-5
182	Luke 6:35	But love ye your enemies, and do good, and lend, hoping for nothing again; and your reward shall be great, and ye shall be the children of the Highest: for he is kind unto the unthankful and to the evil.	Jesus tells us to resist not evil, to love our enemies	430-5

Where'd He Get That? A Biblical Cross-Reference To Ernest Holmes' The Science of Mind

Unique Verse Nr.	Bible Verse	Citation	Ernest Holmes reference	Page in SOM text
183	Luke 6:38	Give, and it shall be given unto you; good measure, pressed down, and shaken together, and running over, shall men give into your bosom. For with the same measure that ye mete withal it shall be measured to you again.	Equivalent: allow the pure spiritual substance to flow through to us, "Pressed down and running over."	
184	Luke 7:47	Wherefore I say unto thee, Her sins, which are many, are forgiven; for she loved much: but to whom little is forgiven, the same loveth little.	To him who hath loved much, much is forgiven	298-4
	Luke 7:47	Wherefore I say unto thee, Her sins, which are many, are forgiven; for she loved much: but to whom little is forgiven, the same loveth little.	To him who loves much, much is forgiven.	458-2
185	Luke 11:2	And he said unto them, When ye pray, say, Our Father which art in heaven, Hallowed be thy name. Thy kingdom come. Thy will be done, as in heaven, so in earth.	Thy will be done	268-4
	Luke 11:2	And he said unto them, When ye pray, say, Our Father which art in heaven, Hallowed be thy name. Thy kingdom come. Thy will be done, as in heaven, so in earth.	Our Father which art in heaven	343-4
186	Luke 11:9	And I say unto you, Ask, and it shall be given you; seek, and ye shall find; knock, and it shall be opened unto you	Ask and it shall be given unto you	157-3
	Luke 11:9	And I say unto you, Ask, and it shall be given you; seek, and ye shall find; knock, and it shall be opened unto you	Everyone who asks receives	175-1
	Luke 11:9	And I say unto you, Ask, and it shall be given you; seek, and ye shall find; knock, and it shall be opened unto you	Ask and it shall be given unto you	307-3
187	Luke 11:11	If a son shall ask bread of any of you that is a father, will he give him a stone? or if he ask a fish, will he for a fish give him a serpent?	If we ask for bread, we shall not receive a stone	435-3
188	Luke 11:18	If Satan also be divided against himself, how shall his kingdom stand? because ye say that I cast out devils through Beelzebub.	If I cast out devils by Beelzebub, the prince of devils, that is a house divided against itself, which cannot stand	076-4
189	Luke 11:34	The light of the body is the eye: therefore when thine eye is single, thy whole body also is full of light; but when thine eye is evil, thy body also is full of darkness.	But if thine eye be evil thy whole body shall be full of darkness	230-1
	Luke 11:34	The light of the body is the eye: therefore when thine eye is single, thy whole body also is full of light; but when thine eye is evil, thy body also is full of darkness.	If our eye is single, we shall be filled with light.	432-2
190	Luke 12:2	For there is nothing covered, that shall not be revealed; neither hid, that shall not be known.	There is nothing covered, that shall not be revealed; and hid, that shall not be known	441-2
191	Luke 12:32	Fear not, little flock; for it is your Father's good pleasure to give you the kingdom.	It is your Father's good pleasure to give you the kingdom.	108-4

Where'd He Get That? A Biblical Cross-Reference To Ernest Holmes' The Science of Mind

Unique Verse Nr.	Bible Verse	Citation	Ernest Holmes reference	Page in SOM text
	Luke 12:32	Fear not, little flock; for it is your Father's good pleasure to give you the kingdom.	Fear not little flock, it is your Father's good pleasure to give you the kingdom.	109-1
	Luke 12:32	Fear not, little flock; for it is your Father's good pleasure to give you the kingdom.	Fear not little flock, it is your Father's good pleasure to give you the kingdom.	404-2
	Luke 12:32	Fear not, little flock; for it is your Father's good pleasure to give you the kingdom.	If it is God's pleasure to give us the Kingdom	405-1
	Luke 12:32	Fear not, little flock; for it is your Father's good pleasure to give you the kingdom.	We are told not to be afraid, for it is the Father's good pleasure to give us the Kingdom.	486-3
	Luke 12:32	Fear not, little flock; for it is your Father's good pleasure to give you the kingdom.	It is the Father's good pleasure to give me the Kingdom of Heaven	556-2
	Luke 12:32	Fear not, little flock; for it is your Father's good pleasure to give you the kingdom.	Fear: "Fear not, little flock, it is your Father's good pleasure to give you the kingdom."	593
192	Luke 14:7-9	And he put forth a parable to those which were bidden, when he marked how they chose out the chief rooms; saying unto them. When thou art bidden of any man to a wedding, sit not down in the highest room; lest a more honourable man than thou be bidden of him; And he that bade thee and him come and say to thee, Give this man place; and thou begin with shame to take the lowest room.	It would be a wonderful experiment if the world would try to solve all of its problems through the power of Spirit. Indeed the time will come when everyone will..."From the highest...to the lowest."	334-3
193	Luke 15:11-12	And he said, A certain man had two sons:	A certain man had two sons.	461-2
	Luke 15:11-12	And the younger of them said to his father, Father, give me the portion of goods that falleth to me. And he divided unto them his living.	And the younger of them said to his father, Father, give me the portion of goods that falleth to me.	461-3
	Luke 15:11-12	And the younger of them said to his father, Father, give me the portion of goods that falleth to me. And he divided unto them his living.	And he divided unto them his living.	461-5
	Luke 15:11-12	And the younger of them said to his father, Father, give me the portion of goods that falleth to me. And he divided unto them his living.	And he divided unto them his living.	462-1
194	Luke 15:13	And not many days after the younger son gathered all together, and took his journey into a far country, and there wasted his substance with riotous living.	And not many days after the younger son gathered all together, and took his journey into a far country, and there wasted his substance with riotous living.	462-2
	Luke 15:13	And not many days after the younger son gathered all together, and took his journey into a far country, and there wasted his substance with riotous living.	The far country	462-3
195	Luke 15:14	And when he had spent all, there arose a mighty famine in that land; and he began to be in want.	And there he wasted his substance with riotous living. And when he had spent all, there arose a mighty famine in that land; and he began to want	462-5

Where'd He Get That? A Biblical Cross-Reference To Ernest Holmes' The Science of Mind

Unique Verse Nr.	Bible Verse	Citation	Ernest Holmes reference	Page in SOM text
196	Luke 15: 15	And he went and joined himself to a citizen of that country; and he sent him into his fields to feed swine.	So the prodigal son "began to be in want. And he went and joined himself to a citizen of that country; and he sent him into his fields to feed swine.	463-3
197	Luke 15:16	And he would fain have filled his belly with the husks that the swine did eat: and no man gave unto him.	And he fain would have filled his belly with the husks that the swine did eat; and no man gave unto him	464-2
198	Luke 15:17	And when he came to himself, he said, How many hired servants of my father's have bread enough and to spare, and I perish with hunger!	And when he came to himself he said, How many hired servants of my father's have bread enough and to spare, and I perish with hunger!	464-6
	Luke 15:17	And when he came to himself, he said, How many hired servants of my father's have bread enough and to spare, and I perish with hunger!	"And when he came to himself." The is the great awakening,	465-1
199	Luke 15:17-18	And when he came to himself, he said, How many hired servants of my father's have bread enough and to spare, and I perish with hunger! I will arise and go to my father, and will say unto him, Father, I have sinned against heaven, and before thee,	The Prodigal Son remained a prodigal as long as he chose to do so. When he chose to, he returned to his "Father's house" and was greeted with outstretched hands.	147-3
	Luke 15:18	I will arise and go to my father, and will say unto him, Father, I have sinned against heaven, and before thee,	They have all agreed that the soul is on the pathway of experience, that is, of self-discovery; that it is on its way back to its Father's House;	333-4
	Luke 15:18	I will arise and go to my father, and will say unto him, Father, I have sinned against heaven, and before thee,	we alone can return to the "Father's House."	464-4
	Luke 15:18	I will arise and go to my father, and will say unto him, Father, I have sinned against heaven, and before thee,	I will arise and go to my father and will say unto him, Father, I have sinned against heaven, and before thee,	465-3
200	Luke 15:19	And am no more worthy to be called thy son: make me as one of thy hired servants.	And am no more worthy to be called thy son: make me as one of thy hired servants.	465-3
201	Luke 15:20	And he arose, and came to his father. But when he was yet a great way off, his father saw him, and had compassion, and ran, and fell on his neck, and kissed him.	And he arose, and came to his father. But when he was yet a great way off, his father saw him, and had compassion, and ran, and fell on his neck, and kissed him.	466-2
	Luke 15:20	And he arose, and came to his father. But when he was yet a great way off, his father saw him, and had compassion, and ran, and fell on his neck, and kissed him.	When he was yet a great way off, his father saw him, and ran, and fell on his neck and kissed him.	466-3
202	Luke 15:21-24	And the son said unto him, Father, I have sinned against heaven, and in thy sight, and am no more worthy to be called thy son. But the father said to his servants, Bring forth the best robe, and put it on him; and put a ring on his hand, and shoes on his feet: And bring hither the fatted calf, and kill it; and let us eat, and be merry: For this my son was dead, and is alive again; he was lost, and is found. And they began to be merry.	And the son said unto him, Father, I have sinned against heaven, and in thy sight, and am no more worthy to be called thy son. But the father said to his servants, Bring forth the best robe, and put it on him; and put a ring on his hand, and shoes on his feet: and bring hither the fatted calf, and kill it; and let us eat, and be merry: For this my son was dead, and is alive again; he was lost, and is found. And they began to be merry.	466-5

Unique Verse Nr.	Bible Verse	Citation	Ernest Holmes reference	Page in SOM text
203	Luke 15:22	But the father said to his servants, Bring forth the best robe, and put it on him; and put a ring on his hand, and shoes on his feet:	"Bring forth quickly the best robe, and put it on him: and put a ring on his hand and shoes on his feet."	467-1
204	Luke 15:23	And bring hither the fatted calf, and kill it; and let us eat, and be merry:	The fatted calf	467-3
205	Luke 15:25	Now his elder son was in the field: and as he came and drew nigh to the house, he heard musick and dancing.	Now his elder son was in the field: and as he came and drew nigh to the house, he heard music and dancing.	468-3
206	Luke 15:26-27	And he called one of the servants, and asked what these things meant. And he said unto him, Thy brother is come; and thy father hath killed the fatted calf, because he hath received him safe and sound.	And he called one of the servants, and asked what these things meant. And he said unto him, Thy brother is come; and thy father hath killed the fatted calf, because he hath received him safe and sound.	468-4
207	Luke 15:28	And he was angry, and would not go in: therefore came his father out, and intreated him.	And he was angry, and would not go in: therefore came his father out, and intreated him.	468-5
208	Luke 15:29	And he answering said to his father, Lo, these many years do I serve thee, neither transgressed I at any time thy commandment: and yet thou never gavest me a kid, that I might make merry with my friends:	And he answering said to his father, Lo, these many years do I serve thee, and yet thou never gavest me a kid, that I might make merry with my friends…	468-6
209	Luke 15:30-31	But as soon as this thy son was come, which hath devoured thy living with harlots, thou hast killed for him the fatted calf. And he said unto him, Son, thou art ever with me, and all that I have is thine.	"All the Father hath is thine."	217-2
	Luke 15:30-31	But as soon as this thy son was come, which hath devoured thy living with harlots, thou hast killed for him the fatted calf. And he said unto him, Son, thou art ever with me, and all that I have is thine.	"And he said unto him, Son, thou art ever with me, and all that I have is thine."	468-7
	Luke 15:31	And he said unto him, Son, thou art ever with me, and all that I have is thine.	He said to the elder son, "Thou art ever with me, and all that I have is thine."	469-1
	Luke 15:31	And he said unto him, Son, thou art ever with me, and all that I have is thine.	Supply: "All that the Father hath."	635
210	Luke 17:19	And he said unto him, Arise, go thy way: thy faith hath made thee whole.	It is done unto you as you believe.	152-1
	Luke 17:19	And he said unto him, Arise, go thy way: thy faith hath made thee whole.	As ye believe, it shall be done unto you	280-1
	Luke 17:19	And he said unto him, Arise, go thy way: thy faith hath made thee whole.	I hear the voice to Truth telling me to arise and walk, for I am healed	506-1
211	Luke 17:20	And when he was demanded of the Pharisees, when the kingdom of God should come, he answered them and said, The kingdom of God cometh not with observation:	The Kingdom of Heaven cometh not by observation	345-3
	Luke 17:20	And when he was demanded of the Pharisees, when the kingdom of God should come, he answered them and said, The kingdom of God cometh not with observation:	The new birth comes not by observation nor by loud proclamation	472-2

Where'd He Get That? A Biblical Cross-Reference To Ernest Holmes' The Science of Mind

Unique Verse Nr.	Bible Verse	Citation	Ernest Holmes reference	Page in SOM text
212	Luke 17:21	Neither shall they say, Lo here! or, lo there! for, behold, the kingdom of God is within you.	Lo here nor Lo there…	124-1
	Luke 17:21	Neither shall they say, Lo here! or, lo there! for, behold, the kingdom of God is within you.	The Kingdom of God is within you.	150-4
	Luke 17:21	Neither shall they say, Lo here! or, lo there! for, behold, the kingdom of God is within you.	The Kingdom of God is within you.	150-5
	Luke 17:21	Neither shall they say, Lo here! or, lo there! for, behold, the kingdom of God is within you.	God is within man	330-3
	Luke 17:21	Neither shall they say, Lo here! or, lo there! for, behold, the kingdom of God is within you.	They have apparently sensed that this Kingdom is within.	335-1
	Luke 17:21	Neither shall they say, Lo here! or, lo there! for, behold, the kingdom of God is within you.	As we enter the One, the One enters into us	343-4
	Luke 17:21	Neither shall they say, Lo here! or, lo there! for, behold, the kingdom of God is within you.	He located God and the Kingdom of Heaven within himself.	362-1
	Luke 17:21	Neither shall they say, Lo here! or, lo there! for, behold, the kingdom of God is within you.	He located and the Kingdom of Heaven within himself.	362-1
	Luke 17:21	Neither shall they say, Lo here! or, lo there! for, behold, the kingdom of God is within you.	Heaven is within man	365-2
	Luke 17:21	Neither shall they say, Lo here! or, lo there! for, behold, the kingdom of God is within you.	The Kingdom of Heaven is within you.	365-2
	Luke 17:21	Neither shall they say, Lo here! or, lo there! for, behold, the kingdom of God is within you.	Heaven is already within	472-4
	Luke 17:21	Neither shall they say, Lo here! or, lo there! for, behold, the kingdom of God is within you.	Kingdom: "The Kingdom of Heaven" is not a place; it is "within".	604
213	Luke 20:25	And he said unto them, Render therefore unto Caesar the things which be Caesar's, and unto God the things which be God's.	Render therefore, unto Caesar the things which are Caesar's; and unto God the things that are God's.	276-3
214	Luke 20:38	For he is not a God of the dead, but of the living: for all live unto him.	God is not a God of the dead but of the living	335-3
	Luke 20:38	For he is not a God of the dead, but of the living: for all live unto him.	Death:" God is not a God of the dead, but of the living, for in His sight, all are alive."	583
215	Luke 24:2	And they found the stone rolled away from the sepulchre.	Roll away the stone	217-2
216	John 1:1, 2, 3	In the beginning was the Word, and the Word was with God, and the Word was God. The same was in the beginning with God. All things were made by him; and without him was not any thing made that was made.	This is what the Bible calls the Word.	038-2

Where'd He Get That? A Biblical Cross-Reference To Ernest Holmes' The Science of Mind

Unique Verse Nr.	Bible Verse	Citation	Ernest Holmes reference	Page in SOM text
	John 1:1, 2, 3	In the beginning was the Word, and the Word was with God, and the Word was God. The same was in the beginning with God. All things were made by him; and without him was not any thing made that was made.	The Word was with God, and the Word was God. All things were made by Him and without Him was not anything made that was made	068-5
	John 1:1, 2, 3	In the beginning was the Word, and the Word was with God, and the Word was God. The same was in the beginning with God. All things were made by him; and without him was not any thing made that was made.	what the Bible calls "The Word."...Absolute Intelligence.	080-3
	John 1:1, 2, 3	In the beginning was the Word, and the Word was with God, and the Word was God. The same was in the beginning with God. All things were made by him; and without him was not any thing made that was made.	"The Word was with God and the Word was God."	145-4
	John 1:1, 2, 3	In the beginning was the Word, and the Word was with God, and the Word was God. The same was in the beginning with God. All things were made by him; and without him was not any thing made that was made.	In the beginning was the Word, and the Word was with God, and the Word was God. All things were made by him; and without him was not any thing made that was made.	310-3
217	John 1:1-5	The Gospel of John also establishes God as First Cause: In the beginning was the Word, and the Word was with God, and the Word was God. The same was in the beginning with God. All things were made through him; and without him was not anything made that hath been made. In him was life; and the life was the light of men. And the light shineth in the darkness; and the darkness apprehended it not. NOTE: Jesus did not say anything specific about Spirit being First Cause. Possibly John 5:26: For as the Father hath life in himself; so hath he given to the Son to have life in himself;	Therefore, we may read Buddha, Jesus, Plato, Socrates, Aristotle, Swedenborg, Emerson, Whitman, Browning or any of the other great mystics, no matter in what age they have lived, and we shall find the same Ultimate [First Cause].	342-1
	John 1:1, 2, 3	In the beginning was the Word, and the Word was with God, and the Word was God. The same was in the beginning with God. All things were made by him; and without him was not any thing made that was made.	Logos: The Word was with God and the Word was God."	608
	John 1:1, 2, 3	In the beginning was the Word, and the Word was with God, and the Word was God. The same was in the beginning with God. All things were made by him; and without him was not any thing made that was made.	Word: The word was with God and the word was God."	646
218	John 1:5	And the light shineth in darkness; and the darkness comprehended it not.	And the light shineth in the darkness and the darkness comprehended it not.	183-2

Where'd He Get That? A Biblical Cross-Reference To Ernest Holmes' The Science of Mind

Unique Verse Nr.	Bible Verse	Citation	Ernest Holmes reference	Page in SOM text
	John 1:5	And the light shineth in darkness; and the darkness comprehended it not.	"The light shines in the darkness and the darkness comprehendeth it not."	345-3
219	John 1:12	But as many as received him, to them gave he power to become the sons of God, even to them that believe on his name:	That is why we are called the "son of God."	036-2
	John 1:12	But as many as received him, to them gave he power to become the sons of God, even to them that believe on his name:	To as many as received him, to them gave he the power.	280-3
	John 1:12	But as many as received him, to them gave he power to become the sons of God, even to them that believe on his name:	To as many as believed, gave he the power.	334-4
	John 1:14	And the Word was made flesh, and dwelt among us, (and we beheld his glory, the glory as of the only begotten of the Father,) full of grace and truth.	The Word becomes flesh.	314-2
220	John 1:18	No man hath seen God at any time, the only begotten Son, which is in the bosom of the Father, he hath declared him.	No one has seen God	072-2
	John 1:18	No man hath seen God at any time, the only begotten Son, which is in the bosom of the Father, he hath declared him.	"No man hath seen God at any time; only the Son, he hath revealed Him."	075-3
	John 1:18	No man hath seen God at any time, the only begotten Son, which is in the bosom of the Father, he hath declared him.	No man has seen God at any time	159-3
221	John 3:3	Jesus answered and said unto him, Verily, verily, I say unto thee, Except a man be born again, he cannot see the kingdom of God.	Except a man be born again, he cannot see the kingdom of God.	471-5
222	John 3:6	That which is born of the flesh is flesh; and that which is born of the Spirit is spirit.	That which is born of the Spirit is Spirit	471-5
223	John 3:13	And no man hath ascended up to heaven, but he that came down from heaven, even the Son of man which is in heaven.	And no man hath ascended up to heaven, but he that came down from heaven, even the Son of man which is in heaven	472-3
224	John 3:14	And as Moses lifted up the serpent in the wilderness, even so must the Son of man be lifted up:	As Moses lifted up the serpent in the wilderness, Jesus tells us must the son of man also be lifted up.	472-5
225	John 3:18	He that believeth on him is not condemned: but he that believeth not is condemned already, because he hath not believed in the name of the only begotten Son of God.	The Son, begotten of the only Father – not "the only begotten Son of God."	357-1
	John 3:18	He that believeth on him is not condemned: but he that believeth not is condemned already, because he hath not believed in the name of the only begotten Son of God.	The Son begotten of the only Father	368-1

Unique Verse Nr.	Bible Verse	Citation	Ernest Holmes reference	Page in SOM text
226	John 4:20,21	Our fathers worshipped in this mountain; and ye say, that in Jerusalem is the place where men ought to worship. Jesus saith unto her, Woman, believe me, the hour cometh, when ye shall neither in this mountain, nor yet at Jerusalem, worship the Father.	Neither in the mountain nor at the temple	150-4
227	John 4:20-24	Our fathers worshipped in this mountain; and ye say, that in Jerusalem is the place where men ought to worship. Jesus saith unto her, Woman, believe me, the hour cometh, when ye shall neither in this mountain, nor yet at Jerusalem, worship the Father. Ye worship ye know not what: we know what we worship: for salvation is of the Jews. But the hour cometh, and now is, when the true worshippers shall worship the Father in spirit and in truth: for the Father seeketh such to worship him. God is a Spirit: and they that worship him must worship him in spirit and in truth.	Jesus said Reality is not in the mountain, nor afar off, but within us	076-3
	John 4:24	God is a Spirit: and they that worship him must worship him in spirit and in truth.	God is spirit and they that worship him must worship him in spirit and in truth	081-2
	John 4:24	God is a Spirit: and they that worship him must worship him in spirit and in truth.	We are told that "God is Spirit, and they that worship Him must worship Him in spirit and in truth."	150-4
228	John 5:19	Then answered Jesus and said unto them, Verily, verily, I say unto you, The Son can do nothing of himself, but what he seeth the Father do: for what things soever he doeth, these also doeth the Son likewise.	The Son can do nothing of himself	475-2
229	John 5:26	For as the Father hath life in himself; so hath he given to the Son to have life in himself;	As the Father has life, so the son has life.	106-3
	John 5:26	For as the Father hath life in himself; so hath he given to the Son to have life in himself;	As the Father has life, so the son has life.	475-6
230	John 6:27	Labour not for the meat which perisheth, but for that meat which endureth unto everlasting life, which the Son of man shall give unto you: for him hath God the Father sealed.	Labour not for the meat which perisheth	476-4
231	John 6:31	Our fathers did eat manna in the desert; as it is written, He gave them bread from heaven to eat.	Manna from heaven	428-4
232	John 6:63	It is the spirit that quickeneth; the flesh profiteth nothing: the words that I speak unto you, they are spirit, and they are life.	Jesus proclaimed that the very words which he spoke were Spirit and were life.	103-3
	John 6:63	It is the spirit that quickeneth; the flesh profiteth nothing: the words that I speak unto you, they are spirit, and they are life.	"The words I have spoken unto you are Spirit, and are life."	262-2

Where'd He Get That? A Biblical Cross-Reference To Ernest Holmes' The Science of Mind

Unique Verse Nr.	Bible Verse	Citation	Ernest Holmes reference	Page in SOM text
	John 6:63	the words that I speak unto you, they are spirit, and they are life.	The words must become "Spirit and Life" if they are to overshadow the thoughts	413-4
233	John 6:69	And we believe and are sure that thou art that Christ, the Son of the living God.	I am the Christ, the Son of the Living God within me	265-2
234	John 7:24	Judge not according to the appearance, but judge righteous judgment.	Judge by appearances	113-2
	John 7:24	Judge not according to the appearance, but judge righteous judgment.	Appearances of	113-2
	John 7:24	Judge not according to the appearance, but judge righteous judgment.	Judge according to appearances.	152-3
	John 7:24	Judge not according to the appearance, but judge righteous judgment.	No matter what the outside appearance…	162-5
	John 7:24	Judge not according to the appearance, but judge righteous judgment.	If, as Jesus said, we "judge not according to appearances, but judge righteous judgment,"	187-3
	John 7:24	Judge not according to the appearance, but judge righteous judgment.	we must see beyond the appearance	189-2
	John 7:24	Judge not according to the appearance, but judge righteous judgment.	we must transcend the appearance	213-3
	John 7:24	Judge not according to the appearance, but judge righteous judgment.	Back of all appearance to the contrary…	222-1
	John 7:24	Judge not according to the appearance, but judge righteous judgment.	no matter what the appearance may be	320-2
	John 7:24	Judge not according to the appearance, but judge righteous judgment.	they have separated the appearance from the reality	337-1
	John 7:24	Judge not according to the appearance, but judge righteous judgment.	Judge not according to appearances.	406-4
	John 7:24	Judge not according to the appearance, but judge righteous judgment.	Judge not according to appearances.	417-2
	John 7:24	Judge not according to the appearance, but judge righteous judgment.	Illusion: "Judge not according to appearances."	599
235	John 8:12	Then spake Jesus again unto them, saying, I am the light of the world: he that followeth me shall not walk in darkness, but shall have the light of life.	I am the light of the world	332-4
	John 8:12	Then spake Jesus again unto them, saying, I am the light of the world: he that followeth me shall not walk in darkness, but shall have the light of life.	"I am the light of the world"	477-5
	John 8:12	Then spake Jesus again unto them, saying, I am the light of the world: he that followeth me shall not walk in darkness, but shall have the light of life.	Light: "I am the light of the world; he that followeth me shall not walk in darkness, but shall have the light of life."	607
236	John 8:32	And ye shall know the truth, and the truth shall make you free.	Ye shall know the truth	032-3
	John 8:32	And ye shall know the truth, and the truth shall make you free.	the Truth will automatically free him	033-2
	John 8:32	And ye shall know the truth, and the truth shall make you free.	I may know the Truth and the Truth may make me free.	057-1
	John 8:32	And ye shall know the truth, and the truth shall make you free.	Ye shall know the truth, and the truth shall make you free.	206-4
	John 8:32	And ye shall know the truth, and the truth shall make you free.	Ye shall know the truth, and the truth shall make you free.	232-5
	John 8:32	And ye shall know the truth, and the truth shall make you free.	Ye shall know the truth, and the truth shall make you free.	248-3
	John 8:32	And ye shall know the truth, and the truth shall make you free.	The Truth makes me free	264-1

Where'd He Get That? A Biblical Cross-Reference To Ernest Holmes' The Science of Mind

Unique Verse Nr.	Bible Verse	Citation	Ernest Holmes reference	Page in SOM text
	John 8:32	And ye shall know the truth, and the truth shall make you free.	Know the truth and the truth shall make you free.	296-1
	John 8:32	And ye shall know the truth, and the truth shall make you free.	truth and truth alone makes us free	474-6
	John 8:32	And ye shall know the truth, and the truth shall make you free.	Truth which alone can make free.	478-2
237	John 9:25	He answered and said, Whether he be a sinner or no, I know not: one thing I know, that, whereas I was blind, now I see.	Whereas I was blind, now I see.	319-2
238	John 10:10	The thief cometh not, but for to steal, and to kill, and to destroy: I am come that they might have life, and that they might have it more abundantly.	I came so they might have life	082-4
239	John 10:30	I and my Father are one.	So with Jesus we may say: "The Father and I are One."	139-2
	John 10:30	I and my Father are one.	The Father and I are one	296-4
	John 10:30	I and my Father are one.	I and the Father are One	330-4
	John 10:30	I and my Father are one.	This is the recognition which Jesus had when he said, "I and the Father are One."	331-2
240	John 11:41-44	Then they took away the stone from the place where the dead was laid. And Jesus lifted up his eyes, and said, Father, I thank thee that thou hast heard me. And I knew that thou hearest me always: but because of the people which stand by I said it, that they may believe that thou hast sent me. And when he thus had spoken, he cried with a loud voice, Lazarus, come forth. And he that was dead came forth, bound hand and foot with graveclothes: and his face was bound about with a napkin. Jesus saith unto them, Loose him, and let him go.	Thanksgiving: Jesus prayed when he raised Lazarus from the tomb: "Father I thank thee…"	637
241	John 11:42	And I knew that thou hearest me always: but because of the people which stand by I said it, that they may believe that thou hast sent me.	I know that thou hearest me always.	331-3
242	John 11:43	And when he thus had spoken, he cried with a loud voice, Lazarus, come forth.	Then he said: "Lazarus, come forth;"	331-3
243	John 11:44	And he that was dead came forth, bound hand and foot with graveclothes: and his face was bound about with a napkin. Jesus saith unto them, Loose him, and let him go.	Loose him and let him go	291-2
	John 11:44	And he that was dead came forth, bound hand and foot with graveclothes: and his face was bound about with a napkin. Jesus saith unto them, Loose him, and let him go.	"Loose him and let him go."	291-2
244	John 12:32	And I, if I be lifted up from the earth, will draw all men unto me.	And I, if I be lifted up,…(not dragged down) will draw all men unto me.	056-1

Unique Verse Nr.	Bible Verse	Citation	Ernest Holmes reference	Page in SOM text
245	John 13:34-35	A new commandment I give unto you, That ye love one another; as I have loved you, that ye also love one another. By this shall all men know that ye are my disciples, if ye have love one to another.	The two great commandments are to love God and our brother man.	459-3
246	John 14:1	Let not your heart be troubled: ye believe in God, believe also in me.	Let not your heart be troubled	238-3
	John 14:1	Let not your heart be troubled: ye believe in God, believe also in me.	Let not your heart be troubled	478-6
247	John 14:2	In my Father's house are many mansions: if it were not so, I would have told you. I go to prepare a place for you.	In my Father's house are many mansions	098-2
	John 14:2	In my Father's house are many mansions: if it were not so, I would have told you. I go to prepare a place for you.	"In my father's house are many mansions."	479-3
	John 14:2	In my Father's house are many mansions: if it were not so, I would have told you. I go to prepare a place for you.	I go to prepare a place for you	479-4
248	John 14:6	Jesus saith unto him, I am the way, the truth, and the life: no man cometh unto the Father, but by me.	I am the way, the truth and the Life. No one cometh to the Father but by me.	358-4
	John 14:6	Jesus saith unto him, I am the way, the truth, and the life: no man cometh unto the Father, but by me.	he [Jesus] proclaimed the Truth to be working through him.	366-2
	John 14:6	Jesus saith unto him, I am the way, the truth, and the life: no man cometh unto the Father, but by me.	"I am the way, the truth and the life."	479-4
	John 14:6	Jesus saith unto him, I am the way, the truth, and the life: no man cometh unto the Father, but by me.	The son is the way to the Father	479-5
	John 14:6	Jesus saith unto him, I am the way, the truth, and the life: no man cometh unto the Father, but by me.	When Jesus said," No man cometh unto the Father but by me," of course he meant the I AM.	564-4
249	John 14:9	Jesus saith unto him, Have I been so long time with you, and yet hast thou not known me, Philip? he that hath seen me hath seen the Father; and how sayest thou then, Shew us the Father?	"Who hath seen me hath seen the Father."	076-4
	John 14:9	Jesus saith unto him, Have I been so long time with you, and yet hast thou not known me, Philip? he that hath seen me hath seen the Father; and how sayest thou then, Shew us the Father?	He that hath seen me hath seen the Father	480-1
	John 14:9	Jesus saith unto him, Have I been so long time with you, and yet hast thou not known me, Philip? he that hath seen me hath seen the Father; and how sayest thou then, Shew us the Father?	He that hath seen me hath seen the Father	480-2
250	John 14:10	Believest thou not that I am in the Father, and the Father in me? the words that I speak unto you I speak not of myself: but the Father that dwelleth in me, he doeth the works.	The Father who dwelleth in me doeth the work.	150-5

Unique Verse Nr.	Bible Verse	Citation	Ernest Holmes reference	Page in SOM text
	John 14:10	Believest thou not that I am in the Father, and the Father in me? the words that I speak unto you I speak not of myself: but the Father that dwelleth in me, he doeth the works.	The Father that dwelleth in me, He doeth the works.	312-4
	John 14:10	Believest thou not that I am in the Father, and the Father in me? the words that I speak unto you I speak not of myself: but the Father that dwelleth in me, he doeth the works.	The Father that dwelleth in me, He doeth the works.	330-4
	John 14:10	Believest thou not that I am in the Father, and the Father in me? the words that I speak unto you I speak not of myself: but the Father that dwelleth in me, he doeth the works.	The Father that dwelleth in me, He doeth the works.	344-2
	John 14:10	Believest thou not that I am in the Father, and the Father in me? the words that I speak unto you I speak not of myself: but the Father that dwelleth in me, he doeth the works.	the Spirit of the Father in me who doeth the work	401-4
	John 14:10	Believest thou not that I am in the Father, and the Father in me? the words that I speak unto you I speak not of myself: but the Father that dwelleth in me, he doeth the works.	It is not I, but the Father Who dwelleth in me, He doeth the works.	507-5
	John 14:10	Believest thou not that I am in the Father, and the Father in me? the words that I speak unto you I speak not of myself: but the Father that dwelleth in me, he doeth the works.	Silence: "the Father within, he doeth the work."	633
	John 14:10	Believest thou not that I am in the Father, and the Father in me? the words that I speak unto you I speak not of myself: but the Father that dwelleth in me, he doeth the works.	Victory: To the metaphysician, every victory is won in the silence of his own soul; by turning to "the Father within."	643
251	John 14:12	Verily, verily, I say unto you, He that believeth on me, the works that I do shall he do also; and greater works than these shall he do; because I go unto my Father.	He that believeth on me, the works that I do shall he do also.	480-4
	John 14:12	Verily, verily, I say unto you, He that believeth on me, the works that I do shall he do also; and greater works than these shall he do; because I go unto my Father.	Savior: "The works that I do shall ye do also; and greater works than these shall ye do; because I go unto my father."	631
252	John 14:13	And whatsoever ye shall ask in my name, that will I do, that the Father may be glorified in the Son.	Whatsoever ye shall ask in my name, that will I do.	151-2
253	John 14:16	And I will pray the Father, and he shall give you another Comforter, that he may abide with you for ever;	The Holy Comforter	480-5
254	John 14:20	At that day ye shall know that I am in my Father, and ye in me, and I in you.	"I am in my Father, and ye in me, and I in you."	480-6
255	John 14:26	But the Comforter, which is the Holy Ghost, whom the Father will send in my name, he shall teach you all things, and bring all things to your remembrance, whatsoever I have said unto you.	This is the one used and expanded on in the text for Holy Comforter. Ernest Holmes misquoted this reference.	480-5

Where'd He Get That? A Biblical Cross-Reference To Ernest Holmes' The Science of Mind

Unique Verse Nr.	Bible Verse	Citation	Ernest Holmes reference	Page in SOM text
	John 14:26	But the Comforter, which is the Holy Ghost, whom the Father will send in my name, he shall teach you all things, and bring all things to your remembrance, whatsoever I have said unto you.	We are told that The Holy Comforter, the Spirit of Truth, will make all things known to us.	480-5
	John 14:26	But the Comforter, which is the Holy Ghost, whom the Father will send in my name, he shall teach you all things, and bring all things to your remembrance, whatsoever I have said unto you.	As the Holy Comforter comes, He makes all things known to us.	480-6
256	John 14:27	Peace I leave with you, my peace I give unto you: not as the world giveth, give I unto you. Let not your heart be troubled, neither let it be afraid.	"Peace I leave with you, my peace I give unto you...Let not your heart be troubled, neither let it be afraid."	247-1
	John 14:27	Peace I leave with you, my peace I give unto you: not as the world giveth, give I unto you. Let not your heart be troubled, neither let it be afraid.	"Peace I leave with you, my peace I give unto you, not as the world giveth, give I unto you."	558-2
	John 14:27	Peace I leave with you, my peace I give unto you: not as the world giveth, give I unto you. Let not your heart be troubled, neither let it be afraid.	Peace: "Peace I leave with you, my peace I give unto you"	617
257	John 14:28	Ye have heard how I said unto you, I go away, and come again unto you. If ye loved me, ye would rejoice, because I said, I go unto the Father: for my Father is greater than I.	But "the Father is greater than I."	417-3
258	John 15:5	I am the vine, ye are the branches: He that abideth in me, and I in him, the same bringeth forth much fruit: for without me ye can do nothing.	I am the vine and ye are the branches	313-4
259	John 15:7	If ye abide In me and my words abide in you, ye shall ask what ye will, and it shall be done unto you.	If ye abide In me and my words abide in you, ye shall ask what ye will, and it shall be done unto you.	481-2
	John 15:7	If ye abide in me, and my words abide in you, ye shall ask what ye will, and it shall be done unto you.	It is done unto you.	034-1
	John 15:7	If ye abide in me, and my words abide in you, ye shall ask what ye will, and it shall be done unto you.	it is done unto us as we believe	148-4
	John 15:7	If ye abide in me, and my words abide in you, ye shall ask what ye will, and it shall be done unto you.	If ye abide in me, and my words abide in you, ye shall ask what ye will, and it shall be done unto you.	150-6
	John 15:7	If ye abide in me, and my words abide in you, ye shall ask what ye will, and it shall be done unto you.	If ye abide in me, and my words abide in you, ye shall ask what ye will, and it shall be done unto you.	151-1
	John 15:7	If ye abide in me, and my words abide in you, ye shall ask what ye will, and it shall be done unto you.	If ye abide in me, and my words abide in you, ye shall ask what ye will, and it shall be done unto you.	313-4
	John 15:7	If ye abide in me, and my words abide in you, ye shall ask what ye will, and it shall be done unto you.	we must first abide in the Spirit of Truth	481-5
	John 15:7	If ye abide in me, and my words abide in you, ye shall ask what ye will, and it shall be done unto you.	I speak into that Law and it is done unto me.	522-1
	John 15:7	If ye abide in me, and my words abide in you, ye shall ask what ye will, and it shall be done unto you.	Now it is done unto me.	524-1

Where'd He Get That? A Biblical Cross-Reference To Ernest Holmes' The Science of Mind

Unique Verse Nr.	Bible Verse	Citation	Ernest Holmes reference	Page in SOM text
	John 15:7	If ye abide in me, and my words abide in you, ye shall ask what ye will, and it shall be done unto you.	Universal Power: "As we believe."	641
260	John 15:8	Herein is my Father glorified, that ye bear much fruit; so shall ye be my disciples.	Except the branch abide in the vine, it shall not bear fruit	313-4
	John 15:8	Herein is my Father glorified, that ye bear much fruit; so shall ye be my disciples.	The Father is glorified in the Son	480-4
	John 15:8	Herein is my Father glorified, that ye bear much fruit; so shall ye be my disciples.	Herein is my Father glorified, that ye bear much fruit	481-7
	John 15:8	Herein is my Father glorified, that ye bear much fruit; so shall ye be my disciples.	I myself am to blame when these "fruits of the Spirit" fail to appear.	557-1
261	John 15:11	These things have I spoken unto you, that my joy might remain in you, and that your joy might be full.	Jesus refers to his joy on the eve of his greatest lesson to mankind.	482-3
262	John 16:20	Most assuredly, I say to you that you will weep and lament, but the world will rejoice; and you will be sorrowful, but your sorrow will be turned into joy.	Despair gives way to joy at the thought of Thee, Indwelling God	537-3
263	John 17:11	And now I am no more in the world, but these are in the world, and I come to thee. Holy Father, keep through thine own name those whom thou hast given me, that they may be one, as we are.	"That they may be One even as we are One," was His prayer	332-2
264	John 17:22	And the glory which You gave Me I have given them, that they may be one just as We are one:	Unity: "That they may all be one, even as Thou, Father, art in me and I in Thee, and they also in us."	641
265	Acts 8:20-21	But Peter said unto him, Thy money perish with thee, because thou hast thought that the gift of God may be purchased with money. Thou hast neither part nor lot in this matter: for thy heart is not right in the sight of God.	Revelation: "But Peter said unto him, Thy money perish with thee, because thou hast thought that the gift of God may be purchased with money. Thou hast neither part nor lot in this matter; for thy heart is not right in the sight of God."	630
266	Acts 9:3	And as he journeyed, he came near Damascus: and suddenly there shined round about him a light from heaven:	All mystics have seen this Cosmic Light. This is why it is said there were illumined. They have all had the same experience, whether it was . . .. Saul on his return to Damascus. . .-where suddenly he became conscious of this light.	344-3
	Acts 9:3	And as he journeyed, he came near Damascus: and suddenly there shined round about him a light from heaven:	The Light of Heaven shines through me and illumines my path	526-2
	Acts 9:3	And as he journeyed, he came near Damascus: and suddenly there shined round about him a light from heaven:	Let Thy light illumine my path, and let Thy wisdom direct my way.	
	Acts 9:3	And as he journeyed, he came near Damascus: and suddenly there shined round about him a light from heaven:	Compel me to follow Thy light that I too may be free and complete	537-4
267	Acts 10:34	Then Peter opened his mouth, and said, Of a truth I perceive that God is no respecter of persons:	Respecter of persons	xvii
	Acts 10:34	Then Peter opened his mouth, and said, Of a truth I perceive that God is no respecter of persons:	Universal principles are never respecters of persons	027-3

Where'd He Get That? A Biblical Cross-Reference To Ernest Holmes' The Science of Mind

Unique Verse Nr.	Bible Verse	Citation	Ernest Holmes reference	Page in SOM text
	Acts 10:34	Then Peter opened his mouth, and said, Of a truth I perceive that God is no respecter of persons:	It is no respecter of persons	041-2
	Acts 10:34	Then Peter opened his mouth, and said, Of a truth I perceive that God is no respecter of persons:	law is no respecter of persons	052-4
	Acts 10:34	Then Peter opened his mouth, and said, Of a truth I perceive that God is no respecter of persons:	It is no respecter of persons	284-2
268	Acts 13:47	For so hath the Lord commanded us, saying, I have set thee to be a light of the Gentiles, that thou shouldest be for salvation unto the ends of the earth.	Light: I have set thee to be a light	607
269	Acts 17:28	For in him we live, and move, and have our being; as certain also of your own poets have said, For we are also his offspring.	Lives, moves and has his being in	032-3
	Acts 17:28	For in him we live, and move, and have our being; as certain also of your own poets have said, For we are also his offspring.	Live, move and have our being in	035-3
	Acts 17:28	For in him we live, and move, and have our being; as certain also of your own poets have said, For we are also his offspring.	"In Him we live, move, and have our being."	076-3
	Acts 17:28	For in him we live, and move, and have our being; as certain also of your own poets have said, For we are also his offspring.	within this One all live	082-2
	Acts 17:28	For in him we live, and move, and have our being; as certain also of your own poets have said, For we are also his offspring.	There is only Mind, in which we all "live and move and have our being."	087-4
	Acts 17:28	For in him we live, and move, and have our being; as certain also of your own poets have said, For we are also his offspring.	that which lives and moves and has Its being where we are	152-5
	Acts 17:28	For in him we live, and move, and have our being; as certain also of your own poets have said, For we are also his offspring.	"In Him we live, move, and have our being."	332-2
	Acts 17:28	For in him we live, and move, and have our being; as certain also of your own poets have said, For we are also his offspring.	the Great Presence in which we live, move and have our being	368-4
270	Romans 1:20	For the invisible things of him from the creation of the world are clearly seen, being understood by the things that are made, even his eternal power and Godhead; so that they are without excuse:	This teaching incorporates the great law of correspondents.	483-1
271	Romans 3:23	For all have sinned, and come short of the glory of God;	Fallen short of	457-4
272	Romans 6:9	Knowing that Christ being raised from the dead dieth no more; death hath no more dominion over him..	Christ triumphs over death and the grave	369-3
273	Romans 8:1	There is therefore now no condemnation to them which are in Christ Jesus, who walk not after the flesh, but after the Spirit.	There is therefore now no condemnation to them	259-4

Where'd He Get That? A Biblical Cross-Reference To Ernest Holmes' The Science of Mind

Unique Verse Nr.	Bible Verse	Citation	Ernest Holmes reference	Page in SOM text
	Romans 8:1	There is therefore now no condemnation to them which are in Christ Jesus, who walk not after the flesh, but after the Spirit.	Know that there is no condemnation	291-2
	Romans 8:1	There is therefore now no condemnation to them which are in Christ Jesus, who walk not after the flesh, but after the Spirit.	There is therefore now no condemnation to them	484-1
	Romans 8:1	There is therefore now no condemnation to them which are in Christ Jesus, who walk not after the flesh, but after the Spirit.	There is no condemnation in me nor operating through me	518-3
274	Romans 8:2	For the law of the Spirit of life in Christ Jesus hath made me free from the law of sin and death.	Righteous prayer sets the "law of the Spirit of Life" in motion for us.	152-3
275	Romans 8:6	For to be carnally minded is death; but to be spiritually minded is life and peace.	"To be spiritually minded is life and peace."	484-3
276	Romans 8:11	But if the Spirit of him that raised up Jesus from the dead dwell in you, he that raised up Christ from the dead shall also quicken your mortal bodies by his Spirit that dwelleth in you.	The Spirit that raised Jesus dwells in all.	484-4
277	Romans 8:15	For ye have not received the spirit of bondage again to fear; but ye have received the Spirit of adoption, whereby we cry, Abba, Father.	We have not received a spirit of bondage but one of adoption	484-5
278	Romans 8:16-17	The Spirit itself beareth witness with our spirit, that we are the children of God: And if children, then heirs; heirs of God, and joint-heirs with Christ; if so be that we suffer with him, that we may be also glorified together.	Joint heirs with Christ	485-2
279	Romans 8:21	Because the creature itself also shall be delivered from the bondage of corruption into the glorious liberty of the children of God.	The creature shall be delivered from bondage	485-4
280	Romans 8:28	And we know that all things work together for good to them that love God, to them who are the called according to his purpose.	All things work for our good	485-5
281	Romans 8:29	For whom he did foreknow, he also did predestinate to be conformed to the image of his Son, that he might be the firstborn among many brethren.	so it is foreknown and predetermined by the Divine Mind that all shall be sons of God.	486-1
282	Romans 8:31	What shall we then say to these things? If God be for us, who can be against us?	If God be for us, who can be against us?	109-4
	Romans 8:31	What shall we then say to these things? If God be for us, who can be against us?	"If God be for us who can be against us?"	146-2
	Romans 8:31	What shall we then say to these things? If God be for us, who can be against us?	"If God be for us who can be against us?"	486-2
	Romans 8:31	What shall we then say to these things? If God be for us, who can be against us?	"If God be for us who can be against us?"	495-5

Where'd He Get That? A Biblical Cross-Reference To Ernest Holmes' The Science of Mind

Unique Verse Nr.	Bible Verse	Citation	Ernest Holmes reference	Page in SOM text
283	Romans 8:38-39	For I am persuaded, that neither death, nor life, nor angels, nor principalities, nor powers, nor things present, nor things to come, Nor height, nor depth, nor any other creature, shall be able to separate us from the love of God, which is in Christ Jesus our Lord.	NOTHING can keep us from the love of God.	486-3
284	Romans 9:1	I say the truth in Christ, I lie not, my conscience also bearing me witness in the Holy Ghost,	We are in Christ when we are in the Truth: we are in the Truth when we live in harmony with It.	484-2
285	Romans 10:8	But what saith it? The word is nigh thee, even in thy mouth, and in thy heart: that is, the word of faith, which we preach;	"The Word is nigh Thee, even in thine own mouth that thou shouldst know it and do it."	146-1
286	Romans 12:2	And be not conformed to this world: but be ye transformed by the renewing of your mind, that ye may prove what is that good, and acceptable, and perfect, will of God.	Transformed by a renewing of the mind.	218-3
	Romans 12:2	And be not conformed to this world: but be ye transformed by the renewing of your mind, that ye may prove what is that good, and acceptable, and perfect, will of God.	Be transformed by the renewing of our minds.	448-1
	Romans 12:2	And be not conformed to this world: but be ye transformed by the renewing of your mind, that ye may prove what is that good, and acceptable, and perfect, will of God.	Be ye transformed by the renewing of your mind.	486-5
	Romans 12:2	And be not conformed to this world: but be ye transformed by the renewing of your mind, that ye may prove what is that good, and acceptable, and perfect, will of God.	The process through which this renewing takes place	487-2
287	Romans 12:14	Bless them which persecute you: bless, and curse not.	Bless and curse not	487-3
288	Romans 12:19	Dearly beloved, avenge not yourselves, but rather give place unto wrath: for it is written, Vengeance is mine; I will repay, saith the Lord.	Vengeance is mine; I will repay saith the Lord	487-4
289	Romans 13:11	And that, knowing the time, that now it is high time to awake out of sleep: for now is our salvation nearer than when we believed.	Now it is high time to awake out of sleep	487-5
290	I Corinth. 2:9	But as it is written, Eye hath not seen, nor ear heard, neither have entered into the heart of man, the things which God hath prepared for them that love him.	The Universe as we see it is not even a fractional part of the Universe that actually is, "Eye hath not seen..."	104-3
291	I Corinth. 2:16	For who hath known the mind of the Lord, that he may instruct him? But we have the mind of Christ.	We have the mind of Christ	273-4
292	I Corinth. 6:19	What? know ye not that your body is the temple of the Holy Ghost which is in you, which ye have of God, and ye are not your own?	Know that you alone are the door-keeper to the "Temple of the Holy Ghost," your body.	243-2
	I Corinth. 6:19	I Cor 6:19: What? know ye not that your body is the temple of the Holy Ghost which is in you, which ye have of God, and ye are not your own?	nor would it set man in the temple of God as God	444-2

Unique Verse Nr.	Bible Verse	Citation	Ernest Holmes reference	Page in SOM text
293	I Corinth. 6:19 and II Corinth. 6:16	I Cor 6:19: What? know ye not that your body is the temple of the Holy Ghost which is in you, which ye have of God, and ye are not your own? II Cor 6:16 And what agreement hath the temple of God with idols? for ye are the temple of the living God; as God hath said, I will dwell in them, and walk in them; and I will be their God, and they shall be my people.	Know ye not that ye are the temple of the Living God?	227-3
294	I Corinth. 13:9	For we know in part, and we prophesy in part.	For we know in part and prophesy in part	098-2
295	I Corinth. 14:33	For God is not the author of confusion, but of peace, as in all churches of the saints.	The Divine Mind is never confused	065-2
	I Corinth. 14:33	For God is not the author of confusion, but of peace, as in all churches of the saints.	God is not the author of confusion but of peace	329-3
296	I Corinth. 15:21	For since by man came death, by man came also the resurrection of the dead.	By man came death, by man came also the resurrection of the dead.	313-3
297	I Corinth. 15:22	For as in Adam all die, even so in Christ shall all be made alive.	As in Adam, all die, even so in Christ all are made alive.	310-4
298	I Corinth. 15:40	There are also celestial bodies, and bodies terrestrial: but the glory of the celestial is one, and the glory of the terrestrial is another.	"There are celestial bodies and bodes terrestrial"	376-1
	I Corinth. 15:40	There are also celestial bodies, and bodies terrestrial: but the glory of the celestial is one, and the glory of the terrestrial is another.	"There are bodies celestial and bodies terrestrial, there is material body and a spiritual body."	583
299	I Corinth. 15:44	It is sown a natural body; it is raised a spiritual body. There is a natural body, and there is a spiritual body.	"There is a natural body and there is a spiritual body"	376-1
300	I Corinth. 15:47	The first man is of the earth, earthy: the second man is the Lord from heaven.	The first man is of the earth, earthy; the second man is the Lord from heaven.	311-1
301	I Corinth. 15:52	In a moment, in the twinkling of an eye, at the last trump: for the trumpet shall sound, and the dead shall be raised incorruptible, and we shall be changed.	The "resurrection body" then, will not be snatched from some cosmic Shelf, as the soul soars aloft.	376-1
302	I Corinth. 15:55	O death, where is thy sting? O grave, where is thy victory?	The experience loses its sting, the grave its victory, when we realize the eternity of our own being.	385-1

Unique Verse Nr.	Bible Verse	Citation	Ernest Holmes reference	Page in SOM text
303	II Corinth. 3:7-12	But if the ministration of death, written and engraven in stones, was glorious, so that the children of Israel could not stedfastly behold the face of Moses for the glory of his countenance; which glory was to be done away: How shall not the ministration of the spirit be rather glorious? For if the ministration of condemnation be glory, much more doth the ministration of righteousness exceed in glory. For even that which was made glorious had no glory in this respect, by reason of the glory that excelleth. For if that which is done away was glorious, much more that which remaineth is glorious. Seeing then that we have such hope, we use great plainness of speech:	The ascending scale of life	490-5
304	II Corinth. 3:17	Now the Lord is that Spirit: and where the Spirit of the Lord is, there is liberty.	The Law of God is One of Liberty	487-2
305	II Corinth. 3:18	But we all, with open face beholding as in a glass the glory of the Lord, are changed into the same image from glory to glory, even as by the Spirit of the Lord.	Being transformed from glory to glory	338-3
	II Corinth. 3:18	But we all, with open face beholding as in a glass the glory of the Lord, are changed into the same image from glory to glory, even as by the Spirit of the Lord.	Being transformed from glory to glory	338-3
	II Corinth. 3:18	But we all, with open face beholding as in a glass the glory of the Lord, are changed into the same image from glory to glory, even as by the Spirit of the Lord.	But we all, with open face beholding as in a glass the glory of the Lord, are changed into the same image from glory to glory, even as by the Spirit of the Lord.	489-5
	II Corinth. 3:18	But we all, with open face beholding as in a glass the glory of the Lord, are changed into the same image from glory to glory, even as by the Spirit of the Lord.	We are changed from glory to glory	490-5
306	II Corinth. 4:8-9	We are troubled on every side, yet not distressed; we are perplexed, but not in despair; Persecuted, but not forsaken; cast down, but not destroyed;	Even in our troubles we are not cast down	491-1

Unique Verse Nr.	Bible Verse	Citation	Ernest Holmes reference	Page in SOM text
307	II Corinth. 5:1-10	For we know that if our earthly house of this tabernacle were dissolved, we have a building of God, an house not made with hands, eternal in the heavens. For in this we groan, earnestly desiring to be clothed upon with our house which is from heaven: If so be that being clothed we shall not be found naked. For we that are in this tabernacle do groan, being burdened: not for that we would be unclothed, but clothed upon, that mortality might be swallowed up of life. Now he that hath wrought us for the selfsame thing is God, who also hath given unto us the earnest of the Spirit. Therefore we are always confident, knowing that, whilst we are at home in the body, we are absent from the Lord: (For we walk by faith, not by sight:) We are confident, I say, and willing rather to be absent from the body, and to be present with the Lord. Wherefore we labour, that, whether present or absent, we may be accepted of him. For we must all appear before the judgment seat of Christ; that every one may receive the things done in his body, according to that he hath done, whether it be good or bad.	This body, which we seem to live is not the eternal body.	491-6
308	II Corinth. 5:16	Wherefore henceforth know we no man after the flesh: yea, though we have known Christ after the flesh, yet now henceforth know we him no more.	Know no man after the flesh	491-8
309	II Corinth. 5:16	Wherefore henceforth know we no man after the flesh: yea, though we have known Christ after the flesh, yet now henceforth know we him no more.	Know no man after the flesh	492-2
310	II Corinth. 6:16	And what agreement hath the temple of God with idols? for ye are the temple of the living God; as God hath said, I will dwell in them, and walk in them; and I will be their God, and they shall be my people.	When the body is the harmonious temple of the Living God	248-3
311	II Corinth. 7:1	Having therefore these promises, dearly beloved, let us cleanse ourselves from all filthiness of the flesh and spirit, perfecting holiness in the fear of God.	To be washed clean by the Spirit should have a real meaning to us	260-3
312	Galatians 3:21	Is the law then against the promises of God? God forbid: for if there had been a law given which could have given life, verily righteousness should have been by the law.	The Bible says: "If there had been any law whereby this freedom could be compelled, then verily by the law would that freedom have been given."	109-2
313	Galatians 5:22-23	But the fruit of the Spirit is love, joy, peace, longsuffering, gentleness, goodness, faith, Meekness, temperance: against such there is no law.	there is but On Ultimate Reality, for "against such there is no law"	121-2
314	Galatians 5:23	Meekness, temperance: against such there is no law.	Against such, there is no law.	494-6

Unique Verse Nr.	Bible Verse	Citation	Ernest Holmes reference	Page in SOM text
315	Galatians 6:7	Be not deceived; God is not mocked: for whatsoever a man soweth, that shall he also reap.	Whatsoever a man soweth, that shall he also reap	039-3
	Galatians 6:7	Be not deceived; God is not mocked: for whatsoever a man soweth, that shall he also reap.	As we sow, so must we reap	195-2
	Galatians 6:7	Be not deceived; God is not mocked: for whatsoever a man soweth, that shall he also reap.	Whatsoever a man soweth, that shall he also reap	269-2
	Galatians 6:7	Be not deceived; God is not mocked: for whatsoever a man soweth, that shall he also reap.	As a man sows, so also shall he reap	340-2
	Galatians 6:7	Be not deceived; God is not mocked: for whatsoever a man soweth, that shall he also reap.	we shall reap as we have sown	429-3
	Galatians 6:7	Be not deceived; God is not mocked: for whatsoever a man soweth, that shall he also reap.	he must reap as he has sown	433-3
	Galatians 6:7	Be not deceived; God is not mocked: for whatsoever a man soweth, that shall he also reap.	Compensation: as you sow you reap.	579
316	Eph. 3:16	That he would grant you, according to the riches of his glory, to be strengthened with might by his Spirit in the inner man;	To be strengthened with might by his Spirit in the inner man	492-3
317	Eph. 3:20-21	Now unto him that is able to do exceeding abundantly above all that we ask or think, according to the power that worketh in us, Unto him be glory in the church by Christ Jesus throughout all ages, world without end. Amen.	World without end	357-2
	Eph. 3:20-21	Now unto him that is able to do exceeding abundantly above all that we ask or think, according to the power that worketh in us.	the Son of God--"the power that worketh in us."	492-6
318	Eph. 3:21	Unto him be glory in the church by Christ Jesus throughout all ages, world without end. Amen.	World without end	492-7
	Eph. 3:21	Unto him be glory in the church by Christ Jesus throughout all ages, world without end. Amen.	"world without end" or worlds without end, are necessary to the expression of Spirit.	493-1
	Eph. 3:21	Unto him be glory in the church by Christ Jesus throughout all ages, world without end. Amen.	Life always was and evermore shall be," World without end."	536-2
319	Eph. 4:1-6	I therefore, the prisoner of the Lord, beseech you that ye walk worthy of the vocation wherewith ye are called, With all lowliness and meekness, with longsuffering, forbearing one another in love; Endeavouring to keep the unity of the Spirit in the bond of peace. There is one body, and one Spirit, even as ye are called in one hope of your calling; One Lord, one faith, one baptism, One God and Father of all, who is above all, and through all, and in you all.	There is one body and one Spirit	493-3

Unique Verse Nr.	Bible Verse	Citation	Ernest Holmes reference	Page in SOM text
	Eph. 4:1-6	I therefore, the prisoner of the Lord, beseech you that ye walk worthy of the vocation wherewith ye are called, With all lowliness and meekness, with longsuffering, forbearing one another in love; Endeavouring to keep the unity of the Spirit in the bond of peace. There is one body, and one Spirit, even as ye are called in one hope of your calling; One Lord, one faith, one baptism, One God and Father of all, who is above all, and through all, and in you all.	One Lord, one faith, one baptism	493-5
320	Eph. 4:6	One God and Father of all, who is above all, and through all, and in you all.	One God and Father of all, who is above all, and through all, and in you all.	493-6
	Eph. 4:6	One God and Father of all, who is above all, and through all, and in you all.	God is "All in all."	103-2
	Eph. 4:6	One God and Father of all, who is above all, and through all, and in you all.	"God is all in all, over all and through all."	398-5
	Eph. 4:6	One God and Father of all, who is above all, and through all, and in you all.	"In all, over all, and through all."	513-1
	Eph. 4:6	One God and Father of all, who is above all, and through all, and in you all.	I proclaim the One Life: "In all and through all."	531-3
	Eph. 4:6	One God and Father of all, who is above all, and through all, and in you all.	"For he is all in all, over all and through all."	546-2
321	Eph. 4:23-24	And be renewed in the spirit of your mind; And that ye put on the new man, which after God is created in righteousness and true holiness.	We are told to be renewed in mind by the Spirit and to put on the new man.	494-1
	Eph. 4:23-24	And be renewed in the spirit of your mind; And that ye put on the new man, which after God is created in righteousness and true holiness.	Christ: each one "puts on the Christ"	579
322	Eph. 5:14	Wherefore he saith, Awake thou that sleepest, and arise from the dead, and Christ shall give thee light.	Awake thou that sleepest and arise from the dead, and Christ shall give thee light.	307-3
323	Eph. 6:10	Finally, my brethren, be strong in the Lord, and in the power of his might.	Be strong in the Lord and in the power of his might	494-3
324	Eph. 6:12	For we wrestle not against flesh and blood, but against principalities, against powers, against the rulers of the darkness of this world, against spiritual wickedness in high places.	Wickedness in high places means an inverted use of the law of righteousness	494-5
325	Eph. 6:13	Wherefore take unto you the whole armour of God, that ye may be able to withstand in the evil day, and having done all, to stand.	The armour of God is faith in the good	494-6
326	Eph. 6:14	Stand therefore, having your loins girt about with truth, and having on the breastplate of righteousness;	The breastplate of righteousness covers and gives sanctuary to the heart of hearts	495-2
327	Eph. 6:15	And your feet shod with the preparation of the gospel of peace;	the feet shod with the gospel of peace	495-2

Where'd He Get That? A Biblical Cross-Reference To Ernest Holmes' The Science of Mind

Unique Verse Nr.	Bible Verse	Citation	Ernest Holmes reference	Page in SOM text
328	Eph. 6:16	Above all, taking the shield of faith, wherewith ye shall be able to quench all the fiery darts of the wicked.	The shield of faith	495-3
329	Eph. 6:17	And take the helmet of salvation, and the sword of the Spirit, which is the word of God:	And the sword of the Spirit is the word of Truth	495-4
330	Phil. 2:5	Let this mind be in you, which was also in Christ Jesus:	we are told to have that Mind in us "which was also in Christ Jesus."	357-3
	Phil. 2:5	Let this mind be in you, which was also in Christ Jesus:	Let this mind be in you which was also in Christ Jesus	364-3
	Phil. 2:5	Let this mind be in you, which was also in Christ Jesus:	We are to let the mind be in us which was in Christ Jesus	495-6
	Phil. 2:5	Let this mind be in you, which was also in Christ Jesus:	To have the same mind that Jesus used	495-7
	Phil. 2:5	Let this mind be in you, which was also in Christ Jesus:	not the name of Jesus, but the Mind of Christ	496-3
	Phil. 2:5	Let this mind be in you, which was also in Christ Jesus:	Assurance: In reality, assurance is having "the mind which was in Christ Jesus."	576
331	Phil. 2:15	That ye may be blameless and harmless, the sons of God, without rebuke, in the midst of a crooked and perverse nation, among whom ye shine as lights in the world;	Light: "The sons of God, without rebuke...ye shine as lights in the world."	607
332	Phil. 3:20	For our conversation is in heaven; from whence also we look for the Saviour, the Lord Jesus Christ:	we will let our "conversation be in Heaven"	055-4
333	Phil. 4:7	And the peace of God, which passeth all understanding, shall keep your hearts and minds through Christ Jesus.	Peace which passeth all understanding	185-2
334	Phil. 4:8	Finally, brethren, whatsoever things are true, whatsoever things are honest, whatsoever things are just, whatsoever things are pure, whatsoever things are lovely, whatsoever things are of good report; if there be any virtue, and if there be any praise, think on these things.	"Whatsoever things are true, whatsoever things are honorable, whatsoever things are just, whatsoever things are pure, whatsoever things are lovely, whatsoever things are of good report."	226-1
	Phil. 4:8	Finally, brethren, whatsoever things are true, whatsoever things are honest, whatsoever things are just, whatsoever things are pure, whatsoever things are lovely, whatsoever things are of good report; if there be any virtue, and if there be any praise, think on these things.	We are to think on those things which are of good report	496-4
335	Phil. 4:19	But my God shall supply all your need according to his riches in glory by Christ Jesus.	And God will supply all our needs.	496-5
336	Col. 3:9	Lie not one to another, seeing that ye have put off the old man with his deeds;	For Christ to be found in us is to put off the old man, with all his mistakes and doubts, and put on a new man, who is always certain he is beloved of the Father.	363-4

Unique Verse Nr.	Bible Verse	Citation	Ernest Holmes reference	Page in SOM text
337	I Thess. 4:16-17	For the Lord himself shall descend from Heaven with a shout, with the voice of the archangel, and the trump of God: and the dead in Christ shall rise first: Then we which are alive, and remain shall be caught up together with them in the clouds, to meet the Lord in the air; and so shall we ever be with the Lord."	The "resurrection body" then, will not be snatched from some cosmic Shelf, as the soul soars aloft.	376-1
338	I Thess. 5:16	Rejoice evermore.	We are to rejoice evermore.	496-6
339	I Thess. 5:17	Pray without ceasing.	Pray without ceasing	497-1
340	I Thess. 5:18	In every thing give thanks: for this is the will of God in Christ Jesus concerning you.	"In everything give thanks"	497-2
341	I Thess. 5:19	Quench not the Spirit.	Quench not the Spirit.	497-3
	I Thess. 5:19	Quench not the Spirit.	Quench not the Spirit.	498-1
342	I Thess. 5:21	Prove all things; hold fast that which is good.	"Prove all things, hold fast to that which is good."	498-2
343	II Thess. 3:15	Yet count him not as an enemy, but admonish him as a brother.	The Bible tells us not to count our enemies.	315-3
344	I Timothy 2:5	For there is one God, and one mediator between God and men, the man Christ Jesus;	There is no mediator between God and man except Christ	272-4
345	II Timothy 1:12	For the which cause I also suffer these things: nevertheless I am not ashamed: for I know whom I have believed, and am persuaded that he is able to keep that which I have committed unto him against that day.	I know in whom I have believed	162-5
346	Hebrews 3:19	So we see that they could not enter in because of unbelief.	They could not enter in because of their unbelief" and they "limited the Holy One of Israel.	304-3
347	Hebrews 4:6	Seeing therefore it remaineth that some must enter therein, and they to whom it was first preached entered not in because of unbelief:	They could not enter because of their unbelief,	037-3
	Hebrews 4:6 and Psalms 78:41	Heb 4:6 Seeing therefore it remaineth that some must enter therein, and they to whom it was first preached entered not in because of unbelief: Ps 78:41 Yea, they turned back and tempted God, and limited the Holy One of Israel.	"They could not enter because of their unbelief, and because they limited the Holy One of Israel."	128-1
	Hebrews 4:6 and Psalms 78:41	Heb 4:6 Seeing therefore it remaineth that some must enter therein, and they to whom it was first preached entered not in because of unbelief: Ps 78:41 Yea, they turned back and tempted God, and limited the Holy One of Israel.	"They could not enter because of their unbelief," and because they "limited the Holy One of Israel."	304-3
	Hebrews 4:6 and Psalms 78:41	Heb 4:6 Seeing therefore it remaineth that some must enter therein, and they to whom it was first preached entered not in because of unbelief: Ps 78:41 Yea, they turned back and tempted God, and limited the Holy One of Israel.	They could not enter because of their unbelief, and because they limited the Holy One of Israel	405-2

Unique Verse Nr.	Bible Verse	Citation	Ernest Holmes reference	Page in SOM text
348	Hebrews 11:1	Now faith is the substance of things hoped for, the evidence of things not seen.	Faith is the substance of things hoped for	156-5
	Hebrews 11:1	Now faith is the substance of things hoped for, the evidence of things not seen.	Faith is the substance of things hoped for, the evidence of things not seen.	178-4
	Hebrews 11:1	Now faith is the substance of things hoped for, the evidence of things not seen.	Faith looks to the invisible	284-3
	Hebrews 11:1	Now faith is the substance of things hoped for, the evidence of things not seen.	We must have a receptive and positive faith in the evidence of things not seen with the physical eye but which are eternal in the heavens.	301-3
	Hebrews 11:1	Now faith is the substance of things hoped for, the evidence of things not seen.	and ever renewing substance of faith	415-1
	Hebrews 11:1	Now faith is the substance of things hoped for, the evidence of things not seen.	Faith: "Faith is the substance of things hoped for, the evidence of things not seen."	591
349	Hebrews 11:3	Through faith we understand that the worlds were framed by the word of God, so that things which are seen were not made of things which do appear.	Things which are seen are not made of things which do appear	057-2
	Hebrews 11:3	Through faith we understand that the worlds were framed by the word of God, so that things which are seen were not made of things which do appear.	Things which are seen are not made of things which do appear	101-3
	Hebrews 11:3	Through faith we understand that the worlds were framed by the word of God, so that things which are seen were not made of things which do appear.	The seen and the unseen	148-4
	Hebrews 11:3	Through faith we understand that the worlds were framed by the word of God, so that things which are seen were not made of things which do appear.	Before our prayer is framed in words, God has already answered.	153-2
	Hebrews 11:3	Through faith we understand that the worlds were framed by the word of God, so that things which are seen were not made of things which do appear.	Before our prayer is framed in words the possibility of its answer already exists.	178-2
	Hebrews 11:3	Through faith we understand that the worlds were framed by the word of God, so that things which are seen were not made of things which do appear.	Things which are seen are not made of things which do appear	187-3
	Hebrews 11:3	Through faith we understand that the worlds were framed by the word of God, so that things which are seen were not made of things which do appear.	Having faith in the unseen	392-4
	Hebrews 11:3	Through faith we understand that the worlds were framed by the word of God, so that things which are seen were not made of things which do appear.	We cannot account for the seen without having faith in the unseen.	407-2

Unique Verse Nr.	Bible Verse	Citation	Ernest Holmes reference	Page in SOM text
	Hebrews 11:3	Through faith we understand that the worlds were framed by the word of God, so that things which are seen were not made of things which do appear.	We understand the unseen by correctly viewing the seen	483-2
	Hebrews 11:3	Through faith we understand that the worlds were framed by the word of God, so that things which are seen were not made of things which do appear.	Effect: "Things which are seen are not made of things which do appear."	588
350	Hebrews 11:33-35	Who through faith subdued kingdoms, wrought righteousness, obtained promises, stopped the mouths of lions. Quenched the violence of fire, escaped the edge of the sword, out of weakness were made strong, waxed valiant in fight, turned to flight the armies of the aliens. Women received their dead raised to life again:	Who through faith subdued kingdoms, wrought righteousness, obtained promises, stopped the mouths of lions, quenched the power of fire, escaped the edge of the sword; out of weakness were made strong, waxed mighty in power, turned to flight armies of aliens, women received their dead raised to life again."	158-2
351	Hebrews 12:1	Wherefore seeing we also are compassed about with so great a cloud of witnesses, let us lay aside every weight, and the sin which doth so easily beset us, and let us run with patience the race that is set before us,	Cast aside all doubt	514-3
352	Hebrews 13:8	Jesus Christ the same yesterday, and to day, and for ever.	He is "the same yesterday, today and forever."	150-3

Unique Verse Nr.	Bible Verse	Citation	Ernest Holmes reference	Page in SOM text
353	James 1:5-18	If any of you lack wisdom, let him ask of God, that giveth to all men liberally, and upbraideth not; and it shall be given him. But let him ask in faith, nothing wavering. For he that wavereth is like a wave of the sea driven with the wind and tossed. For let not that man think that he shall receive any thing of the Lord. A double minded man is unstable in all his ways. Let the brother of low degree rejoice in that he is exalted: But the rich, in that he is made low: because as the flower of the grass he shall pass away. For the sun is no sooner risen with a burning heat, but it withereth the grass, and the flower thereof falleth, and the grace of the fashion of it perisheth: so also shall the rich man fade away in his ways. Blessed is the man that endureth temptation: for when he is tried, he shall receive the crown of life, which the Lord hath promised to them that love him. Let no man say when he is tempted, I am tempted of God: for God cannot be tempted with evil, neither tempteth he any man: But every man is tempted, when he is drawn away of his own lust, and enticed. Then when lust hath conceived, it bringeth forth sin: and sin, when it is finished, bringeth forth death. Do not err, my beloved brethren. Every good gift and every perfect gift is from above, and cometh down from the Father of lights, with whom is no variableness, neither shadow of turning. Of his own will begat he us with the word of truth, that we should be a kind of firstfruits of his creatures.	Ask in Faith, Believing	498-3
	James 1:5-18	If any of you lack wisdom, let him ask of God, that giveth to all men liberally, and upbraideth not; and it shall be given him.	When we ask for anything, we are to believe that we have it	498-5
354	James 1:6	But let him ask in faith, nothing wavering. For he that wavereth is like a wave of the sea driven with the wind and tossed.	Anything that is not of faith is sin, or a mistake.	498-4
355	James 1:8	A double minded man is unstable in all his ways.	The double-minded man gets nowhere	498-3
356	James 1:13	Let no man say when he is tempted, I am tempted of God: for God cannot be tempted with evil, neither tempteth he any man:	God never tempts	498-6
	James 1:13	Let no man say when he is tempted, I am tempted of God: for God cannot be tempted with evil, neither tempteth he any man:	God cannot be tempted	498-6

Unique Verse Nr.	Bible Verse	Citation	Ernest Holmes reference	Page in SOM text
357	James 1:22	But be ye doers of the word, and not hearers only, deceiving your own selves.	"Be ye doers of the word, and not hearers only, deceiving your own selves."	499-5
358	James 2:1-11	My brethren, have not the faith of our Lord Jesus Christ, the Lord of glory, with respect of persons. For if there come unto your assembly a man with a gold ring, in goodly apparel, and there come in also a poor man in vile raiment; And ye have respect to him that weareth the gay clothing, and say unto him, Sit thou here in a good place; and say to the poor, Stand thou there, or sit here under my footstool: Are ye not then partial in yourselves, and are become judges of evil thoughts? Hearken, my beloved brethren, Hath not God chosen the poor of this world rich in faith, and heirs of the kingdom which he hath promised to them that love him? But ye have despised the poor. Do not rich men oppress you, and draw you before the judgment seats? Do not they blaspheme that worthy name by the which ye are called? If ye fulfil the royal law according to the scripture, Thou shalt love thy neighbour as thyself, ye do well: But if ye have respect to persons, ye commit sin, and are convinced of the law as transgressors. For whosoever shall keep the whole law, and yet offend in one point, he is guilty of all. For he that said, Do not commit adultery, said also, Do not kill. Now if thou commit no adultery, yet if thou kill, thou art become a transgressor of the law.	The Law is No Respecter of Persons	500-2
359	James 2:9	But if ye have respect to persons, ye commit sin, and are convinced of the law as transgressors.	James speaks of being convinced of the law as transgressors	500-2
360	James 4:3	Ye ask, and receive not, because ye ask amiss, that ye may consume it upon your lusts.	We shall no longer "ask amiss"	150-5
	James 4:3	Ye ask, and receive not, because ye ask amiss, that ye may consume it upon your lusts.	When we abide in the One, we cannot ask amiss	481-4
361	James 5:15	And the prayer of faith shall save the sick, and the Lord shall raise him up; and if he have committed sins, they shall be forgiven him.	The prayer of faith is the unconditional belief in both the ability and desire of Spirit to hear and answer	500-5
362	James 5:16	Confess your faults one to another, and pray one for another, that ye may be healed. The effectual fervent prayer of a righteous man availeth much.	James tells us to confess our faults.	501-5
363	I Peter 3:4	But let it be the hidden man of the heart, in that which is not corruptible, even the ornament of a meek and quiet spirit, which is in the sight of God of great price.	This is what the mystics call "The Man of the Heart"	306-4

Unique Verse Nr.	Bible Verse	Citation	Ernest Holmes reference	Page in SOM text
364	I John 2:10	He that loveth his brother abideth in the light, and there is none occasion of stumbling in him.	Light: He that loveth his brother abideth in the light	607
365	I John 3:2	Beloved, now are we the sons of God, and it doth not yet appear what we shall be: but we know that, when he shall appear, we shall be like him; for we shall see him as he is.	All men are the Sons of God	162-1
	I John 3:2	Beloved, now are we the sons of God, and it doth not yet appear what we shall be: but we know that, when he shall appear, we shall be like him; for we shall see him as he is.	Beloved, now are we the Sons of God	335-3
	I John 3:2	Beloved, now are we the sons of God, and it doth not yet appear what we shall be: but we know that, when he shall appear, we shall be like him; for we shall see him as he is.	Beloved, now are we the Sons of God and it doth not yet appear what we shall be but we know that when he shall appear, we shall be like Him for we shall see Him as He is.	338-3
	I John 3:2	Beloved, now are we the sons of God, and it doth not yet appear what we shall be: but we know that, when he shall appear, we shall be like him; for we shall see him as he is.	God's love is complete in us, in that we are His sons	502-7
	I John 3:2	Beloved, now are we the sons of God, and it doth not yet appear what we shall be: but we know that, when he shall appear, we shall be like him; for we shall see him as he is.	Now are we the Sons of God	503-1
	I John 3:2	Beloved, now are we the sons of God, and it doth not yet appear what we shall be: but we know that, when he shall appear, we shall be like him; for we shall see him as he is.	"We shall see him as he is"	503-3
366	I John 3:7	Little children, let no man deceive you: he that doeth righteousness is righteous, even as he is righteous	Who doeth right, is right, even as He is right.	503-4
367	I John 3:9	Whosoever is born of God doth not commit sin; for his seed remaineth in him: and he cannot sin, because he is born of God.	"Who is born of love is born of God, for God is Love."	503-6
368	I John 4:8	He that loveth not knoweth not God; for God is love.	It is written that God is love	478-3
	I John 4:8	He that loveth not knoweth not God; for God is love.	Love: "He that loveth not, knoweth not God; for God is Love."	608
369	I John 4:12	No man hath seen God at any time. If we love one another, God dwelleth in us, and his love is perfected in us.	No one has seen God	072-2
	I John 4:12	No man hath seen God at any time. If we love one another, God dwelleth in us, and his love is perfected in us.	No man has seen God at any time	159-3
370	I John 4:16	And we have known and believed the love that God hath to us. God is love; and he that dwelleth in love dwelleth in God, and God in him.	"Who is born of love is born of God, for God is Love."	503-6
371	I John 4:18	There is no fear in love; but perfect love casteth out fear: because fear hath torment. He that feareth is not made perfect in love.	Perfect love casteth out fear	238-4

Where'd He Get That? A Biblical Cross-Reference To Ernest Holmes' The Science of Mind

Unique Verse Nr.	Bible Verse	Citation	Ernest Holmes reference	Page in SOM text
	I John 4:18	There is no fear in love; but perfect love casteth out fear: because fear hath torment. He that feareth is not made perfect in love.	Perfect love casts out fear	404-4
	I John 4:18	There is no fear in love; but perfect love casteth out fear: because fear hath torment. He that feareth is not made perfect in love.	Love dissolves all fear, casts out all doubt and sets the captive free	522-3
	I John 4:18	There is no fear in love; but perfect love casteth out fear: because fear hath torment. He that feareth is not made perfect in love.	Perfect Love casteth out all fear.	528-2
	I John 4:18	There is no fear in love; but perfect love casteth out fear: because fear hath torment. He that feareth is not made perfect in love.	We are no longer afraid, for love casts out fear.	560-2
	I John 4:18	There is no fear in love; but perfect love casteth out fear: because fear hath torment. He that feareth is not made perfect in love.	Fear: "Perfect love casteth out fear:	593
372	II John 1:7	For many deceivers are entered into the world, who confess not that Jesus Christ is come in the flesh. This is a deceiver and an antichrist.	The spirit of the Antichrist means	120-3
	II John 1:7	For many deceivers are entered into the world, who confess not that Jesus Christ is come in the flesh. This is a deceiver and an antichrist.	The spirit of the Antichrist is the destructive use of the Law.	127-2
373	Rev. 1:8	I am Alpha and Omega, the beginning and the ending, saith the Lord, which is, and which was, and which is to come, the Almighty.	I AM Alpha and Omega	144-2
	Rev. 1:8	I am Alpha and Omega, the beginning and the ending, saith the Lord, which is, and which was, and which is to come, the Almighty.	I AM Alpha and Omega	289-2
374	Rev. 3:20	Behold, I stand at the door, and knock: if any man hear my voice, and open the door, I will come in to him, and will sup with him, and he with me.	Behold, I stand at the door and knock.	109-2
	Rev. 3:20	Behold, I stand at the door, and knock: if any man hear my voice, and open the door, I will come in to him, and will sup with him, and he with me.	"Behold I stand at the door and knock."	342-3
	Rev. 3:20	Behold, I stand at the door, and knock: if any man hear my voice, and open the door, I will come in to him, and will sup with him, and he with me.	He stands at the door and knocks	369-1
	Rev. 3:20	Behold, I stand at the door, and knock: if any man hear my voice, and open the door, I will come in to him, and will sup with him, and he with me.	It shall be opened to us when we knock.	435-3
375	Rev. 21:5	And he that sat upon the throne said, Behold, I make all things new. And he said unto me, Write: for these words are true and faithful.	Behold, I make all things new.	275-2
	Rev. 21:5	And he that sat upon the throne said, Behold, I make all things new. And he said unto me, Write: for these words are true and faithful.	Behold, He maketh all things new	540-2

Unique Verse Nr.	Bible Verse	Citation	Ernest Holmes reference	Page in SOM text
376	Rev. 21:21	And the twelve gates were twelve pearls: every several gate was of one pearl: and the street of the city was pure gold, as it were transparent glass.	Heaven: Heaven is not a place, a locality "with streets of gold and gates of pearl."	598
377	Rev. 22:17	And the Spirit and the bride say, Come. And let him that heareth say, Come. And let him that is athirst come. And whosoever will, let him take the water of life freely.	And let him that is athirst come. And whosoever will, let him take the water of life freely.	027-3

TABLE II: BIBLE VERSES CITED IN *THE SCIENCE OF MIND* BY ORDER OF APPEARANCE

Ref. Nr.	Bible Verse	Citation	Ernest Holmes Reference	Page in SOM Text
1	Matthew 8:13	And Jesus said unto the centurion, Go thy way; and as thou hast believed, so be it done unto thee. And his servant was healed in the selfsame hour.	It Is Done Unto Us	x
2	Matthew 6:22-23	The light of the body is the eye: if therefore thine eye be single, thy whole body shall be full of light. But if thine eye be evil, thy whole body shall be full of darkness. If therefore the light that is in thee be darkness, how great is that darkness!	The Single Eye –	xv
3	Acts 10:34	Then Peter opened his mouth, and said, Of a truth I perceive that God is no respecter of persons:	Respecter of persons	xvii
4	Acts 10:34	Then Peter opened his mouth, and said, Of a truth I perceive that God is no respecter of persons:	Universal principles are never respecters of persons	027-3
5	Revelations 22:17	And the Spirit and the bride say, Come. And let him that heareth say, Come. And let him that is athirst come. And whosoever will, let him take the water of life freely.	And let him that is athirst come. And whosoever will, let him take the water of life freely.	027-3
6	Matthew 5:45	That ye may be the children of your Father which is in heaven: for he maketh his sun to rise on the evil and on the good, and sendeth rain on the just and on the unjust.	God "maketh His sun to rise on the evil and on the good, and sendeth rain on the just and on the unjust."	028-1
7	Matthew 9:27-29	And when Jesus departed thence, two blind men followed him, crying, and saying, Thou Son of David, have mercy on us. And when he was come into the house, the blind men came to him: and Jesus saith unto them, Believe ye that I am able to do this? They said unto him, Yea, Lord. Then touched he their eyes, saying, According to your faith be it unto you.	According to our beliefs and faith	032-1
8	Matthew 5:26	Verily I say unto thee, Thou shalt by no means come out thence, till thou hast paid the uttermost farthing.	There is a Law in the Universe which exacts the uttermost farthing	032-3
9	John 8:32	And ye shall know the truth, and the truth shall make you free.	Ye shall know the truth	032-3
10	Acts 17:28	For in him we live, and move, and have our being; as certain also of your own poets have said, For we are also his offspring.	Lives, moves and has his being in	032-3
11	John 8:32	And ye shall know the truth, and the truth shall make you free.	the Truth will automatically free him	033-2
12	John 15:7	If ye abide in me, and my words abide in you, ye shall ask what ye will, and it shall be done unto you.	It is done unto you.	034-1
13	Acts 17:28	For in him we live, and move, and have our being; as certain also of your own poets have said, For we are also his offspring.	Live, move and have our being in	035-3
14	Malachi 3:8	Will a man rob God? Yet ye have robbed me. But ye say, Wherein have we robbed thee? In tithes and offerings.	Robbing God	036-1
15	John 1:12	But as many as received him, to them gave he power to become the sons of God, even to them that believe on his name:	That is why we are called the "son of God."	036-2

Where'd He Get That? A Biblical Cross-Reference To Ernest Holmes' The Science of Mind

Ref. Nr.	Bible Verse	Citation	Ernest Holmes Reference	Page in SOM Text
16	Matthew 8:13	And Jesus said unto the centurion, Go thy way; and as thou hast believed, so be it done unto thee. And his servant was healed in the selfsame hour.	It is done unto you as you believe	037-1
17	Hebrews 4:6	Seeing therefore it remaineth that some must enter therein, and they to whom it was first preached entered not in because of unbelief:	They could not enter because of their unbelief,	037-3
18	Matthew 8:13	And Jesus said unto the centurion, Go thy way; and as thou hast believed, so be it done unto thee. And his servant was healed in the selfsame hour.	AS MUCH AS WE CAN BELIEVE will be done unto us	038-1
19	John 1:1, 2, 3	In the beginning was the Word, and the Word was with God, and the Word was God. The same was in the beginning with God. All things were made by him; and without him was not any thing made that was made.	This is what the Bible calls the Word.	038-2
20	Galatians 6:7	Be not deceived; God is not mocked: for whatsoever a man soweth, that shall he also reap.	Whatsoever a man soweth, that shall he also reap	039-3
21	Psalms 23:6	Surely goodness and mercy shall follow me all the days of my life: and I will dwell in the house of the LORD for ever.	Only good and loving-kindness shall "follow me all the days of my life."	039-4
22	Acts 10:34	Then Peter opened his mouth, and said, Of a truth I perceive that God is no respecter of persons:	It is no respecter of persons	041-2
23	Luke 2:12-14	And suddenly there was with the angel a multitude of the heavenly host praising God, and saying, Glory to God in the highest, and on earth peace, good will toward men.	The farmer has seen the Heavenly Host in his fields.	041-3
24	Acts 10:34	Then Peter opened his mouth, and said, Of a truth I perceive that God is no respecter of persons:	law is no respecter of persons	052-4
25	Matthew 5:48	Be ye therefore perfect, even as your Father which is in heaven is perfect.	Be ye therefore perfect, even as your Father…	053-5
26	Psalms 19:7	The law of the LORD is perfect, converting the soul: the testimony of the LORD is sure, making wise the simple.	The law of the Lord is perfect	054-1
27	Matthew 24:35	Heaven and earth shall pass away, but my words shall not pass away.	Heaven and earth shall pass away	054-1
28	Genesis 3:1-5	Now the serpent was more subtil than any beast of the field which the LORD God had made. And he said unto the woman, Yea, hath God said, Ye shall not eat of every tree of the garden? And the woman said unto the serpent, We may eat of the fruit of the trees of the garden: But of the fruit of the tree which is in the midst of the garden, God hath said, Ye shall not eat of it, neither shall ye touch it, lest ye die. And the serpent said unto the woman, Ye shall not surely die: For God doth know that in the day ye eat thereof, then your eyes shall be opened, and ye shall be as gods, knowing good and evil.	should he listen to this "tale of the serpent"	055-3

Ref. Nr.	Bible Verse	Citation	Ernest Holmes Reference	Page in SOM Text
29	Philippians 3:20	For our conversation is in heaven; from whence also we look for the Saviour, the Lord Jesus Christ:	we will let our "conversation be in Heaven"	055-4
30	Matthew 15:14	Let them alone: they be blind leaders of the blind. And if the blind lead the blind, both shall fall into the ditch.	The blind leading the blind	055-4
31	John 12:32	And I, if I be lifted up from the earth, will draw all men unto me.	And I, if I be lifted up,…(not dragged down) will draw all men unto me.	056-1
32	Isaiah 55:11	So shall my word be that goeth forth out of my mouth: it shall not return unto me void, but it shall accomplish that which I please, and it shall prosper in the thing whereto I sent it.	That, unto where it was sent	057-1
33	John 8:32	And ye shall know the truth, and the truth shall make you free.	I may know the Truth and the Truth may make me free.	057-1
34	Hebrews 11:3	Through faith we understand that the worlds were framed by the word of God, so that things which are seen were not made of things which do appear.	Things which are seen are not made of things which do appear	057-2
35	Genesis 1:1	1In the beginning God created the heaven and the earth.	In the beginning God!	063-2
36	Genesis 1:2	And the earth was without form, and void; and darkness was upon the face of the deep. And the Spirit of God moved upon the face of the waters.	the Spirit, had not yet moved upon the waters	063-2
37	Genesis 1:1-31	In the beginning God created the heaven and the earth. And the earth was without form, and void; and darkness was upon the face of the deep. And the Spirit of God moved upon the face of the waters. And God said, Let there be light: and there was light. And God saw the light, that it was good: and God divided the light from the darkness. And God called the light Day, and the darkness he called Night. And the evening and the morning were the first day. . . . And God blessed them, and God said unto them, Be fruitful, and multiply, and replenish the earth, and subdue it: and have dominion over the fish of the sea, and over the fowl of the air, and over every living thing that moveth upon the earth. . . . And God saw every thing that he had made, and, behold, it was very good. And the evening and the morning were the sixth day.	Without repeating the well-known account (rather accounts, for there are two) of Creation, as given in the Bible	064-3

Ref. Nr.	Bible Verse	Citation	Ernest Holmes Reference	Page in SOM Text
38	Genesis: 2:6-25	And the LORD God formed man of the dust of the ground, and breathed into his nostrils the breath of life; and man became a living soul. And the LORD God planted a garden eastward in Eden; and there he put the man whom he had formed And out of the ground made the LORD God to grow every tree that is pleasant to the sight, and good for food; the tree of life also in the midst of the garden, and the tree of knowledge of good and evil... And the LORD God caused a deep sleep to fall upon Adam, and he slept: and he took one of his ribs, and closed up the flesh instead thereof; And the rib, which the LORD God had taken from man, made he a woman, and brought her unto the man. And Adam said, This is now bone of my bones, and flesh of my flesh: she shall be called Woman, because she was taken out of Man. Therefore shall a man leave his father and his mother, and shall cleave unto his wife: and they shall be one flesh. And they were both naked, the man and his wife, and were not ashamed.	Without repeating the well-known account (rather accounts, for there are two) of Creation, as given in the Bible	064-3
39	Genesis 2:19-20	And out of the ground the LORD God formed every beast of the field, and every fowl of the air; and brought them unto Adam to see what he would call them: and whatsoever Adam called every living creature, that was the name thereof. And Adam gave names to all cattle, and to the fowl of the air, and to every beast of the field;	I will let him name everything I have created	065-5
40	Genesis 1:26	And God said, Let us make man in our image, after our likeness: and let them have dominion over the fish of the sea, and over the fowl of the air, and over the cattle, and over all the earth, and over every creeping thing that creepeth upon the earth.	So God gave man dominion over all earthly things.	065-6
41	Genesis 1:28	And God blessed them, and God said unto them, Be fruitful, and multiply, and replenish the earth, and subdue it: and have dominion over the fish of the sea, and over the fowl of the air, and over every living thing that moveth upon the earth.	he was given the power to have dominion	065-6
42	I Corinthians 14:33	For God is not the author of confusion, but of peace, as in all churches of the saints.	The Divine Mind is never confused	065-2
43	Genesis 1:31	And God saw every thing that he had made, and, behold, it was very good. And the evening and the morning were the sixth day.	And God viewing all that He had created saw that it was it was good, "very good."	065-7

Ref. Nr.	Bible Verse	Citation	Ernest Holmes Reference	Page in SOM Text
44	Genesis 1:26	And God said, Let us make man in our image, after our likeness: and let them have dominion over the fish of the sea, and over the fowl of the air, and over the cattle, and over all the earth, and over every creeping thing that creepeth upon the earth.	He must make him in His own image and likeness	065-3
45	Genesis 1:1	In the beginning God created the heaven and the earth.	In the beginning God created the heavens and the earth	067-2
46	Psalm 33:9	For he spake, and it was done; he commanded, and it stood fast.	He spake and it was done	068-5
47	John I: 1-3	In the beginning was the Word, and the Word was with God, and the Word was God. The same was in the beginning with God. All things were made by him; and without him was not any thing made that was made.	The Word was with God, and the Word was God. All things were made by Him and without Him was not anything made that was made	068-5
48	Psalm 33:9	For he spake, and it was done; he commanded, and it stood fast.	GOD SPEAKS AND IT IS DONE!	069-3
49	Exodus 3:14	And God said unto Moses, I AM THAT I AM: and he said, Thus shalt thou say unto the children of Israel, I AM hath sent me unto you.	I AM - I AM-ness -The I AM	069-3
50	John 1:18	No man hath seen God at any time, the only begotten Son, which is in the bosom of the Father, he hath declared him.	No one has seen God	072-2
51	I John 4:12	No man hath seen God at any time. If we love one another, God dwelleth in us, and his love is perfected in us.	No one has seen God	072-2
52	Exodus 3:14	And God said unto Moses, I AM THAT I AM: and he said, Thus shalt thou say unto the children of Israel, I AM hath sent me unto you.	the day when he first said "I am"	072-3
53	I Kings 19:12	And after the earthquake a fire; but the LORD was not in the fire: and after the fire a still small voice.	Little attention has been given to that still, small voice	072-4
54	John 1:18	No man hath seen God at any time, the only begotten Son, which is in the bosom of the Father, he hath declared him.	"No man hath seen God at any time; only the Son, he hath revealed Him."	075-3
55	Acts 17:28	For in him we live, and move, and have our being; as certain also of your own poets have said, For we are also his offspring.	"In Him we live, move, and have our being."	076-3
56	John 4:20-24	Our fathers worshipped in this mountain; and ye say, that in Jerusalem is the place where men ought to worship. Jesus saith unto her, Woman, believe me, the hour cometh, when ye shall neither in this mountain, nor yet at Jerusalem, worship the Father. Ye worship ye know not what: we know what we worship: for salvation is of the Jews. But the hour cometh, and now is, when the true worshippers shall worship the Father in spirit and in truth: for the Father seeketh such to worship him. God is a Spirit: and they that worship him must worship him in spirit and in truth.	Jesus said Reality is not in the mountain, nor afar off, but within us	076-3

Where'd He Get That? A Biblical Cross-Reference To Ernest Holmes' The Science of Mind

Ref. Nr.	Bible Verse	Citation	Ernest Holmes Reference	Page in SOM Text
57	Luke 11:18	If Satan also be divided against himself, how shall his kingdom stand? because ye say that I cast out devils through Beelzebub.	If I cast out devils by Beelzebub, the prince of devils, that is a house divided against itself, which cannot stand	076-4
58	John 14:9	Jesus saith unto him, Have I been so long time with you, and yet hast thou not known me, Philip? he that hath seen me hath seen the Father; and how sayest thou then, Shew us the Father?	"Who hath seen me hath seen the Father."	076-4
59	John 1:1, 2, 3	In the beginning was the Word, and the Word was with God, and the Word was God. The same was in the beginning with God. All things were made by him; and without him was not any thing made that was made.	what the Bible calls "The Word.". . .Absolute Intelligence.	080-3
60	John 4:24	God is a Spirit: and they that worship him must worship him in spirit and in truth.	God is spirit and they that worship him must worship him in spirit and in truth	081-2
61	Acts 17:28	For in him we live, and move, and have our being; as certain also of your own poets have said, For we are also his offspring.	within this One all live	082-2
62	Deuteronomy 6:4	Hear, O Israel: The LORD our God is one LORD: (Old Testament)	The fundamental premise upon which the philosophy of the Bible is develop is that Spirit is One.	082-3
63	Mark 12:29	And Jesus answered him, The first of all the commandments is, Hear, O Israel; The Lord our God is one Lord: (New Testament)	The fundamental premise upon which the philosophy of the Bible is develop is that Spirit is One.	082-3
64	John 10:10	The thief cometh not, but for to steal, and to kill, and to destroy: I am come that they might have life, and that they might have it more abundantly.	I came so they might have life	082-4
65	Acts 17:28	For in him we live, and move, and have our being; as certain also of your own poets have said, For we are also his offspring.	There is only Mind, in which we all "live and move and have our being."	087-4
66	John 14:2	In my Father's house are many mansions: if it were not so, I would have told you. I go to prepare a place for you.	In my Father's house are many mansions	098-2
67	I Corinthians 13:9	For we know in part, and we prophesy in part.	For we know in part and prophesy in part	098-2
68	Hebrews 11:3	Through faith we understand that the worlds were framed by the word of God, so that things which are seen were not made of things which do appear.	Things which are seen are not made of things which do appear	101-3
69	Ephesians 4:6	One God and Father of all, who is above all, and through all, and in you all.	God is "All in all."	103-2
70	John 6:63	It is the spirit that quickeneth; the flesh profiteth nothing: the words that I speak unto you, they are spirit, and they are life.	Jesus proclaimed that the very words which he spoke were Spirit and were life.	103-3
71	I Corinthians 2:9	But as it is written, Eye hath not seen, nor ear heard, neither have entered into the heart of man, the things which God hath prepared for them that love him.	The Universe as we see it is not even a fractional part of the Universe that actually is, "Eye hath not seen. . ."	104-3
72	John 5:26	For as the Father hath life in himself; so hath he given to the Son to have life in himself;	As the Father has life, so the son has life.	106-3

Where'd He Get That? A Biblical Cross-Reference To Ernest Holmes' The Science of Mind

Ref. Nr.	Bible Verse	Citation	Ernest Holmes Reference	Page in SOM Text
73	Job 14:14	If a man die, shall he live again? all the days of my appointed time will I wait, till my change come.	something rises from within and says with Job: "Though I die, yet shall I live."	108-2
74	Luke 12:32	Fear not, little flock; for it is your Father's good pleasure to give you the kingdom.	It is your Father's good pleasure to give you the kingdom.	108-4
75	Luke 12:32	Fear not, little flock; for it is your Father's good pleasure to give you the kingdom.	Fear not little flock, it is your Father's good pleasure to give you the kingdom.	109-1
76	Revelations 3:20	Behold, I stand at the door, and knock: if any man hear my voice, and open the door, I will come in to him, and will sup with him, and he with me.	Behold, I stand at the door and knock.	109-2
77	Galatians 3:21	Is the law then against the promises of God? God forbid: for if there had been a law given which could have given life, verily righteousness should have been by the law.	The Bible says: "If there had been any law whereby this freedom could be compelled, then verily by the law would that freedom have been given."	109-2
78	Romans 8:31	What shall we then say to these things? If God be for us, who can be against us?	If God be for us, who can be against us?	109-4
79	Matthew 1:23	Behold, a virgin shall be with child, and shall bring forth a son, and they shall call his name Emmanuel, which being interpreted is, God with us.	Emmanuel or God with us	113-1
80	John 7:24	Judge not according to the appearance, but judge righteous judgment.	Judge by appearances	113-2
81	John 7:24	Judge not according to the appearance, but judge righteous judgment.	Appearances of	113-2
82	Genesis 1:2	And the earth was without form, and void; and darkness was upon the face of the deep.	In the theoretical beginning of creation, the world was "without form and void."	117-1
83	II John 1:7	For many deceivers are entered into the world, who confess not that Jesus Christ is come in the flesh. This is a deceiver and an antichrist.	The spirit of the Antichrist means	120-3

Ref. Nr.	BIBLE Verse	Citation	Ernest Holmes Reference	Page in SOM Text
84	Genesis 7:17-24	And the flood was forty days upon the earth; and the waters increased, and bare up the ark, and it was lift up above the earth. And the waters prevailed, and were increased greatly upon the earth; and the ark went upon the face of the waters. And the waters prevailed exceedingly upon the earth; and all the high hills, that were under the whole heaven, were covered. Fifteen cubits upward did the waters prevail; and the mountains were covered. And all flesh died that moved upon the earth, both of fowl, and of cattle, and of beast, and of every creeping thing that creepeth upon the earth, and every man: All in whose nostrils was the breath of life, of all that was in the dry land, died. And every living substance was destroyed which was upon the face of the ground, both man, and cattle, and the creeping things, and the fowl of the heaven; and they were destroyed from the earth: and Noah only remained alive, and they that were with him in the ark. And the waters prevailed upon the earth an hundred and fifty days.	The meaning of the Flood or Deluge (which is recorded in every sacred scripture we have ever heard of or read)	120-3
85	Galatians 5:22-23	But the fruit of the Spirit is love, joy, peace, longsuffering, gentleness, goodness, faith, Meekness, temperance: against such there is no law.	there is but On Ultimate Reality, for "against such there is no law"	121-2
86	Luke 17:21	Neither shall they say, Lo here! or, lo there! for, behold, the kingdom of God is within you.	Lo here nor Lo there…	124-1
87	Matthew 9:27-29	And when Jesus departed thence, two blind men followed him, crying, and saying, Thou Son of David, have mercy on us. And when he was come into the house, the blind men came to him: and Jesus saith unto them, Believe ye that I am able to do this? They said unto him, Yea, Lord. Then touched he their eyes, saying, According to your faith be it unto you.	Jesus said: "As thou has believed, so be it done unto thee"	127-1
88	II John 1:7	For many deceivers are entered into the world, who confess not that Jesus Christ is come in the flesh. This is a deceiver and an antichrist.	The spirit of the Antichrist is the destructive use of the Law.	127-2
89	Matthew 26:52	Then said Jesus unto him, Put up again thy sword into his place: for all they that take the sword shall perish with the sword.	All that take the sword shall die by the sword	127-3
90	Hebrews 4:6 and Psalms 78:41	Heb 4:6 Seeing therefore it remaineth that some must enter therein, and they to whom it was first preached entered not in because of unbelief: Ps 78:41 Yea, they turned back and tempted God, and limited the Holy One of Israel.	"They could not enter because of their unbelief, and because they limited the Holy One of Israel."	128-1
91	Proverbs 23:7	For as he thinketh in his heart, so is he: Eat and drink, saith he to thee; but his heart is not with thee.	As a man thinketh in his heart, so is he.	137-1

Ref. Nr.	Bible Verse	Citation	Ernest Holmes Reference	Page in SOM Text
92	Genesis 1:26	And God said, Let us make man in our image, after our likeness: and let them have dominion over the fish of the sea, and over the fowl of the air, and over the cattle, and over all the earth, and over every creeping thing that creepeth upon the earth.	incredible possibilities of dominion	138-1
93	John 10:30	I and my Father are one.	So with Jesus we may say: "The Father and I are One."	139-2
94	Matthew 8:13	And Jesus said unto the centurion, Go thy way; and as thou hast believed, so be it done unto thee. And his servant was healed in the selfsame hour.	It is done unto you AS you believe.	140-2
95	Revelation 1:8	I am Alpha and Omega, the beginning and the ending, saith the Lord, which is, and which was, and which is to come, the Almighty.	I AM Alpha and Omega	144-2
96	John 1:1, 2, 3	In the beginning was the Word, and the Word was with God, and the Word was God. The same was in the beginning with God. All things were made by him; and without him was not any thing made that was made.	"The Word was with God and the Word was God."	145-4
97	Romans 10:8	But what saith it? The word is nigh thee, even in thy mouth, and in thy heart: that is, the word of faith, which we preach;	"The Word is nigh Thee, even in thine own mouth that thou shouldst know it and do it."	146-1
98	Romans 8:31	What shall we then say to these things? If God be for us, who can be against us?	"If God be for us who can be against us?"	146-2
99	Isaiah 55:11	So shall my word be that goeth forth out of my mouth: it shall not return unto me void, but it shall accomplish that which I please, and it shall prosper in the thing whereto I sent it.	So shall my word that goeth forth not return unto me void.	146-3
100	Luke 15:17-18	And when he came to himself, he said, How many hired servants of my father's have bread enough and to spare, and I perish with hunger! I will arise and go to my father, and will say unto him, Father, I have sinned against heaven, and before thee,	The Prodigal Son remained a prodigal as long as he chose to do so. When he chose to, he returned to his "Father's house" and was greeted with outstretched hands.	147-3
101	Jeremiah 33:2-3	Thus saith the LORD the maker thereof, the LORD that formed it, to establish it; the LORD is his name; Call unto me, and I will answer thee, and shew thee great and mighty things, which thou knowest not.	In that day they call upon me, I will answer	148-4
102	John 15:7	If ye abide in me, and my words abide in you, ye shall ask what ye will, and it shall be done unto you.	it is done unto us as we believe	148-4
103	Hebrews 11:3	Through faith we understand that the worlds were framed by the word of God, so that things which are seen were not made of things which do appear.	The seen and the unseen	148-4
104	Hebrews 13:8	Jesus Christ the same yesterday, and to day, and for ever.	He is "the same yesterday, today and forever."	150-3
105	John 4:24	God is a Spirit: and they that worship him must worship him in spirit and in truth.	We are told that "God is Spirit, and they that worship Him must worship Him in spirit and in truth."	150-4

Ref. Nr.	Bible Verse	Citation	Ernest Holmes Reference	Page in SOM Text
106	John 4:20,21	Our fathers worshipped in this mountain; and ye say, that in Jerusalem is the place where men ought to worship. Jesus saith unto her, Woman, believe me, the hour cometh, when ye shall neither in this mountain, nor yet at Jerusalem, worship the Father.	Neither in the mountain nor at the temple	150-4
107	Luke 17:21	Neither shall they say, Lo here! or, lo there! for, behold, the kingdom of God is within you.	The Kingdom of God is within you.	150-4
108	John 14:10	Believest thou not that I am in the Father, and the Father in me? the words that I speak unto you I speak not of myself: but the Father that dwelleth in me, he doeth the works.	The Father who dwelleth in me doeth the work.	150-5
109	Luke 17:21	Neither shall they say, Lo here! or, lo there! for, behold, the kingdom of God is within you.	The Kingdom of God is within you.	150-5
110	James 4:3	Ye ask, and receive not, because ye ask amiss, that ye may consume it upon your lusts.	We shall no longer "ask amiss"	150-5
111	John 15:7	If ye abide in me, and my words abide in you, ye shall ask what ye will, and it shall be done unto you.	If ye abide in me, and my words abide in you, ye shall ask what ye will, and it shall be done unto you.	150-6
112	John 15:7	If ye abide in me, and my words abide in you, ye shall ask what ye will, and it shall be done unto you.	If ye abide in me, and my words abide in you, ye shall ask what ye will, and it shall be done unto you.	151-1
113	John 14:13	And whatsoever ye shall ask in my name, that will I do, that the Father may be glorified in the Son.	Whatsoever ye shall ask in my name, that will I do.	151-2
114	Luke 17:19	And he said unto him, Arise, go thy way: thy faith hath made thee whole.	It is done unto you as you believe.	152-1
115	John 7:24	Judge not according to the appearance, but judge righteous judgment.	Judge according to appearances.	152-3
116	Romans 8:2	For the law of the Spirit of life in Christ Jesus hath made me free from the law of sin and death.	Righteous prayer sets the "law of the Spirit of Life" in motion for us.	152-3
117	Acts 17:28	For in him we live, and move, and have our being; as certain also of your own poets have said, For we are also his offspring.	that which lives and moves and has Its being where we are	152-5
118	Isaiah 65:24	And it shall come to pass, that before they call, I will answer; and while they are yet speaking, I will hear.	Before they call, I will answer	153-2
119	Hebrews 11:3	Through faith we understand that the worlds were framed by the word of God, so that things which are seen were not made of things which do appear.	Before our prayer is framed in words, God has already answered.	153-2
120	Psalms 66:18	If I regard iniquity in my heart, the Lord will not hear me:	Someone has said that the entire world is suffering from one big fear. . .the fear that God will not answer our prayers	156-3
121	Hebrews 11:1	Now faith is the substance of things hoped for, the evidence of things not seen.	Faith is the substance of things hoped for	156-5
122	Psalms 145:16	Thou openest thine hand, and satisfiest the desire of every living thing.	He openeth his hand and satisfieth the desire of every living creature	157-3

Ref. Nr.	Bible Verse	Citation	Ernest Holmes Reference	Page in SOM Text
123	Matthew 7:7	Ask, and it shall be given you; seek, and ye shall find; knock, and it shall be opened unto you:	And I say unto you, ask and it shall be given unto you.	157-3
124	Luke 11:9	And I say unto you, Ask, and it shall be given you; seek, and ye shall find; knock, and it shall be opened unto you	Ask and it shall be given unto you	157-3
125	Psalms 145:16	Thou openest thine hand, and satisfiest the desire of every living thing.	"He openeth his hand and satisfieth the desire of every living thing."	157-3
126	Exodus 3:14	And God said unto Moses, I AM THAT I AM: and he said, Thus shalt thou say unto the children of Israel, I AM hath sent me unto you.	It only knows "I AM."	157-4
127	Matthew 8:13	And Jesus said unto the centurion, Go thy way; and as thou hast believed, so be it done unto thee. And his servant was healed in the selfsame hour.	It is done unto you as you believe.	157-4
128	Psalms 78:8	And might not be as their fathers, a stubborn and rebellious generation; a generation that set not their heart aright, and whose spirit was not stedfast with God.	Prays aright	158-1
129	Hebrews 11:33-35	Who through faith subdued kingdoms, wrought righteousness, obtained promises, stopped the mouths of lions. Quenched the violence of fire, escaped the edge of the sword, out of weakness were made strong, waxed valiant in fight, turned to flight the armies of the aliens. Women received their dead raised to life again:	Who through faith subdued kingdoms, wrought righteousness, obtained promises, stopped the mouths of lions, quenched the power of fire, escaped the edge of the sword; out of weakness were made strong, waxed mighty in power, turned to flight armies of aliens, women received their dead raised to life again."	158-2
130	John 1:18	No man hath seen God at any time, the only begotten Son, which is in the bosom of the Father, he hath declared him.	No man has seen God at any time	159-3
131	I John 4:12	No man hath seen God at any time. If we love one another, God dwelleth in us, and his love is perfected in us.	No man has seen God at any time	159-3
132	Matthew 8:13	And Jesus said unto the centurion, Go thy way; and as thou hast believed, so be it done unto thee. And his servant was healed in the selfsame hour.	Go thy way; and as thou hast believed, so be it done unto thee.	161-1
133	Matthew 8:10	When Jesus heard it, he marveled, and said to them that followed, Verily I say unto you, I have not found so great faith, no, not in Israel.	Jesus said, "I have not found so great faith, no, not in all Israel."	161-1
134	Matthew 12:25	And Jesus knew their thoughts, and said unto them, Every kingdom divided against itself is brought to desolation; and every city or house divided against itself shall not stand:	We should be careful not to divide our mental house against itself	161-4
135	I John 3:2	Beloved, now are we the sons of God, and it doth not yet appear what we shall be: but we know that, when he shall appear, we shall be like him; for we shall see him as he is.	All men are the Sons of God	162-1

Ref. Nr.	Bible Verse	Citation	Ernest Holmes Reference	Page in SOM Text
136	Matthew 17:20	And Jesus said unto them, Because of your unbelief: for verily I say unto you, If ye have faith as a grain of mustard seed, ye shall say unto this mountain, Remove hence to yonder place; and it shall remove; and nothing shall be impossible unto you.	If ye have faith as a grain of mustard seed	162-2
137	John 7:24	Judge not according to the appearance, but judge righteous judgment.	No matter what the outside appearance…	162-5
138	II Timothy 1:12	For the which cause I also suffer these things: nevertheless I am not ashamed: for I know whom I have believed, and am persuaded that he is able to keep that which I have committed unto him against that day.	I know in whom I have believed	162-5
139	Matthew 19:26	But Jesus beheld them, and said unto them, With men this is impossible; but with God all things are possible.	With God all things are possible	169-3
140	Psalms 91:1	He that dwelleth in the secret place of the most High shall abide under the shadow of the Almighty.	The secret place of the Most High	169-3
141	Isaiah 55:11	So shall my word be that goeth forth out of my mouth: it shall not return unto me void, but it shall accomplish that which I please, and it shall prosper in the thing whereto I sent it.	that his word is the law of that whereunto it was spoken	169-3
142	Matthew 24:35	Heaven and earth shall pass away, but my words shall not pass away.	And Jesus said, "Heaven and earth shall pass away, but my words shall not pass away."	173-4
143	Isaiah 65:24	And it shall come to pass, that before they call, I will answer; and while they are yet speaking, I will hear.	Before they call, I will answer is the divine promise	174-2
144	Luke 11:9	And I say unto you, Ask, and it shall be given you; seek, and ye shall find; knock, and it shall be opened unto you	Everyone who asks receives	175-1
145	Isaiah 55:11	So shall my word be that goeth forth out of my mouth: it shall not return unto me void, but it shall accomplish that which I please, and it shall prosper in the thing whereto I sent it.	that our word has accomplished "that, whereunto it was sent."	176-1
146	Hebrews 11:3	Through faith we understand that the worlds were framed by the word of God, so that things which are seen were not made of things which do appear.	Before our prayer is framed in words the possibility of its answer already exists.	178-2
147	Hebrews 11:1	Now faith is the substance of things hoped for, the evidence of things not seen.	Faith is the substance of things hoped for, the evidence of things not seen.	178-4
148	John 1:5	And the light shineth in darkness; and the darkness comprehended it not.	And the light shineth in the darkness and the darkness comprehended it not.	183-2
149	Isaiah 55:11	So shall my word be that goeth forth out of my mouth: it shall not return unto me void, but it shall accomplish that which I please, and it shall prosper in the thing whereto I sent it.	This word is the law unto the thing whereunto it is spoken	184-3
150	Philippians 4:7	And the peace of God, which passeth all understanding, shall keep your hearts and minds through Christ Jesus.	Peace which passeth all understanding	185-2

Ref. Nr.	Bible Verse	Citation	Ernest Holmes Reference	Page in SOM Text
151	Matthew 5:48	Be ye therefore perfect, even as your Father which is in heaven is perfect.	Be ye therefore perfect, even as your Father…	185-2
152	Matthew 18:10	Take heed that ye despise not one of these little ones; for I say unto you, That in heaven their angels do always behold the face of my Father which is in heaven.	"Behold thou my face forevermore"	185-3
153	Isaiah 45:22	Look unto me, and be ye saved, all the ends of the earth: for I am God, and there is none else.	Look unto me and be ye saved, all the ends of the earth.	185-3
154	John 7:24	Judge not according to the appearance, but judge righteous judgment.	If, as Jesus said, we "judge not according to appearances, but judge righteous judgment,"	187-3
155	Hebrews 11:3	Through faith we understand that the worlds were framed by the word of God, so that things which are seen were not made of things which do appear.	Things which are seen are not made of things which do appear	187-3
156	Isaiah 55:11	So shall my word be that goeth forth out of my mouth: it shall not return unto me void, but it shall accomplish that which I please, and it shall prosper in the thing whereto I sent it.	The Law unto the thing whereto they are spoken	188-2
157	John 7:24	Judge not according to the appearance, but judge righteous judgment.	we must see beyond the appearance	189-2
158	Matthew 6:27	Which of you by taking thought can add one cubit unto his stature?	Who by taking thought can add one cubit to his stature?	194-3
159	Galatians 6:7	Be not deceived; God is not mocked: for whatsoever a man soweth, that shall he also reap.	As we sow, so must we reap	195-2
160	Ecclesiastes 7:29 or 30	Lo, this only have I found, that God hath made man upright; but they have sought out many inventions.	The Scriptures say: "God hath made man upright; but they have sought out many inventions."	196-1
161	Exodus 3:14	And God said unto Moses, I AM THAT I AM: and he said, Thus shalt thou say unto the children of Israel, I AM hath sent me unto you.	God creates by contemplating His own I-AM-NESS	196-4
162	Isaiah 55:11	So shall my word be that goeth forth out of my mouth: it shall not return unto me void, but it shall accomplish that which I please, and it shall prosper in the thing whereto I sent it.	Your word is the law unto the thing unto which it is spoken	203-3
163	Mark 1:22	And they were astonished at his doctrine: for he taught them as one that had authority, and not as the scribes.	For He taught them as one having authority, and not as the scribes	203-3
164	John 8:32	And ye shall know the truth, and the truth shall make you free.	Ye shall know the truth, and the truth shall make you free.	206-4
165	Matthew 24:35	Heaven and earth shall pass away, but my words shall not pass away.	Jesus said: "Heaven and earth shall pass away, but my words shall not pass away."	212-2
166	Isaiah 55:11	So shall my word be that goeth forth out of my mouth: it shall not return unto me void, but it shall accomplish that which I please, and it shall prosper in the thing whereto I sent it.	So shall my word be that goeth forth out of my mouth: it shall not return unto me void	212-2

Ref. Nr.	Bible Verse	Citation	Ernest Holmes Reference	Page in SOM Text
167	Matthew 12:13	Then saith he to the man, Stretch forth thine hand. And he stretched it forth; and it was restored whole, like as the other.	When Jesus said to the man, "Stretch forth thine hand,"	212-3
168	John 7:24	Judge not according to the appearance, but judge righteous judgment.	we must transcend the appearance	213-3
169	Mark 12:32	And the scribe said unto him, Well, Master, thou hast said the truth: for there is one God; and there is none other but he:	which is God, "beside which there is none other."	216-1
170	Isaiah 55:11	So shall my word be that goeth forth out of my mouth: it shall not return unto me void, but it shall accomplish that which I please, and it shall prosper in the thing whereto I sent it.	This word is the law unto the thing whereunto it is spoken	216-2
171	Exodus 14:13	And Moses said unto the people, Fear ye not, stand still, and see the salvation of the LORD, which he will shew to you to day: for the Egyptians whom ye have seen to day, ye shall see them again no more for ever.	Stand still and watch the sure salvation of the Lord	217-1
172	Exodus 3:14	And God said unto Moses, I AM THAT I AM: and he said, Thus shalt thou say unto the children of Israel, I AM hath sent me unto you.	an incarnation of the Universal "I Am."	217-1
173	Luke 15:30-31	But as soon as this thy son was come, which hath devoured thy living with harlots, thou hast killed for him the fatted calf. And he said unto him, Son, thou art ever with me, and all that I have is thine.	"All the Father hath is thine."	217-2
174	Matthew 3:2	And saying, Repent ye: for the kingdom of heaven is at hand.	Behold! The Kingdom of Heaven is at hand.	217-2
175	Matthew 4:17	From that time Jesus began to preach, and to say, Repent: for the kingdom of heaven is at hand.	Behold! The Kingdom of Heaven is at hand.	217-2
176	Matthew 6:6	But thou, when thou prayest, enter into thy closet, and when thou hast shut thy door, pray to thy Father which is in secret; and thy Father which seeth in secret shall reward thee openly.	Pray to Father who is in secret	217-2
177	Matthew 28:2	And, behold, there was a great earthquake: for the angel of the Lord descended from heaven, and came and rolled back the stone from the door, and sat upon it.	Roll away the stone	217-2
178	Luke 24:2	And they found the stone rolled away from the sepulchre.	Roll away the stone	217-2
179	Psalms 91:1	He that dwelleth in the secret place of the most High shall abide under the shadow of the Almighty.	"Heavenly Consciousness" which is the "secret place of the Most High" in man	218-1
180	Romans 12:2	And be not conformed to this world: but be ye transformed by the renewing of your mind, that ye may prove what is that good, and acceptable, and perfect, will of God.	Transformed by a renewing of the mind.	218-3
181	Matthew 14:25	And in the fourth watch of the night Jesus went unto them, walking on the sea.	Since we can not walk on water we take a boat.	219-2
182	Exodus 3:14	And God said unto Moses, I AM THAT I AM: and he said, Thus shalt thou say unto the children of Israel, I AM hath sent me unto you.	the soul recognizes its own I-Am-ness	220-3
183	John 7:24	Judge not according to the appearance, but judge righteous judgment.	Back of all appearance to the contrary…	222-1

Ref. Nr.	Bible Verse	Citation	Ernest Holmes Reference	Page in SOM Text
184	Matthew 5:6	Blessed are they which do hunger and thirst after righteousness: for they shall be filled.	Blessed are they who hunger and thirst after righteousness (right living) for they shall be filled	223-2
185	Philippians 4:8	Finally, brethren, whatsoever things are true, whatsoever things are honest, whatsoever things are just, whatsoever things are pure, whatsoever things are lovely, whatsoever things are of good report; if there be any virtue, and if there be any praise, think on these things.	"Whatsoever things are true, whatsoever things are honorable, whatsoever things are just, whatsoever things are pure, whatsoever things are lovely, whatsoever things are of good report."	226-1
186	I Corinthians 6:19, and II Corinthians 6:16 (combined)	I Cor 6:19: What? know ye not that your body is the temple of the Holy Ghost which is in you, which ye have of God, and ye are not your own? II Cor 6:16 And what agreement hath the temple of God with idols? for ye are the temple of the living God; as God hath said, I will dwell in them, and walk in them; and I will be their God, and they shall be my people.	Know ye not that ye are the temple of the Living God?	227-3
187	Matthew 15:14	Let them alone: they be blind leaders of the blind. And if the blind lead the blind, both shall fall into the ditch.	he would be truly "the blind leading the blind.".	228-1
188	Matthew 6:22-23	The light of the body is the eye: if therefore thine eye be single, thy whole body shall be full of light. But if thine eye be evil, thy whole body shall be full of darkness. If therefore the light that is in thee be darkness, how great is that darkness!	The mind and body must be kept pure – must be kept "single"	229-5
189	Luke 11:34	The light of the body is the eye: therefore when thine eye is single, thy whole body also is full of light; but when thine eye is evil, thy body also is full of darkness.	But if thine eye be evil thy whole body shall be full of darkness	230-1
190	Psalms 121:1	I will lift up mine eyes unto the hills, from whence cometh my help.	I will lift up my eyes unto God from whom comes my perfect sight	231-3
191	Proverbs 11:17	The merciful man doeth good to his own soul: but he that is cruel troubleth his own flesh.	Solomon tells us that "he that is cruel troubleth his own flesh"	232-3
192	Luke 2:12-14	And suddenly there was with the angel a multitude of the heavenly host praising God, and saying, Glory to God in the highest, and on earth peace, good will toward men.	Thoughts of peace and good will…will produce harmony	232-3
193	John 8:32	And ye shall know the truth, and the truth shall make you free.	Ye shall know the truth, and the truth shall make you free.	232-5
194	Matthew 15:13	But he answered and said, Every plant, which my heavenly Father hath not planted, shall be rooted up.	Declare: "every plant which my Heavenly Father hath not planted, shall be rooted up."	234-5
195	Mark 2:5	When Jesus saw their faith, he said unto the sick of the palsy, Son, thy sins be forgiven thee.	This explains why Jesus said: "Thy sins be forgiven thee."	237-2

Where'd He Get That? A Biblical Cross-Reference To Ernest Holmes' The Science of Mind

Ref. Nr.	Bible Verse	Citation	Ernest Holmes Reference	Page in SOM Text
196	Matthew 9:2	And, behold, they brought to him a man sick of the palsy, lying on a bed: and Jesus seeing their faith said unto the sick of the palsy; Son, be of good cheer; thy sins be forgiven thee.	This explains why Jesus said: "Thy sins be forgiven thee."	237-2
197	John 14:1	Let not your heart be troubled: ye believe in God, believe also in me.	Let not your heart be troubled	238-3
198	Proverbs 4:23	Keep thy heart with all diligence; for out of it are the issues of life.	Keep thy heart with all diligence; for out of it are the issues of life.	238-4
199	I John 4:18	There is no fear in love; but perfect love casteth out fear: because fear hath torment. He that feareth is not made perfect in love.	Perfect love casteth out fear	238-4
200	Matthew 5:8	Blessed are the pure in heart: for they shall see God.	Blessed are the pure in heart: for they shall see God.	240-2
201	I Corinthians 6:19	What? know ye not that your body is the temple of the Holy Ghost which is in you, which ye have of God, and ye are not your own?	Know that you alone are the door-keeper to the "Temple of the Holy Ghost," your body.	243-2
202	John 14:27	Peace I leave with you, my peace I give unto you: not as the world giveth, give I unto you. Let not your heart be troubled, neither let it be afraid.	"Peace I leave with you, my peace I give unto you…Let not your heart be troubled, neither let it be afraid."	247-1
203	John 8:32	And ye shall know the truth, and the truth shall make you free.	Ye shall know the truth, and the truth shall make you free.	248-3
204	II Corinthians 6:16	And what agreement hath the temple of God with idols? for ye are the temple of the living God; as God hath said, I will dwell in them, and walk in them; and I will be their God, and they shall be my people.	When the body is the harmonious temple of the Living God	248-3
205	Genesis 1:26	And God said, Let us make man in our image, after our likeness: and let them have dominion over the fish of the sea, and over the fowl of the air, and over the cattle, and over all the earth, and over every creeping thing that creepeth upon the earth.	Claim our power and dominion	250-6
206	Genesis 1:26	And God said, Let us make man in our image, after our likeness: and let them have dominion over the fish of the sea, and over the fowl of the air, and over the cattle, and over all the earth, and over every creeping thing that creepeth upon the earth.	We should claim our dominion and power in Spirit.	252-5
207	Isaiah 50:5	The Lord GOD hath opened mine ear, and I was not rebellious, neither turned away back.	The Lord Jehovah hath opened thine ear	257-6
208	I Samuel 3:9	Therefore Eli said unto Samuel, Go, lie down: and it shall be, if he call thee, that thou shalt say, Speak, LORD; for thy servant heareth. So Samuel went and lay down in his place.	Speak Lord for thy servant heareth	258-1
209	Romans 8:1	There is therefore now no condemnation to them which are in Christ Jesus, who walk not after the flesh, but after the Spirit.	There is therefore now no condemnation to them	259-4

Where'd He Get That? A Biblical Cross-Reference To Ernest Holmes' The Science of Mind

Ref. Nr.	Bible Verse	Citation	Ernest Holmes Reference	Page in SOM Text
210	II Corinthians 7:1	Having therefore these promises, dearly beloved, let us cleanse ourselves from all filthiness of the flesh and spirit, perfecting holiness in the fear of God.	To be washed clean by the Spirit should have a real meaning to us	260-3
211	Mark 8:23-25	And he took the blind man by the hand, and led him out of the town; and when he had spit on his eyes, and put his hands upon him, he asked him if he saw ought. And he looked up, and said, I see men as trees, walking. After that he put his hands again upon his eyes, and made him look up: and he was restored, and saw every man clearly.	how else could Jesus have told the blind man to look up--He said up and not down.	2603
212	Isaiah 55:11	So shall my word be that goeth forth out of my mouth: it shall not return unto me void, but it shall accomplish that which I please, and it shall prosper in the thing whereto I sent it.	the words he uses are the Law unto the thing whereto they are spoken	262-2
213	John 6:63	It is the spirit that quickeneth; the flesh profiteth nothing: the words that I speak unto you, they are spirit, and they are life.	"The words I have spoken unto you are Spirit, and are life."	262-2
214	Isaiah 55:11	So shall my word be that goeth forth out of my mouth: it shall not return unto me void, but it shall accomplish that which I please, and it shall prosper in the thing whereto I sent it.	it is the law unto that thing where unto it is spoken	263-4
215	John 8:32	And ye shall know the truth, and the truth shall make you free.	The Truth makes me free	264-1
216	Psalms 46:10	Be still, and know that I am God: I will be exalted among the heathen, I will be exalted in the earth.	Be still and know that I am God.	264-4
217	John 6:69	And we believe and are sure that thou art that Christ, the Son of the living God.	I am the Christ, the Son of the Living God within me	265-2
218	Matthew 6:10	Thy kingdom come, Thy will be done in earth, as it is in heaven.	Thy will be done	268-4
219	Luke 11:2	And he said unto them, When ye pray, say, Our Father which art in heaven, Hallowed be thy name. Thy kingdom come. Thy will be done, as in heaven, so in earth.	Thy will be done	268-4
220	Galatians 6:7	Be not deceived; God is not mocked: for whatsoever a man soweth, that shall he also reap.	Whatsoever a man soweth, that shall he also reap	269-2
221	Psalms 23:3	He restoreth my soul: he leadeth me in the paths of righteousness for his name's sake.	Do ultimately compel experience into the path of true righteousness	270-1
222	I Timothy 2:5	For there is one God, and one mediator between God and men, the man Christ Jesus;	There is no mediator between God and man except Christ	272-4
223	I Corinthians 2:16	For who hath known the mind of the Lord, that he may instruct him? But we have the mind of Christ.	We have the mind of Christ	273-4
224	Revelations 21:5	And he that sat upon the throne said, Behold, I make all things new. And he said unto me, Write: for these words are true and faithful.	Behold, I make all things new.	275-2
225	Luke 20:25	And he said unto them, Render therefore unto Caesar the things which be Caesar's, and unto God the things which be God's.	Render therefore, unto Caesar the things which are Caesar's; and unto God the things that are God's.	276-3

Where'd He Get That? A Biblical Cross-Reference To Ernest Holmes' The Science of Mind

Ref. Nr.	Bible Verse	Citation	Ernest Holmes Reference	Page in SOM Text
226	Mark 12:17	And Jesus answering said unto them, Render to Caesar the things that are Caesar's, and to God the things that are God's. And they marveled at him.	Render therefore, unto Caesar the things which are Caesar's; and unto God the things that are God's.	276-3
227	Matthew 26:39	And he went a little farther, and fell on his face, and prayed, saying, O my Father, if it be possible, let this cup pass from me: nevertheless not as I will, but as thou wilt.	Let this cup pass from me	277-2
228	Matthew 9:27-29	And when Jesus departed thence, two blind men followed him, crying, and saying, Thou Son of David, have mercy on us. And when he was come into the house, the blind men came to him: and Jesus saith unto them, Believe ye that I am able to do this? They said unto him, Yea, Lord. Then touched he their eyes, saying, According to your faith be it unto you.	It is done unto us	280-1
229	Luke 17:19	And he said unto him, Arise, go thy way: thy faith hath made thee whole.	As ye believe, it shall be done unto you	280-1
230	Matthew 7:1,2	Judge not, that ye be not judged. For with what judgment ye judge, ye shall be judged: and with what measure ye mete, it shall be measured to you again.	It must be measured out to us according to our own measuring.	280-2
231	Matthew 9:27-29	And when Jesus departed thence, two blind men followed him, crying, and saying, Thou Son of David, have mercy on us. And when he was come into the house, the blind men came to him: and Jesus saith unto them, Believe ye that I am able to do this? They said unto him, Yea, Lord. Then touched he their eyes, saying, According to your faith be it unto you.	According to your faith	280-2
232	John 1:12	But as many as received him, to them gave he power to become the sons of God, even to them that believe on his name:	To as many as received him, to them gave he the power.	280-3
233	Psalms 78:8	And might not be as their fathers, a stubborn and rebellious generation; a generation that set not their heart aright, and whose spirit was not stedfast with God.	To pray aright	281-2
234	Matthew 9:5,6	For whether is easier, to say, Thy sins be forgiven thee; or to say, Arise, and walk? But that ye may know that the Son of man hath power on earth to forgive sins, (then saith he to the sick of the palsy,) Arise, take up thy bed, and go unto thine house.	Why is it that Jesus could say to the paralyzed man, "Take up thy bed and walk"?	281-3
235	Acts 10:34	Then Peter opened his mouth, and said, Of a truth I perceive that God is no respecter of persons:	It is no respecter of persons	284-2
236	Hebrews 11:1	Now faith is the substance of things hoped for, the evidence of things not seen.	Faith looks to the invisible	284-3
237	Matthew 5:23-24	Therefore if thou bring thy gift to the altar, and there rememberest that thy brother hath ought against thee; Leave there thy gift before the altar, and go thy way; first be reconciled to thy brother, and then come and offer thy gift.	Therefore if thou bring thy gift to the altar, and there rememberest that thy brother hath ought against thee; leave there thy gift before the altar, and go thy way; first be reconciled to thy brother, and then come and offer thy gift.	285-4

Ref. Nr.	Bible Verse	Citation	Ernest Holmes Reference	Page in SOM Text
238	Matthew 6:11	Give us this day our daily bread.	Jesus said, "Give us this day our daily bread'"	286-1
239	Mark 3:25	And if a house be divided against itself, that house cannot stand.	The Spiritual Universe should no longer be divided against Itself.	286-1
240	Revelation 1:8	I am Alpha and Omega, the beginning and the ending, saith the Lord, which is, and which was, and which is to come, the Almighty.	I AM Alpha and Omega	289-2
241	Isaiah 65:24	And it shall come to pass, that before they call, I will answer; and while they are yet speaking, I will hear.	Before they call, I will answer	289-4
242	Mark 11:24	Therefore I say unto you, What things soever ye desire, when ye pray, believe that ye receive them, and ye shall have them.	When ye pray, believe that ye have and ye shall receive	290-1
243	John 11:44	And he that was dead came forth, bound hand and foot with graveclothes: and his face was bound about with a napkin. Jesus saith unto them, Loose him, and let him go.	Loose him and let him go	291-2
244	Romans 8:1	There is therefore now no condemnation to them which are in Christ Jesus, who walk not after the flesh, but after the Spirit.	Know that there is no condemnation	291-2
245	John 11:44	And he that was dead came forth, bound hand and foot with graveclothes: and his face was bound about with a napkin. Jesus saith unto them, Loose him, and let him go.	"Loose him and let him go."	291-2
246	John 8:32	And ye shall know the truth, and the truth shall make you free.	Know the truth and the truth shall make you free.	296-1
247	John 10:30	I and my Father are one.	The Father and I are one	296-4
248	Luke 7:47	Wherefore I say unto thee, Her sins, which are many, are forgiven; for she loved much: but to whom little is forgiven, the same loveth little.	To him who hath loved much, much is forgiven	298-4
249	Matthew 8:13	And Jesus said unto the centurion, Go thy way; and as thou hast believed, so be it done unto thee. And his servant was healed in the selfsame hour.	"It is done unto you as you believe."	301-2
250	Hebrews 11:1	Now faith is the substance of things hoped for, the evidence of things not seen.	We must have a receptive and positive faith in the evidence of things not seen with the physical eye but which are eternal in the heavens.	301-3
251	Matthew 5:39	But I say unto you, That ye resist not evil: but whosoever shall smite thee on thy right cheek, turn to him the other also.	When Jesus said: "Resist not"	303-2
252	Isaiah 55:11	So shall my word be that goeth forth out of my mouth: it shall not return unto me void, but it shall accomplish that which I please, and it shall prosper in the thing whereto I sent it.	Our word becomes a law unto the thing for which it is spoken	304-1
253	Hebrews 3:19	So we see that they could not enter in because of unbelief.	They could not enter in because of their unbelief" and they "limited the Holy One of Israel.	304-3

Where'd He Get That? A Biblical Cross-Reference To Ernest Holmes' The Science of Mind

Ref. Nr.	Bible Verse	Citation	Ernest Holmes Reference	Page in SOM Text
254	Hebrews 4:6 and Psalms 78:41	Heb 4:6 Seeing therefore it remaineth that some must enter therein, and they to whom it was first preached entered not in because of unbelief: Ps 78:41 Yea, they turned back and tempted God, and limited the Holy One of Israel.	"They could not enter because of their unbelief," and because they "limited the Holy One of Israel."	304-3
255	I Peter 3:4	But let it be the hidden man of the heart, in that which is not corruptible, even the ornament of a meek and quiet spirit, which is in the sight of God of great price.	This is what the mystics call "The Man of the Heart"	306-4
256	Luke 1:19	And the angel answering said unto him, I am Gabriel, that stand in the presence of God; and am sent to speak unto thee, and to shew thee these glad tidings.	[This is what the mystics call] "The Angel of God's Presence."	306-4
257	Ephesians 5:14	Wherefore he saith, Awake thou that sleepest, and arise from the dead, and Christ shall give thee light.	Awake thou that sleepest and arise from the dead, and Christ shall give thee light.	307-3
258	Malachi 3:10	Bring ye all the tithes into the storehouse, that there may be meat in mine house, and prove me now herewith, saith the LORD of hosts, if I will not open you the windows of heaven, and pour you out a blessing, that there shall not be room enough to receive it.	Prove me now herewith, saith the Lord of Hosts, if I will not open you the windows of heaven, and pour you out a blessing, that there shall not be room to receive it.	307-3
259	Matthew 8:13	And Jesus said unto the centurion, Go thy way; and as thou hast believed, so be it done unto thee. And his servant was healed in the selfsame hour.	As thou hast believed, so be it done.	307-3
260	Luke 11:9	And I say unto you, Ask, and it shall be given you; seek, and ye shall find; knock, and it shall be opened unto you	Ask and it shall be given unto you	307-3
261	Isaiah 7:9	If ye be not firm in faith, ye shall surely not be made firm. [*The Bible*, English Standard Version]	"Be firm and ye shall be made firm"	307-3
262	Isaiah 55:11	So shall my word be that goeth forth out of my mouth: it shall not return unto me void, but it shall accomplish that which I please, and it shall prosper in the thing whereto I sent it.	"So shall my word be that goeth forth out of my mouth--it shall prosper."	307-3
263	John 1:1, 2, 3	In the beginning was the Word, and the Word was with God, and the Word was God. The same was in the beginning with God. All things were made by him; and without him was not any thing made that was made.	In the beginning was the Word, and the Word was with God, and the Word was God. All things were made by him; and without him was not any thing made that was made.	310-3
264	Ecclesiastes 7:29 or 30	Lo, this only have I found, that God hath made man upright; but they have sought out many inventions.	God hath made man upright; but they have sought out many inventions.	310-4
265	I Corinthians 15:22	For as in Adam all die, even so in Christ shall all be made alive.	As in Adam, all die, even so in Christ all are made alive.	310-4
266	Ecclesiastes 7:29 or 30	Lo, this only have I found, that God hath made man upright; but they have sought out many inventions.	Inventions of the human mind	310-4

Where'd He Get That? A Biblical Cross-Reference To Ernest Holmes' The Science of Mind

Ref. Nr.	Bible Verse	Citation	Ernest Holmes Reference	Page in SOM Text
267	Ecclesiastes 7:29 or 30	Lo, this only have I found, that God hath made man upright; but they have sought out many inventions.	In the beginning God made man perfect, but he has sought out many inventions.	310-4
268	I Corinthians 15:47	The first man is of the earth, earthy: the second man is the Lord from heaven.	The first man is of the earth, earthy; the second man is the Lord from heaven.	311-1
269	Matthew 22:32	I am the God of Abraham, and the God of Isaac, and the God of Jacob? God is not the God of the dead, but of the living.	God is not a God of the dead but of the living for in His sight all are alive.	311-1
270	John 14:10	Believest thou not that I am in the Father, and the Father in me? the words that I speak unto you I speak not of myself: but the Father that dwelleth in me, he doeth the works.	The Father that dwelleth in me, He doeth the works.	312-4
271	I Corinthians 15:21	For since by man came death, by man came also the resurrection of the dead.	By man came death, by man came also the resurrection of the dead.	313-3
272	Matthew 22:32	I am the God of Abraham, and the God of Isaac, and the God of Jacob? God is not the God of the dead, but of the living.	God is not a God of the dead but of the living: for all live unto Him.	313-3
273	John 15:5	I am the vine, ye are the branches: He that abideth in me, and I in him, the same bringeth forth much fruit: for without me ye can do nothing.	I am the vine and ye are the branches	313-4
274	John 15:7	If ye abide in me, and my words abide in you, ye shall ask what ye will, and it shall be done unto you.	If ye abide in me, and my words abide in you, ye shall ask what ye will, and it shall be done unto you.	313-4
275	John 15:8	Herein is my Father glorified, that ye bear much fruit; so shall ye be my disciples.	Except the branch abide in the vine, it shall not bear fruit	313-4
276	John 1:14	And the Word was made flesh, and dwelt among us, (and we beheld his glory, the glory as of the only begotten of the Father,) full of grace and truth.	The Word becomes flesh.	314-2
277	II Thessalonians 3:15	Yet count him not as an enemy, but admonish him as a brother.	The Bible tells us not to count our enemies.	315-3
278	Matthew 17:19-20	Then came the disciples to Jesus apart, and said, Why could not we cast him out? And Jesus said unto them, Because of your unbelief: for verily I say unto you, If ye have faith as a grain of mustard seed, ye shall say unto this mountain, Remove hence to yonder place; and it shall remove; and nothing shall be impossible unto you.	When Jesus explained to his disciples that they had failed to heal because of lack of faith, they protested that they did have faith in God. Jesus explained to them that this was insufficient; they must have the faith of God.	317-3
279	John 9:25	He answered and said, Whether he be a sinner or no, I know not: one thing I know, that, whereas I was blind, now I see.	Whereas I was blind, now I see.	319-2
280	John 7:24	Judge not according to the appearance, but judge righteous judgment.	no matter what the appearance may be	320-2
281	Exodus 3:14	And God said unto Moses, I AM THAT I AM: and he said, Thus shalt thou say unto the children of Israel, I AM hath sent me unto you.	every time man says "I am"	323-3
282	I Corinthians 14:33	For God is not the author of confusion, but of peace, as in all churches of the saints.	God is not the author of confusion but of peace	329-3

Ref. Nr.	Bible Verse	Citation	Ernest Holmes Reference	Page in SOM Text
283	Deuteronomy 6:4	Hear, O Israel: The LORD our God is one LORD:	Hear O Israel, the Lord our God is One Lord	330-2
284	Luke 17:21	Neither shall they say, Lo here! or, lo there! for, behold, the kingdom of God is within you.	God is within man	330-3
285	Psalms 19:4	Their line is gone out through all the earth, and their words to the end of the world. In them hath he set a tabernacle for the sun,	"His lines have gone out into all places."	330-3
286	Jeremiah 23:24	Can any hide himself in secret places that I shall not see him? saith the LORD. Do not I fill heaven and earth? saith the LORD.	There is no place where God is not.	330-3
287	Job 19:26	And though after my skin worms destroy this body, yet in my flesh shall I see God:	In my flesh shall I see God	330-4
288	John 10:30	I and my Father are one.	I and the Father are One	330-4
289	John 14:10	Believest thou not that I am in the Father, and the Father in me? the words that I speak unto you I speak not of myself: but the Father that dwelleth in me, he doeth the works.	The Father that dwelleth in me, He doeth the works.	330-4
290	John 10:30	I and my Father are one.	This is the recognition which Jesus had when he said, "I and the Father are One."	331-2
291	John 11:42	And I knew that thou hearest me always: but because of the people which stand by I said it, that they may believe that thou hast sent me.	I know that thou hearest me always.	331-3
292	John 11:43	And when he thus had spoken, he cried with a loud voice, Lazarus, come forth.	Then he said: "Lazarus, come forth;"	331-3
293	John 17:11	And now I am no more in the world, but these are in the world, and I come to thee. Holy Father, keep through thine own name those whom thou hast given me, that they may be one, as we are.	"That they may be One even as we are One," was His prayer	332-2
294	Acts 17:28	For in him we live, and move, and have our being; as certain also of your own poets have said, For we are also his offspring.	"In Him we live, move, and have our being."	332-2
295	John 8:12	Then spake Jesus again unto them, saying, I am the light of the world: he that followeth me shall not walk in darkness, but shall have the light of life.	I am the light of the world	332-4
296	Luke 15:18	I will arise and go to my father, and will say unto him, Father, I have sinned against heaven, and before thee,	They have all agreed that the soul is on the pathway of experience, that is, of self-discovery; that it is on its way back to its Father's House;	333-4
297	Psalms 82:6	I have said, Ye are gods; and all of you are children of the most High.	I have said, Ye are Gods and all of you are the children of the most high	333-5

Where'd He Get That? A Biblical Cross-Reference To Ernest Holmes' The Science of Mind

Ref. Nr.	Bible Verse	Citation	Ernest Holmes Reference	Page in SOM Text
298	Luke 14:7-9	And he put forth a parable to those which were bidden, when he marked how they chose out the chief rooms; saying unto them. When thou art bidden of any man to a wedding, sit not down in the highest room; lest a more honourable man than thou be bidden of him; And he that bade thee and him come and say to thee, Give this man place; and thou begin with shame to take the lowest room.	It would be a wonderful experiment if the world would try to solve all of its problems through the power of Spirit. Indeed the time will come when everyone will…"From the highest…to the lowest."	334-3
299	John 1:12	But as many as received him, to them gave he power to become the sons of God, even to them that believe on his name:	To as many as believed, gave he the power.	334-4
300	Luke 17:21	Neither shall they say, Lo here! or, lo there! for, behold, the kingdom of God is within you.	They have apparently sensed that this Kingdom is within.	335-1
301	I John 3:2	Beloved, now are we the sons of God, and it doth not yet appear what we shall be: but we know that, when he shall appear, we shall be like him; for we shall see him as he is.	Beloved, now are we the Sons of God	335-3
302	Luke 20:38	For he is not a God of the dead, but of the living: for all live unto him.	God is not a God of the dead but of the living	335-3
303	Matthew 11:28	Come unto me, all ye that labour and are heavy laden, and I will give you rest.	Come unto me all ye that labor and are heavy laden and I will give ye rest.	335-4
304	Exodus 3:14	And God said unto Moses, I AM THAT I AM: and he said, Thus shalt thou say unto the children of Israel, I AM hath sent me unto you.	when a man says "I am"	336-2
305	Exodus 3:14	And God said unto Moses, I AM THAT I AM: and he said, Thus shalt thou say unto the children of Israel, I AM hath sent me unto you.	recognizing the I-Am-ness	336-3
306	John 7:24	Judge not according to the appearance, but judge righteous judgment.	they have separated the appearance from the reality	337-1
307	II Corinthians 3:18	But we all, with open face beholding as in a glass the glory of the Lord, are changed into the same image from glory to glory, even as by the Spirit of the Lord.	Being transformed from glory to glory	338-3
308	I John 3:2	Beloved, now are we the sons of God, and it doth not yet appear what we shall be: but we know that, when he shall appear, we shall be like him; for we shall see him as he is.	Beloved, now are we the Sons of God and it doth not yet appear what we shall be but we know that when he shall appear, we shall be like Him for we shall see Him as He is.	338-3
309	II Corinthians 3:18	But we all, with open face beholding as in a glass the glory of the Lord, are changed into the same image from glory to glory, even as by the Spirit of the Lord.	Being transformed from glory to glory	338-3
310	Galatians 6:7	Be not deceived; God is not mocked: for whatsoever a man soweth, that shall he also reap.	As a man sows, so also shall he reap	340-2

Ref. Nr.	Bible Verse	Citation	Ernest Holmes Reference	Page in SOM Text
311	Isaiah 45.5-7	The Old Testament establishes God as First Cause: I am the LORD, and there is none else, there is no God beside me: I girded thee, though thou hast not known me: That they may know from the rising of the sun, and from the west, that there is none beside me. I am the LORD, and there is none else. form the light, and create darkness: I make peace, and create evil: I the LORD do all these things.	Therefore, we may read Buddha, Jesus, Plato, Socrates, Aristotle, Swedenborg, Emerson, Whitman, Browning or any of the other great mystics, no matter in what age they have lived, and we shall find the same Ultimate [First Cause].	342-1
312	John 1:1-5	The Gospel of John also establishes God as First Cause: In the beginning was the Word, and the Word was with God, and the Word was God. The same was in the beginning with God. All things were made through him; and without him was not anything made that hath been made. In him was life; and the life was the light of men. And the light shineth in the darkness; and the darkness apprehended it not. NOTE: Jesus did not say anything specific about Spirit being First Cause. Possibly John 5:26: For as the Father hath life in himself; so hath he given to the Son to have life in himself;	Therefore, we may read Buddha, Jesus, Plato, Socrates, Aristotle, Swedenborg, Emerson, Whitman, Browning or any of the other great mystics, no matter in what age they have lived, and we shall find the same Ultimate [First Cause].	342-1
313	Revelations 3:20	Behold, I stand at the door, and knock: if any man hear my voice, and open the door, I will come in to him, and will sup with him, and he with me.	"Behold I stand at the door and knock."	342-3
314	Matthew 6:9	After this manner therefore pray ye: Our Father which art in heaven, Hallowed be thy name.	Our Father which art in heaven	343-4
315	Luke 11:2	And he said unto them, When ye pray, say, Our Father which art in heaven, Hallowed be thy name. Thy kingdom come. Thy will be done, as in heaven, so in earth.	Our Father which art in heaven	343-4
316	Luke 17:21	Neither shall they say, Lo here! or, lo there! for, behold, the kingdom of God is within you.	As we enter the One, the One enters into us	343-4
317	Exodus 3:14	And God said unto Moses, I AM THAT I AM: and he said, Thus shalt thou say unto the children of Israel, I AM hath sent me unto you.	The greater a man's consciousness of this Indwelling I AM	344-2
318	John 14:10	Believest thou not that I am in the Father, and the Father in me? the words that I speak unto you I speak not of myself: but the Father that dwelleth in me, he doeth the works.	The Father that dwelleth in me, He doeth the works.	344-2

Where'd He Get That? A Biblical Cross-Reference To Ernest Holmes' The Science of Mind

Ref. Nr.	Bible Verse	Citation	Ernest Holmes Reference	Page in SOM Text
319	Matthew 17:1-2	And after six days Jesus taketh Peter, James, and John his brother, and bringeth them up into an high mountain apart, And was transfigured before them: and his face did shine as the sun, and his raiment was white as the light.	Jesus was the greatest of all the mystics and, once at least, after a period of illumination, his face was so bright that his followers could not look upon it.	344-3
320	Exodus 34:29-30	And it came to pass, when Moses came down from mount Sinai with the two tables of testimony in Moses' hand, when he came down from the mount, that Moses wist not that the skin of his face shone while he talked with him. And when Aaron and all the children of Israel saw Moses, behold, the skin of his face shone; and they were afraid to come nigh him.	All mystics have seen this Cosmic Light. This is why it is said there were illumined. They have all had the same experience, whether it was Moses coming down from the mountain, . . .-where suddenly he became conscious of this light.	344-3
321	Acts 9:3	And as he [Saul] journeyed, he came near Damascus: and suddenly there shined round about him a light from heaven:	All mystics have seen this Cosmic Light. This is why it is said there were illumined. They have all had the same experience, whether it was . . . . Saul on his return to Damascus. . .-where suddenly he became conscious of this light.	344-3
322	John 1:5	And the light shineth in darkness; and the darkness comprehended it not.	"The light shines in the darkness and the darkness comprehendeth it not."	345-3
323	Luke 17:20	And when he was demanded of the Pharisees, when the kingdom of God should come, he answered them and said, The kingdom of God cometh not with observation:	The Kingdom of Heaven cometh not by observation	345-3
324	John 3:18	He that believeth on him is not condemned: but he that believeth not is condemned already, because he hath not believed in the name of the only begotten Son of God.	The Son, begotten of the only Father – not "the only begotten Son of God."	357-1
325	Ephesians 3:20-21	Now unto him that is able to do exceeding abundantly above all that we ask or think, according to the power that worketh in us, Unto him be glory in the church by Christ Jesus throughout all ages, world without end. Amen.	World without end	357-2
326	Philippians 2:5	Let this mind be in you, which was also in Christ Jesus:	we are told to have that Mind in us "which was also in Christ Jesus."	357-3
327	John 14:6	Jesus saith unto him, I am the way, the truth, and the life: no man cometh unto the Father, but by me.	I am the way, the truth and the Life. No one cometh to the Father but by me.	358-4
328	Luke 17:21	Neither shall they say, Lo here! or, lo there! for, behold, the kingdom of God is within you.	He located God and the Kingdom of Heaven within himself.	362-1
329	Luke 17:21	Neither shall they say, Lo here! or, lo there! for, behold, the kingdom of God is within you.	He located and the Kingdom of Heaven within himself.	362-1
330	Matthew 5:14	Ye are the light of the world. A city that is set on an hill cannot be hid.	Ye are the light of the world	362-4

Where'd He Get That? A Biblical Cross-Reference To Ernest Holmes' The Science of Mind

Ref. Nr.	Bible Verse	Citation	Ernest Holmes Reference	Page in SOM Text
331	Colossians 3:9	Lie not one to another, seeing that ye have put off the old man with his deeds;	For Christ to be found in us is to put off the old man, with all his mistakes and doubts, and put on a new man, who is always certain he is beloved of the Father.	363-4
332	Psalms 82:6	I have said, Ye are gods; and all of you are children of the most High.	I have said, Ye are Gods and all of you are the children of the most high	364-2
333	Philippians 2:5	Let this mind be in you, which was also in Christ Jesus:	Let this mind be in you which was also in Christ Jesus	364-3
334	Luke 17:21	Neither shall they say, Lo here! or, lo there! for, behold, the kingdom of God is within you.	Heaven is within man	365-2
335	Matthew 6:9	After this manner therefore pray ye: Our Father which art in heaven, Hallowed be thy name.	Our Father which art in heaven	365-2
336	Luke 17:21	Neither shall they say, Lo here! or, lo there! for, behold, the kingdom of God is within you.	The Kingdom of Heaven is within you.	365-2
337	Matthew 25:31	When the Son of man shall come in his glory, and all the holy angels with him, then shall he sit upon the throne of his glory:	an arbitrary God, sending some to heaven and some to hell, all "for His glory."	365-3
338	John 14:6	Jesus saith unto him, I am the way, the truth, and the life: no man cometh unto the Father, but by me.	he [Jesus] proclaimed the Truth to be working through him.	366-2
339	Matthew 3:17	And lo a voice from heaven, saying, This is my beloved Son, in whom I am well pleased.	there is a voice ever proclaiming: "This is my Beloved Son."	367-1
340	Exodus 3:14	And God said unto Moses, I AM THAT I AM: and he said, Thus shalt thou say unto the children of Israel, I AM hath sent me unto you.	To the illumined, has ever come self-realization and I-AM-NESS	367-5
341	John 3:18	He that believeth on him is not condemned: but he that believeth not is condemned already, because he hath not believed in the name of the only begotten Son of God.	The Son begotten of the only Father	368-1
342	Acts 17:28	For in him we live, and move, and have our being; as certain also of your own poets have said, For we are also his offspring.	the Great Presence in which we live, move and have our being	368-4
343	Psalms 46:10	Be still, and know that I am God: I will be exalted among the heathen, I will be exalted in the earth.	to be still and know that the inner light shines	369-1
344	Revelations 3:20	Behold, I stand at the door, and knock: if any man hear my voice, and open the door, I will come in to him, and will sup with him, and he with me.	He stands at the door and knocks	369-1
345	Mark 4:39	And he arose, and rebuked the wind, and said unto the sea, Peace, be still. And the wind ceased, and there was a great calm.	Be still O soul and know	369-2
346	Romans 6:9	Knowing that Christ being raised from the dead dieth no more; death hath no more dominion over him..	Christ triumphs over death and the grave	369-3

Ref. Nr.	Bible Verse	Citation	Ernest Holmes Reference	Page in SOM Text
347	Matthew 14:29-31	And he said, Come. And when Peter was come down out of the ship, he walked on the water, to go to Jesus. But when he saw the wind boisterous, he was afraid; and beginning to sink, he cried, saying, Lord, save me. And immediately Jesus stretched forth his hand, and caught him, and said unto him, O thou of little faith, wherefore didst thou doubt?	Christ places His hand in the outstretched hand of the Universe, and walks unafraid through life.	370-1
348	Exodus 3:14	And God said unto Moses, I AM THAT I AM: and he said, Thus shalt thou say unto the children of Israel, I AM hath sent me unto you.	"I am that I am."	372-3
349	Exodus 3:14	And God said unto Moses, I AM THAT I AM: and he said, Thus shalt thou say unto the children of Israel, I AM hath sent me unto you.	this I Am appears no longer to be	374-2
350	I Corinthians 15:40	There are also celestial bodies, and bodies terrestrial: but the glory of the celestial is one, and the glory of the terrestrial is another.	"There are celestial bodies and bodes terrestrial"	376-1
351	I Corinthians 15:44	It is sown a natural body; it is raised a spiritual body. There is a natural body, and there is a spiritual body.	"There is a natural body and there is a spiritual body"	376-1
352	I Corinthians 15:52	In a moment, in the twinkling of an eye, at the last trump: for the trumpet shall sound, and the dead shall be raised incorruptible, and we shall be changed.	The "resurrection body" then, will not be snatched from some cosmic Shelf, as the soul soars aloft.	376-1
353	I Thessalonians 4:16-17	For the Lord himself shall descend from Heaven with a shout, with the voice of the archangel, and the trump of God: and the dead in Christ shall rise first: Then we which are alive, and remain shall be caught up together with them in the clouds, to meet the Lord in the air; and so shall we ever be with the Lord."	The "resurrection body" then, will not be snatched from some cosmic Shelf, as the soul soars aloft.	376-1
354	Matthew 12:25	And Jesus knew their thoughts, and said unto them, Every kingdom divided against itself is brought to desolation; and every city or house divided against itself shall not stand:	Such a house can not stand.	383-1
355	I Corinthians 15:55	O death, where is thy sting? O grave, where is thy victory?	The experience loses its sting, the grave its victory, when we realize the eternity of our own being.	385-1
356	Hebrews 11:3	Through faith we understand that the worlds were framed by the word of God, so that things which are seen were not made of things which do appear.	Having faith in the unseen	392-4
357	Mark 11:24	Therefore I say unto you, What things soever ye desire, when ye pray, believe that ye receive them, and ye shall have them.	"Whatsoever things we desire" when we pray we should "Believe that we have them."	398-3
358	Ephesians 4:6	One God and Father of all, who is above all, and through all, and in you all.	"God is all in all, over all and through all."	398-5

Ref. Nr.	Bible Verse	Citation	Ernest Holmes Reference	Page in SOM Text
359	John 14:10	Believest thou not that I am in the Father, and the Father in me? the words that I speak unto you I speak not of myself: but the Father that dwelleth in me, he doeth the works.	the Spirit of the Father in me who doeth the work	401-4
360	Psalms 18:26	With the pure thou wilt shew thyself pure; and with the froward thou wilt shew thyself froward.	To the pure thou wilt show thyself pure: to the froward thou wilt show thyself froward	402-3
361	Luke 12:32	Fear not, little flock; for it is your Father's good pleasure to give you the kingdom.	Fear not little flock, it is your Father's good pleasure to give you the kingdom.	404-2
362	I John 4:18	There is no fear in love; but perfect love casteth out fear: because fear hath torment. He that feareth is not made perfect in love.	Perfect love casts out fear	404-4
363	Luke 12:32	Fear not, little flock; for it is your Father's good pleasure to give you the kingdom.	If it is God's pleasure to give us the Kingdom	405-1
364	Hebrews 4:6 and Psalms 78:41	Heb 4:6 Seeing therefore it remaineth that some must enter therein, and they to whom it was first preached entered not in because of unbelief: Ps 78:41 Yea, they turned back and tempted God, and limited the Holy One of Israel.	They could not enter because of their unbelief, and because they limited the Holy One of Israel	405-2
365	John 7:24	Judge not according to the appearance, but judge righteous judgment.	Judge not according to appearances.	406-4
366	Hebrews 11:3	Through faith we understand that the worlds were framed by the word of God, so that things which are seen were not made of things which do appear.	We cannot account for the seen without having faith in the unseen.	407-2
367	Genesis 2:19-20	And out of the ground the LORD God formed every beast of the field, and every fowl of the air; and brought them unto Adam to see what he would call them: and whatsoever Adam called every living creature, that was the name thereof. And Adam gave names to all cattle, and to the fowl of the air, and to every beast of the field;	Adam was permitted to name all creation and man was supposed to exercise an authority over all that is below him	410-3
368	Genesis 1:26	And God said, Let us make man in our image, after our likeness: and let them have dominion over the fish of the sea, and over the fowl of the air, and over the cattle, and over all the earth, and over every creeping thing that creepeth upon the earth.	Adam was permitted to name all creation and man was supposed to exercise an authority over all that is below him	410-3
369	Psalm 51:1	Have mercy upon me, O God, according to thy lovingkindness: according unto the multitude of thy tender mercies blot out my transgressions.	"I will blot out their transgressions and remember them no longer against them	412-2
370	Exodus 3:14	And God said unto Moses, I AM THAT I AM: and he said, Thus shalt thou say unto the children of Israel, I AM hath sent me unto you.	The "I AM" is both individual and universal	413-1
371	Zechariah 2:10	Sing and rejoice, O daughter of Zion: for, lo, I come, and I will dwell in the midst of thee, saith the LORD.	"I Am is in the midst of thee"	413-3

Where'd He Get That? A Biblical Cross-Reference To Ernest Holmes' The Science of Mind

Ref. Nr.	Bible Verse	Citation	Ernest Holmes Reference	Page in SOM Text
372	john 6:63	the words that I speak unto you, they are spirit, and they are life.	The words must become "Spirit and Life" if they are to overshadow the thoughts	413-4
373	Hebrews 11:1	Now faith is the substance of things hoped for, the evidence of things not seen.	and ever renewing substance of faith	415-1
374	Matthew 15:14	Let them alone: they be blind leaders of the blind. And if the blind lead the blind, both shall fall into the ditch.	But the blind cannot lead the blind.	415-2
375	John 7:24	Judge not according to the appearance, but judge righteous judgment.	Judge not according to appearances.	417-2
376	Exodus 3:14	And God said unto Moses, I AM THAT I AM: and he said, Thus shalt thou say unto the children of Israel, I AM hath sent me unto you.	The individual "I" is a complement to the universal "I AM."	417-3
377	John 14:28	Ye have heard how I said unto you, I go away, and come again unto you. If ye loved me, ye would rejoice, because I said, I go unto the Father: for my Father is greater than I.	But "the Father is greater than I."	417-3
378	Matthew 6:9	After this manner therefore pray ye: Our Father which art in heaven, Hallowed be thy name.	We cannot come unto the "Father Which Art in Heaven"	422-3
379	Exodus 3:14	And God said unto Moses, I AM THAT I AM: and he said, Thus shalt thou say unto the children of Israel, I AM hath sent me unto you.	I am that which thou art; thou art that which I am	423-3
380	Matthew 4:4	But he answered and said, It is written, Man shall not live by bread alone, but by every word that proceedeth out of the mouth of God.	It is written that man shall not live by bread alone, but by every word that proceedeth out of the mouth of God.	427-3
381	Matthew 5:5	Blessed are the meek: for they shall inherit the earth.	The meek shall inherit the earth	427-5
382	Matthew 5:6	Blessed are they which do hunger and thirst after righteousness: for they shall be filled.	They who hunger and thirst after righteousness shall be filled.	428-4
383	Matthew 7:9	Or what man is there of you, whom if his son ask bread, will he give him a stone?	They have not received a stone when they asked for bread	428-5
384	Matthew 5:7	Blessed are the merciful: for they shall obtain mercy.	Blessed are the merciful; for they shall obtain mercy	429-1
385	John 6:31	Our fathers did eat manna in the desert; as it is written, He gave them bread from heaven to eat.	Manna from heaven	428-4
386	Galatians 6:7	Be not deceived; God is not mocked: for whatsoever a man soweth, that shall he also reap.	we shall reap as we have sown	429-3
387	Matthew 5:8	Blessed are the pure in heart: for they shall see God.	The pure in heart shall see God	429-4
388	Matthew 5:9	Blessed are the peacemakers: for they shall be called the children of God.	The peacemakers are called the children of God	429-5
389	Matthew 5:14	Ye are the light of the world. A city that is set on an hill cannot be hid.	Ye are the light of the world	430-2
390	Matthew 5:39	But I say unto you, That ye resist not evil: but whosoever shall smite thee on thy right cheek, turn to him the other also.	Jesus tells us to resist not evil	430-5
391	Matthew 5:44	But I say unto you, Love your enemies, bless them that curse you, do good to them that hate you, and pray for them which despitefully use you, and persecute you;	Jesus tells us...to love our enemies	430-5

Where'd He Get That? A Biblical Cross-Reference To Ernest Holmes' The Science of Mind

Ref. Nr.	Bible Verse	Citation	Ernest Holmes Reference	Page in SOM Text
392	Luke 6:27	But I say unto you which hear, Love your enemies, do good to them which hate you,	Jesus tells us to resist not evil, to love our enemies	430-5
393	Luke 6:35	But love ye your enemies, and do good, and lend, hoping for nothing again; and your reward shall be great, and ye shall be the children of the Highest: for he is kind unto the unthankful and to the evil.	Jesus tells us to resist not evil, to love our enemies	430-5
394	Matthew 6:4	so that your giving may be in secret. Then your Father, who sees what is done in secret, will reward you.	The Father who seeth in secret	430-6
395	Matthew 6:6	But thou, when thou prayest, enter into thy closet, and when thou hast shut thy door, pray to thy Father which is in secret; and thy Father which seeth in secret shall reward thee openly.	And this Father who seeth in secret	431-1
396	Matthew 6:6	But thou, when thou prayest, enter into thy closet, and when thou hast shut thy door, pray to thy Father which is in secret; and thy Father which seeth in secret shall reward thee openly.	Our prayers are to be made to God in the secret place of our own being.	431-1
397	Matthew 6:14-15	For if ye forgive men their trespasses, your heavenly Father will also forgive you: But if ye forgive not men their trespasses, neither will your Father forgive your trespasses.	We are told God will forgive us after we have forgiven others.	431-4
398	Psalms 91:1	He that dwelleth in the secret place of the most High shall abide under the shadow of the Almighty.	Shall we not learn to enter the "secret place of the Most High"	431-5
399	Matthew 6:20	But lay up for yourselves treasures in heaven, where neither moth nor rust doth corrupt, and where thieves do not break through nor steal:	Our treasure is already in heaven	432-1
400	Matthew 6:22-23	The light of the body is the eye: if therefore thine eye be single, thy whole body shall be full of light. But if thine eye be evil, thy whole body shall be full of darkness. If therefore the light that is in thee be darkness, how great is that darkness!	"If our eye is single, we shall be filled with light."	432-2
401	Matthew 6:26	Behold the fowls of the air: for they sow not, neither do they reap, nor gather into barns; yet your heavenly Father feedeth them. Are ye not much better than they?	birds, who do not gather into barns	432-2
402	Matthew 6:28	And why take ye thought for raiment? Consider the lilies of the field, how they grow; they toil not, neither do they spin:	They toil not nor do they spin.	432-2
403	Luke 11:34	The light of the body is the eye: therefore when thine eye is single, thy whole body also is full of light; but when thine eye is evil, thy body also is full of darkness.	If our eye is single, we shall be filled with light.	432-2
404	Matthew 6:33	But seek ye first the kingdom of God, and his righteousness; and all these things shall be added unto you.	But we are to seek the kingdom first	432-3
405	Matthew 7:1,2	Judge not, that ye be not judged. For with what judgment ye judge, ye shall be judged: and with what measure ye mete, it shall be measured to you again.	Judge not that ye be not judged, for with what judgment ye judge ye shall be judged, and with what measure ye mete, it shall be measured to you again.	433-2
406	Galatians 6:7	Be not deceived; God is not mocked: for whatsoever a man soweth, that shall he also reap.	he must reap as he has sown	433-3

Ref. Nr.	Bible Verse	Citation	Ernest Holmes Reference	Page in SOM Text
407	Ezra 9:5	And at the evening sacrifice I arose up from my heaviness; and having rent my garment and my mantle, I fell upon my knees, and spread out my hands unto the LORD my God,	Jesus tears the mantle of unreality from the shoulders of hypocrisy	435-2
408	Matthew 7:7	Ask, and it shall be given you; seek, and ye shall find; knock, and it shall be opened unto you:	It shall be opened to us when we knock	435-3
409	Luke 11:11	If a son shall ask bread of any of you that is a father, will he give him a stone? or if he ask a fish, will he for a fish give him a serpent?	If we ask for bread, we shall not receive a stone	435-3
410	Revelations 3:20	Behold, I stand at the door, and knock: if any man hear my voice, and open the door, I will come in to him, and will sup with him, and he with me.	It shall be opened to us when we knock.	435-3
411	Psalms 78:8	And might not be as their fathers, a stubborn and rebellious generation; a generation that set not their heart aright, and whose spirit was not stedfast with God.	We do not "pray aright" when we are in opposition	436-1
412	Matthew 7:21	Not every one that saith unto me, Lord, Lord, shall enter into the kingdom of heaven; but he that doeth the will of my Father which is in heaven.	It is not everyone who says "Lord, Lord," who enters the kingdom of harmony;	436-3
413	Matthew 7:24	Therefore whosoever heareth these sayings of mine, and doeth them, I will liken him unto a wise man, which built his house upon a rock:	The wise man builds his house on the solid rock of Truth	436-5
414	Matthew 8:8	The centurion answered and said, Lord, I am not worthy that thou shouldest come under my roof: but speak the word only, and my servant shall be healed.	The Centurion would not allow Jesus to come to his house, but asked him to speak the word only.	437-2
415	Matthew 8:8	The centurion answered and said, Lord, I am not worthy that thou shouldest come under my roof: but speak the word only, and my servant shall be healed.	"Speak the word only, and my servant shall be healed."	437-3
416	Matthew 8:13	And Jesus said unto the centurion, Go thy way; and as thou hast believed, so be it done unto thee. And his servant was healed in the selfsame hour.	Go thy way; and as thou hast believed, so be it done unto thee.	437-3
417	Matthew 8:10	When Jesus heard it, he marveled, and said to them that followed, Verily I say unto you, I have not found so great faith, no, not in Israel.	no wonder Jesus marveled at his faith	437-3
418	Matthew 9:5,6	For whether is easier, to say, Thy sins be forgiven thee; or to say, Arise, and walk? But that ye may know that the Son of man hath power on earth to forgive sins, (then saith he to the sick of the palsy,) Arise, take up thy bed, and go unto thine house.	Jesus Forgives a Man and Heals Him	437-5
419	Matthew 9:5,6	For whether is easier, to say, Thy sins be forgiven thee; or to say, Arise, and walk? But that ye may know that the Son of man hath power on earth to forgive sins, (then saith he to the sick of the palsy,) Arise, take up thy bed, and go unto thine house.	For whether is easier, to say, Thy sins be forgiven thee; or to say, Arise, take up thy bed, and go unto thine house.	438-1

Where'd He Get That? A Biblical Cross-Reference To Ernest Holmes' The Science of Mind

Ref. Nr.	Bible Verse	Citation	Ernest Holmes Reference	Page in SOM Text
420	Matthew 9:16,17	No man putteth a piece of new cloth unto an old garment, for that which is put in to fill it up taketh from the garment, and the rent is made worse. Neither do men put new wine into old bottles: else the bottles break, and the wine runneth out, and the bottles perish: but they put new wine into new bottles, and both are preserved.	No man puts a piece of new cloth on an old garment or new wine into old bottles	439-2
421	Matthew 9:20	And, behold, a woman, which was diseased with an issue of blood twelve years, came behind him, and touched the hem of his garment:	And, behold, a woman, which was diseased with an issue of blood twelve years, came behind him, and touched the hem of his garment:	439-4
422	Matthew 9:21	For she said within herself, If I may but touch his garment, I shall be whole.	For she said within herself, If I may but touch his garment, I shall be whole.	439-4
423	Matthew 9:22	But Jesus turned him about, and when he saw her, he said, Daughter, be of good comfort; thy faith hath made thee whole. And the woman was made whole from that hour.	And the woman was made whole from that hour	439-4
424	Matthew 9:27-29	And when Jesus departed thence, two blind men followed him, crying, and saying, Thou Son of David, have mercy on us. And when he was come into the house, the blind men came to him: and Jesus saith unto them, Believe ye that I am able to do this? They said unto him, Yea, Lord. Then touched he their eyes, saying, According to your faith be it unto you.	"According to your faith be it unto you."	439-6
425	Matthew 10:8	Heal the sick, cleanse the lepers, raise the dead, cast out devils: freely ye have received, freely give.	Freely ye have received, freely give.	440-2
426	Matthew 10:39	He that findeth his life shall lose it: and he that loseth his life for my sake shall find it.	"he that findeth his life shall lose it; and he that loseth his life, shall find it."	440-3
427	Matthew 10:12,13	And when ye come into an house, salute it. And if the house be worthy, let your peace come upon it: but if it be not worthy, let your peace return to you.	And when ye come into an house, salute it. And if the house be worthy, let your peace come upon it: but if it be not worthy, let your peace return to you.	440-5
428	Matthew 10:20	For it is not ye that speak, but the Spirit of your Father which speaketh in you.	For it is not ye that speak, but the Spirit of your Father which speaketh in you	441-1
429	Luke 12:2	For there is nothing covered, that shall not be revealed; neither hid, that shall not be known.	There is nothing covered, that shall not be revealed; and hid, that shall not be known	441-2
430	Matthew 10:36	And a man's foes shall be they of his own household.	And a man's foes shall be they of his own household	441-3
431	Matthew 10:41	He that receiveth a prophet in the name of a prophet shall receive a prophet's reward; and he that receiveth a righteous man in the name of a righteous man shall receive a righteous man's reward.	He that receiveth a prophet in the name of a prophet shall receive a prophet's reward; and he that receiveth a righteous man in the name of a righteous man shall receive a righteous man's reward.	442-1

Where'd He Get That? A Biblical Cross-Reference To Ernest Holmes' The Science of Mind

Ref. Nr.	Bible Verse	Citation	Ernest Holmes Reference	Page in SOM Text
432	Matthew 11:18,19	For John came neither eating nor drinking, and they say, He hath a devil.: The Son of man came eating and drinking, and they say, Behold a man gluttonous, and a winebibber, a friend of publicans and sinners. But wisdom is justified of her children.	"For John came neither eating nor drinking, and they say, He hath a devil.: The Son of man came eating and drinking, and they say, Behold a man gluttonous, and a winebibber, a friend of publicans and sinners. But wisdom is justified of her children.	442-2
433	Matthew 11:19	The Son of man came eating and drinking, and they say, Behold a man gluttonous, and a winebibber, a friend of publicans and sinners. But wisdom is justified of her children	Wisdom is justified of her children."	442-3
434	Matthew 18:3	And said, Verily I say unto you, Except ye be converted, and become as little children, ye shall not enter into the kingdom of heaven.	The child-like faith	443-1
435	Matthew 11:27	All things are delivered unto me of my Father: and no man knoweth the Son, but the Father; neither knoweth any man the Father, save the Son, and he to whomsoever the Son will reveal him.	And no man knoweth the Son, but the Father; neither knoweth any many the Father, save the Son, and he to whomsoever the Son will reveal him.	443-2
436	Matthew 11:28	Come unto me, all ye that labour and are heavy laden, and I will give you rest.	Come unto me all ye that labor and are heavy laden and I will give you rest.	444-1
437	I Corinthians 6:19	I Cor 6:19: What? know ye not that your body is the temple of the Holy Ghost which is in you, which ye have of God, and ye are not your own?	nor would it set man in the temple of God as God	444-2
438	Romans 12:2	And be not conformed to this world: but be ye transformed by the renewing of your mind, that ye may prove what is that good, and acceptable, and perfect, will of God.	Be transformed by the renewing of our minds.	448-1
439	Matthew 12:25	And Jesus knew their thoughts, and said unto them, Every kingdom divided against itself is brought to desolation; and every city or house divided against itself shall not stand:	And Jesus knew their thoughts	448-2
440	Matthew 12:25	And Jesus knew their thoughts, and said unto them, Every kingdom divided against itself is brought to desolation; and every city or house divided against itself shall not stand:	Jesus understanding what was in their minds, told them that a house divided against itself cannot stand;	448-3
441	Matthew 12:28	But if I cast out devils by the Spirit of God, then the kingdom of God is come unto you.	If I cast out devils by the spirit of God, then the Kingdom of God has come unto you	448-3
442	Matthew 7:17,18	Even so every good tree bringeth forth good fruit; but a corrupt tree bringeth forth evil fruit. A good tree cannot bring forth evil fruit, neither can a corrupt tree bring forth good fruit.	Good thoughts and a good harvest	448-5

Ref. Nr.	Bible Verse	Citation	Ernest Holmes Reference	Page in SOM Text
443	Matthew 12:47,48	Then one said unto him, Behold, thy mother and thy brethren stand without, desiring to speak with thee. But he answered and said unto him that told him, Who is my mother? and who are my brethren?	But he answering said unto him that told him, Who is my mother? And who are my brethren?	449-4
444	Matthew 13:12	For whosoever hath, to him shall be given, and he shall have more abundance: but whosoever hath not, from him shall be taken away even that he hath.	Whosoever hath, to him shall be given, and he shall have more abundance; but whosoever hath not, from him shall be taken away even that he hath	449-6
445	Matthew 13:16	But blessed are your eyes, for they see: and your ears, for they hear.	Blessed are your eyes, for they see; and your ears, for they hear	451-2
446	Matthew 13:31-32	Another parable put he forth unto them, saying, The kingdom of heaven is like to a grain of mustard seed, which a man took, and sowed in his field: Which indeed is the least of all seeds: but when it is grown, it is the greatest among herbs, and becometh a tree, so that the birds of the air come and lodge in the branches thereof.	The kingdom of heaven is like a grain of mustard seed	451-4
447	Matthew 13:33	Another parable spake he unto them; The kingdom of heaven is like unto leaven, which a woman took, and hid in three measures of meal, till the whole was leavened.	The kingdom of heaven is like leaven.	451-5
448	Matthew 13:33	Another parable spake he unto them; The kingdom of heaven is like unto leaven, which a woman took, and hid in three measures of meal, till the whole was leavened.	"Leaven the whole lump of subjectivity"	451-5
449	Matthew 13:45-46	Again, the kingdom of heaven is like unto a merchant man, seeking goodly pearls: Who, when he had found one pearl of great price, went and sold all that he had, and bought it.	The kingdom of heaven is likened unto a pearl of great price, for which a man will sell all that he has, that he may possess it.	452-2
450	Matthew 15:18-20	But those things which proceed out of the mouth come forth from the heart; and they defile the man. For out of the heart proceed evil thoughts, murders, adulteries, fornications, thefts, false witness, blasphemies: These are the things which defile a man: but to eat with unwashen hands defileth not a man.	Not what we eat or drink, but what we think, defiles.	453-1
451	Matthew 15:14	Let them alone: they be blind leaders of the blind. And if the blind lead the blind, both shall fall into the ditch.	If the blind lead the blind, both shall fall into the ditch.	453-5
452	Deuteronomy 6:4	Hear, O Israel: The LORD our God is one LORD:	Remember the teachings of Moses, the "god is One."	453-6

Where'd He Get That? A Biblical Cross-Reference To Ernest Holmes' The Science of Mind

Ref. Nr.	Bible Verse	Citation	Ernest Holmes Reference	Page in SOM Text
453	Matthew 16:24-27	Then said Jesus unto his disciples, If any man will come after me, let him deny himself, and take up his cross, and follow me. For whosoever will save his life shall lose it: and whosoever will lose his life for my sake shall find it. For what is a man profited, if he shall gain the whole world, and lose his own soul? or what shall a man give in exchange for his soul? For the Son of man shall come in the glory of his Father with his angels; and then he shall reward every man according to his works.	Who would save his life would lose it	454-2
454	Matthew 17:21	Howbeit this kind goeth not out but by prayer and fasting.	Fasting and prayer	455-3
455	Matthew 17:15	Lord, have mercy on my son: for he is lunatick, and sore vexed: for ofttimes he falleth into the fire, and oft into the water.	Healing the Lunatic	456-1
456	Matthew 17:17	Then Jesus answered and said, O faithless and perverse generation, how long shall I be with you? how long shall I suffer you? bring him hither to me.	Bring him hither to me.	456-1
457	Matthew 17:18	And Jesus rebuked the devil; and he departed out of him: and the child was cured from that very hour.	And Jesus rebuked the devil; and he departed out of him.	456-1
458	Matthew 18:3	And said, Verily I say unto you, Except ye be converted, and become as little children, ye shall not enter into the kingdom of heaven.	We must become as little children	456-3
459	Matthew 18:18	Verily I say unto you, Whatsoever ye shall bind on earth shall be bound in heaven: and whatsoever ye shall loose on earth shall be loosed in heaven.	Whatsoever ye shall bind on earth shall be bound in heaven; and whatsoever ye shall loose on earth shall be loosed in heaven.	457-1
460	Matthew 18:21-22	Then came Peter to him, and said, Lord, how oft shall my brother sin against me, and I forgive him? till seven times? Jesus saith unto him, I say not unto thee, Until seven times: but, Until seventy times seven.	He says we should forgive until seventy times seven.	457-4
461	Romans 3:23	For all have sinned, and come short of the glory of God;	Fallen short of	457-4
462	Matthew 21:21-22	Jesus answered and said unto them, Verily I say unto you, If ye have faith, and doubt not, ye shall not only do this which is done to the fig tree, but also if ye shall say unto this mountain, Be thou removed, and be thou cast into the sea; it shall be done. And all things, whatsoever ye shall ask in prayer, believing, ye shall receive.	The things we need we are to ask for—and we are to believe that we receive them!	458-2
463	Luke 7:47	Wherefore I say unto thee, Her sins, which are many, are forgiven; for she loved much: but to whom little is forgiven, the same loveth little.	To him who loves much, much is forgiven.	458-2

Where'd He Get That? A Biblical Cross-Reference To Ernest Holmes' The Science of Mind

Ref. Nr.	Bible Verse	Citation	Ernest Holmes Reference	Page in SOM Text
464	Matthew 22:36-40	Jesus said unto him, Thou shalt love the Lord thy God with all thy heart, and with all thy soul, and with all thy mind. This is the first and great commandment. And the second is like unto it, Thou shalt love thy neighbour as thyself. On these two commandments hang all the law and the prophets.	The two great commandments are to love God and our brother man.	459-3
465	John 13:34-35	A new commandment I give unto you, That ye love one another; as I have loved you, that ye also love one another. By this shall all men know that ye are my disciples, if ye have love one to another.	The two great commandments are to love God and our brother man.	459-3
466	Matthew 21:9	And the multitudes that went before, and that followed, cried, saying, Hosanna to the son of David: Blessed is he that cometh in the name of the Lord; Hosanna in the highest.	The student of Truth will receive all that comes in the name of the Lord*	459-6
467	Matthew 26:52	Then said Jesus unto him, Put up again thy sword into his place: for all they that take the sword shall perish with the sword.	"...for all they that take the sword shall perish with the sword."	460-1
468	Job 38:33	Knowest thou the ordinances of heaven? canst thou set the dominion thereof in the earth?	Love alone overcomes all and justifies the eternity of her dominion	460-3
469	Deuteronomy 11:25-27	There shall no man be able to stand before you: for the LORD your God shall lay the fear of you and the dread of you upon all the land that ye shall tread upon, as he hath said unto you. Behold, I set before you this day a blessing and a curse; A blessing, if ye obey the commandments of the LORD your God, which I command you this day:	Moses referred to the same thing when he said that he had set a blessing and a curse before the Children of Israel	461-2
470	Joshua 24:15	And if it seem evil unto you to serve the LORD, choose you this day whom ye will serve;	they must *choose* whom they would serve.	461-2
471	Luke 15:11-12	And he said, A certain man had two sons:	A certain man had two sons.	461-2
472	Luke 15:11-12	And the younger of them said to his father, Father, give me the portion of goods that falleth to me. And he divided unto them his living.	And the younger of them said to his father, Father, give me the portion of goods that falleth to me.	461-3
473	Luke 15:11-12	And the younger of them said to his father, Father, give me the portion of goods that falleth to me. And he divided unto them his living.	And he divided unto them his living.	461-5
474	Luke 15:11-12	And the younger of them said to his father, Father, give me the portion of goods that falleth to me. And he divided unto them his living.	And he divided unto them his living.	462-1
475	Luke 15:13	And not many days after the younger son gathered all together, and took his journey into a far country, and there wasted his substance with riotous living.	And not many days after the younger son gathered all together, and took his journey into a far country, and there wasted his substance with riotous living.	462-2

Where'd He Get That? A Biblical Cross-Reference To Ernest Holmes' The Science of Mind

Ref. Nr.	Bible Verse	Citation	Ernest Holmes Reference	Page in SOM Text
476	Luke 15:13	And not many days after the younger son gathered all together, and took his journey into a far country, and there wasted his substance with riotous living.	The far country	462-3
477	Luke 15:14	And when he had spent all, there arose a mighty famine in that land; and he began to be in want.	And there he wasted his substance with riotous living. And when he had spent all, there arose a mighty famine in that land; and he began to want	462-5
478	Luke 15: 15	And he went and joined himself to a citizen of that country; and he sent him into his fields to feed swine.	So the prodigal son "began to be in want. And he went and joined himself to a citizen of that country; and he sent him into his fields to feed swine.	463-3
479	Luke 15:16	And he would fain have filled his belly with the husks that the swine did eat: and no man gave unto him.	And he fain would have filled his belly with the husks that the swine did eat; and no man gave unto him	464-2
480	Luke 15:18	I will arise and go to my father, and will say unto him, Father, I have sinned against heaven, and before thee,	we alone can return to the "Father's House."	464-4
481	Luke 15:17	And when he came to himself, he said, How many hired servants of my father's have bread enough and to spare, and I perish with hunger!	And when he came to himself he said, How many hired servants of my father's have bread enough and to spare, and I perish with hunger!	464-6
482	Luke 15:17	And when he came to himself, he said, How many hired servants of my father's have bread enough and to spare, and I perish with hunger!	"And when he came to himself." The is the great awakening,	465-1
483	Luke 15:18	I will arise and go to my father, and will say unto him, Father, I have sinned against heaven, and before thee,	I will arise and go to my father and will say unto him, Father, I have sinned against heaven, and before thee,	465-3
484	Luke 15:19	And am no more worthy to be called thy son: make me as one of thy hired servants.	And am no more worthy to be called thy son: make me as one of thy hired servants.	465-3
485	Luke 15:20	And he arose, and came to his father. But when he was yet a great way off, his father saw him, and had compassion, and ran, and fell on his neck, and kissed him.	And he arose, and came to his father. But when he was yet a great way off, his father saw him, and had compassion, and ran, and fell on his neck, and kissed him.	466-2
486	Luke 15:20	And he arose, and came to his father. But when he was yet a great way off, his father saw him, and had compassion, and ran, and fell on his neck, and kissed him.	When he was yet a great way off, his father saw him, and ran, and fell on his neck and kissed him.	466-3
487	Matthew 8:13	And Jesus said unto the centurion, Go thy way; and as thou hast believed, so be it done unto thee. And his servant was healed in the selfsame hour.	"It is done unto us as we believe."	466-3

Ref. Nr.	Bible Verse	Citation	Ernest Holmes Reference	Page in SOM Text
488	Luke 15:21-24	And the son said unto him, Father, I have sinned against heaven, and in thy sight, and am no more worthy to be called thy son. But the father said to his servants, Bring forth the best robe, and put it on him; and put a ring on his hand, and shoes on his feet: And bring hither the fatted calf, and kill it; and let us eat, and be merry: For this my son was dead, and is alive again; he was lost, and is found. And they began to be merry.	And the son said unto him, Father, I have sinned against heaven, and in thy sight, and am no more worthy to be called thy son. But the father said to his servants, Bring forth the best robe, and put it on him; and put a ring on his hand, and shoes on his feet: and bring hither the fatted calf, and kill it; and let us eat, and be merry: For this my son was dead, and is alive again; he was lost, and is found. And they began to be merry.	466-5
489	Luke 15:22	But the father said to his servants, Bring forth the best robe, and put it on him; and put a ring on his hand, and shoes on his feet:	"Bring forth quickly the best robe, and put it on him: and put a ring on his hand and shoes on his feet."	467-1
490	Luke 15:23	And bring hither the fatted calf, and kill it; and let us eat, and be merry:	The fatted calf	467-3
491	Luke 15:25	Now his elder son was in the field: and as he came and drew nigh to the house, he heard musick and dancing.	Now his elder son was in the field: and as he came and drew nigh to the house, he heard music and dancing.	468-3
492	Luke 15:26-27	And he called one of the servants, and asked what these things meant. And he said unto him, Thy brother is come; and thy father hath killed the fatted calf, because he hath received him safe and sound.	And he called one of the servants, and asked what these things meant. And he said unto him, Thy brother is come; and thy father hath killed the fatted calf, because he hath received him safe and sound.	468-4
493	Luke 15:28	And he was angry, and would not go in: therefore came his father out, and intreated him.	And he was angry, and would not go in: therefore came his father out, and intreated him.	468-5
494	Luke 15:29	And he answering said to his father, Lo, these many years do I serve thee, neither transgressed I at any time thy commandment: and yet thou never gavest me a kid, that I might make merry with my friends:	And he answering said to his father, Lo, these many years do I serve thee, and yet thou never gavest me a kid, that I might make merry with my friends…	468-6
495	Luke 15:30-31	But as soon as this thy son was come, which hath devoured thy living with harlots, thou hast killed for him the fatted calf. And he said unto him, Son, thou art ever with me, and all that I have is thine.	"And he said unto him, Son, thou art ever with me, and all that I have is thine."	468-7
496	Luke 15:31	And he said unto him, Son, thou art ever with me, and all that I have is thine.	He said to the elder son, "Thou art ever with me, and all that I have is thine."	469-1
497	John 3:3	Jesus answered and said unto him, Verily, verily, I say unto thee, Except a man be born again, he cannot see the kingdom of God.	Except a man be born again, he cannot see the kingdom of God.	471-5
498	John 3:6	That which is born of the flesh is flesh; and that which is born of the Spirit is spirit.	That which is born of the Spirit is Spirit	471-5

Ref. Nr.	Bible Verse	Citation	Ernest Holmes Reference	Page in SOM Text
499	Luke 17:20	And when he was demanded of the Pharisees, when the kingdom of God should come, he answered them and said, The kingdom of God cometh not with observation:	The new birth comes not by observation nor by loud proclamation	472-2
500	John 3:13	And no man hath ascended up to heaven, but he that came down from heaven, even the Son of man which is in heaven.	And no man hath ascended up to heaven, but he that came down from heaven, even the Son of man which is in heaven	472-3
501	Luke 17:21	Neither shall they say, Lo here! or, lo there! for, behold, the kingdom of God is within you.	Heaven is already within	472-4
502	John 3:14	And as Moses lifted up the serpent in the wilderness, even so must the Son of man be lifted up:	As Moses lifted up the serpent in the wilderness, Jesus tells us must the son of man also be lifted up.	472-5
503	Numbers 21:8-9	And the LORD said unto Moses, Make thee a fiery serpent, and set it upon a pole: and it shall come to pass, that every one that is bitten, when he looketh upon it, shall live. And Moses made a serpent of brass, and put it upon a pole, and it came to pass, that if a serpent had bitten any man, when he beheld the serpent of brass, he lived.	When Moses lifted up the serpent, those who looked upon it were healed.	472-6
504	Genesis 3:23-24	Therefore the LORD God sent him forth from the garden of Eden, to till the ground from whence he was taken. So he drove out the man; and he placed at the east of the garden of Eden Cherubims, and a flaming sword which turned every way, to keep the way of the tree of life.	We are reminded here of another symbol, one used in the Old Testament, that of the serpent which cast Adam and Eve out of the Garden of Eden. *NOTE: The serpent did not cast out Adam and Eve, God did. God cursed the serpent and made him eat dust all the days of his life.*	473-2
505	Genesis 2:22	And the rib, which the LORD God had taken from man, made he a woman, and brought her unto the man.	Eve, the woman in the case, was made from a rib of Adam.	473-5
506	Genesis 3:22	And the LORD God said, Behold, the man is become as one of us, to know good and evil: and now, lest he put forth his hand, and take also of the tree of life, and eat, and live for ever:	He shall become as one of us and live forever	474-1
507	Genesis 3:8	And they heard the voice of the LORD God walking in the garden in the cool of the day: and Adam and his wife hid themselves from the presence of the LORD God amongst the trees of the garden.	The Voice of God, "walking in the garden in the cool of the day," means the introspective and meditative part of us	474-3
508	John 8:32	And ye shall know the truth, and the truth shall make you free.	truth and truth alone makes us free	474-6
509	John 5:19	Then answered Jesus and said unto them, Verily, verily, I say unto you, The Son can do nothing of himself, but what he seeth the Father do: for what things soever he doeth, these also doeth the Son likewise.	The Son can do nothing of himself	475-2

Where'd He Get That? A Biblical Cross-Reference To Ernest Holmes' The Science of Mind

Ref. Nr.	Bible Verse	Citation	Ernest Holmes Reference	Page in SOM Text
510	John 5:26	For as the Father hath life in himself; so hath he given to the Son to have life in himself;	As the Father has life, so the son has life.	475-6
511	John 6:27	Labour not for the meat which perisheth, but for that meat which endureth unto everlasting life, which the Son of man shall give unto you: for him hath God the Father sealed.	Labour not for the meat which perisheth	476-4
512	John 8:12	Then spake Jesus again unto them, saying, I am the light of the world: he that followeth me shall not walk in darkness, but shall have the light of life.	"I am the light of the world"	477-5
513	Exodus 3:14	And God said unto Moses, I AM THAT I AM: and he said, Thus shalt thou say unto the children of Israel, I AM hath sent me unto you.	"I Am" has a dual meaning	477-6
514	Exodus 3:14	And God said unto Moses, I AM THAT I AM: and he said, Thus shalt thou say unto the children of Israel, I AM hath sent me unto you.	God was revealed to Moses as the great "I AM"	477-6
515	Exodus 3:14	And God said unto Moses, I AM THAT I AM: and he said, Thus shalt thou say unto the children of Israel, I AM hath sent me unto you.	Moses taught that "I AM" is the First Principle of all life	477-6
516	Exodus 3:14	And God said unto Moses, I AM THAT I AM: and he said, Thus shalt thou say unto the children of Israel, I AM hath sent me unto you.	unto the perfect "I AM"	478-1
517	John 8:32	And ye shall know the truth, and the truth shall make you free.	Truth which alone can make free.	478-2
518	I John 4:8	He that loveth not knoweth not God; for God is love.	It is written that God is love	478-3
519	John 14:1	Let not your heart be troubled: ye believe in God, believe also in me.	Let not your heart be troubled	478-6
520	John 14:2	In my Father's house are many mansions: if it were not so, I would have told you. I go to prepare a place for you.	"In my father's house are many mansions."	479-3
521	John 14:2	In my Father's house are many mansions: if it were not so, I would have told you. I go to prepare a place for you.	I go to prepare a place for you	479-4
522	John 14:6	Jesus saith unto him, I am the way, the truth, and the life: no man cometh unto the Father, but by me.	"I am the way, the truth and the life."	479-4
523	Exodus 3:14	And God said unto Moses, I AM THAT I AM: and he said, Thus shalt thou say unto the children of Israel, I AM hath sent me unto you.	the individual "I" the son of the eternal "I AM."	479-5
524	John 14:6	Jesus saith unto him, I am the way, the truth, and the life: no man cometh unto the Father, but by me.	The son is the way to the Father	479-5
525	John 14:9	Jesus saith unto him, Have I been so long time with you, and yet hast thou not known me, Philip? he that hath seen me hath seen the Father; and how sayest thou then, Shew us the Father?	He that hath seen me hath seen the Father	480-1
526	John 14:9	Jesus saith unto him, Have I been so long time with you, and yet hast thou not known me, Philip? he that hath seen me hath seen the Father; and how sayest thou then, Shew us the Father?	He that hath seen me hath seen the Father	480-2

Where'd He Get That? A Biblical Cross-Reference To Ernest Holmes' The Science of Mind

Ref. Nr.	Bible Verse	Citation	Ernest Holmes Reference	Page in SOM Text
527	John 14:12	Verily, verily, I say unto you, He that believeth on me, the works that I do shall he do also; and greater works than these shall he do; because I go unto my Father.	He that believeth on me, the works that I do shall he do also.	480-4
528	John 15:8	Herein is my Father glorified, that ye bear much fruit; so shall ye be my disciples.	The Father is glorified in the Son	480-4
529	John 14:16	And I will pray the Father, and he shall give you another Comforter, that he may abide with you for ever;	The Holy Comforter	480-5
530	John 14:26	But the Comforter, which is the Holy Ghost, whom the Father will send in my name, he shall teach you all things, and bring all things to your remembrance, whatsoever I have said unto you.	This is the one used and expanded on in the text for Holy Comforter. Ernest Holmes misquoted this reference.	480-5
531	John 14:26	But the Comforter, which is the Holy Ghost, whom the Father will send in my name, he shall teach you all things, and bring all things to your remembrance, whatsoever I have said unto you.	We are told that The Holy Comforter, the Spirit of Truth, will make all things known to us.	480-5
532	John 14:26	But the Comforter, which is the Holy Ghost, whom the Father will send in my name, he shall teach you all things, and bring all things to your remembrance, whatsoever I have said unto you.	As the Holy Comforter comes, He makes all things known to us.	480-6
533	John 14:20	At that day ye shall know that I am in my Father, and ye in me, and I in you.	"I am in my Father, and ye in me, and I in you."	480-6
534	John 15:7	If ye abide In me and my words abide in you, ye shall ask what ye will, and it shall be done unto you.	If ye abide In me and my words abide in you, ye shall ask what ye will, and it shall be done unto you.	481-2
535	James 4:3	Ye ask, and receive not, because ye ask amiss, that ye may consume it upon your lusts.	When we abide in the One, we cannot ask amiss	481-4
536	John 15:7	If ye abide in me, and my words abide in you, ye shall ask what ye will, and it shall be done unto you.	we must first abide in the Spirit of Truth	481-5
537	John 15:8	Herein is my Father glorified, that ye bear much fruit; so shall ye be my disciples.	Herein is my Father glorified, that ye bear much fruit	481-7
538	John 15:11	These things have I spoken unto you, that my joy might remain in you, and that your joy might be full.	Jesus refers to his joy on the eve of his greatest lesson to mankind.	482-3
539	Romans 1:20	For the invisible things of him from the creation of the world are clearly seen, being understood by the things that are made, even his eternal power and Godhead; so that they are without excuse:	This teaching incorporates the great law of correspondents.	483-1
540	Hebrews 11:3	Through faith we understand that the worlds were framed by the word of God, so that things which are seen were not made of things which do appear.	We understand the unseen by correctly viewing the seen	483-2
541	Romans 8:1	There is therefore now no condemnation to them which are in Christ Jesus, who walk not after the flesh, but after the Spirit.	There is therefore now no condemnation to them	484-1
542	Romans 9:1	I say the truth in Christ, I lie not, my conscience also bearing me witness in the Holy Ghost,	We are in Christ when we are in the Truth: we are in the Truth when we live in harmony with It.	484-2
543	Romans 8:6	For to be carnally minded is death; but to be spiritually minded is life and peace.	"To be spiritually minded is life and peace."	484-3

Where'd He Get That? A Biblical Cross-Reference To Ernest Holmes' The Science of Mind

Ref. Nr.	Bible Verse	Citation	Ernest Holmes Reference	Page in SOM Text
544	Romans 8:11	But if the Spirit of him that raised up Jesus from the dead dwell in you, he that raised up Christ from the dead shall also quicken your mortal bodies by his Spirit that dwelleth in you.	The Spirit that raised Jesus dwells in all.	484-4
545	Romans 8:15	For ye have not received the spirit of bondage again to fear; but ye have received the Spirit of adoption, whereby we cry, Abba, Father.	We have not received a spirit of bondage but one of adoption	484-5
546	Romans 8:16-17	The Spirit itself beareth witness with our spirit, that we are the children of God: And if children, then heirs; heirs of God, and joint-heirs with Christ; if so be that we suffer with him, that we may be also glorified together.	Joint heirs with Christ	485-2
547	Romans 8:21	Because the creature itself also shall be delivered from the bondage of corruption into the glorious liberty of the children of God.	The creature shall be delivered from bondage	485-4
548	Romans 8:28	And we know that all things work together for good to them that love God, to them who are the called according to his purpose.	All things work for our good	485-5
549	Romans 8:29	For whom he did foreknow, he also did predestinate to be conformed to the image of his Son, that he might be the firstborn among many brethren.	so it is foreknown and predetermined by the Divine Mind that all shall be sons of God.	486-1
550	Romans 8:31	What shall we then say to these things? If God be for us, who can be against us?	"If God be for us who can be against us?"	486-2
551	Romans 8:38-39	For I am persuaded, that neither death, nor life, nor angels, nor principalities, nor powers, nor things present, nor things to come, Nor height, nor depth, nor any other creature, shall be able to separate us from the love of God, which is in Christ Jesus our Lord.	NOTHING can keep us from the love of God.	486-3
552	Luke 12:32	Fear not, little flock; for it is your Father's good pleasure to give you the kingdom.	We are told not to be afraid, for it is the Father's good pleasure to give us the Kingdom.	486-3
553	Romans 12:2	And be not conformed to this world: but be ye transformed by the renewing of your mind, that ye may prove what is that good, and acceptable, and perfect, will of God.	Be ye transformed by the renewing of your mind.	486-5
554	Romans 12:2	And be not conformed to this world: but be ye transformed by the renewing of your mind, that ye may prove what is that good, and acceptable, and perfect, will of God.	The process through which this renewing takes place	487-2
555	Romans 12:14	Bless them which persecute you: bless, and curse not.	Bless and curse not	487-3
556	Romans 12:19	Dearly beloved, avenge not yourselves, but rather give place unto wrath: for it is written, Vengeance is mine; I will repay, saith the Lord.	Vengeance is mine; I will repay saith the Lord	487-4
557	Romans 13:11	And that, knowing the time, that now it is high time to awake out of sleep: for now is our salvation nearer than when we believed.	Now it is high time to awake out of sleep	487-5

Where'd He Get That? A Biblical Cross-Reference To Ernest Holmes' The Science of Mind

Ref. Nr.	Bible Verse	Citation	Ernest Holmes Reference	Page in SOM Text
558	II Corinthians 3:17	Now the Lord is that Spirit: and where the Spirit of the Lord is, there is liberty.	The Law of God is One of Liberty	487-2
559	Matthew 6:27	Which of you by taking thought can add one cubit unto his stature?	By taking thought, you do not add one cubit to Reality	489-3
560	II Corinthians 3:18	But we all, with open face beholding as in a glass the glory of the Lord, are changed into the same image from glory to glory, even as by the Spirit of the Lord.	But we all, with open face beholding as in a glass the glory of the Lord, are changed into the same image from glory to glory, even as by the Spirit of the Lord.	489-5
561	Matthew 6:33	But seek ye first the kingdom of God, and his righteousness; and all these things shall be added unto you.	And Jesus tells us to seek the Kingdom of God first and that all else will be added unto us.	490-1
562	II Corinthians 3:7-12	But if the ministration of death, written and engraven in stones, was glorious, so that the children of Israel could not stedfastly behold the face of Moses for the glory of his countenance; which glory was to be done away: How shall not the ministration of the spirit be rather glorious? For if the ministration of condemnation be glory, much more doth the ministration of righteousness exceed in glory. For even that which was made glorious had no glory in this respect, by reason of the glory that excelleth. For if that which is done away was glorious, much more that which remaineth is glorious. Seeing then that we have such hope, we use great plainness of speech:	The ascending scale of life	490-5
563	II Corinthians 3:18	But we all, with open face beholding as in a glass the glory of the Lord, are changed into the same image from glory to glory, even as by the Spirit of the Lord.	We are changed from glory to glory	490-5
564	II Corinthians 4:8-9	We are troubled on every side, yet not distressed; we are perplexed, but not in despair; Persecuted, but not forsaken; cast down, but not destroyed;	Even in our troubles we are not cast down	491-1

Ref. Nr.	BIBLE VERSE	Citation	Ernest Holmes Reference	Page in SOM Text
565	II Corinthians 5:1-10	For we know that if our earthly house of this tabernacle were dissolved, we have a building of God, an house not made with hands, eternal in the heavens. For in this we groan, earnestly desiring to be clothed upon with our house which is from heaven: If so be that being clothed we shall not be found naked. For we that are in this tabernacle do groan, being burdened: not for that we would be unclothed, but clothed upon, that mortality might be swallowed up of life. Now he that hath wrought us for the selfsame thing is God, who also hath given unto us the earnest of the Spirit. Therefore we are always confident, knowing that, whilst we are at home in the body, we are absent from the Lord: (For we walk by faith, not by sight:) We are confident, I say, and willing rather to be absent from the body, and to be present with the Lord. Wherefore we labour, that, whether present or absent, we may be accepted of him. For we must all appear before the judgment seat of Christ; that every one may receive the things done in his body, according to that he hath done, whether it be good or bad.	This body, which we seem to live is not the eternal body.	491-6
566	II Corinthians 5:16	Wherefore henceforth know we no man after the flesh: yea, though we have known Christ after the flesh, yet now henceforth know we him no more.	Know no man after the flesh	491-8
567	II Corinthians 5:16	Wherefore henceforth know we no man after the flesh: yea, though we have known Christ after the flesh, yet now henceforth know we him no more.	Know no man after the flesh	492-2
568	Ephesians 3:16	That he would grant you, according to the riches of his glory, to be strengthened with might by his Spirit in the inner man;	To be strengthened with might by his Spirit in the inner man	492-3
569	Ephesians 3:20-21	Now unto him that is able to do exceeding abundantly above all that we ask or think, according to the power that worketh in us.	the Son of God--"the power that worketh in us."	492-6
570	Ephesians 3:21	Unto him be glory in the church by Christ Jesus throughout all ages, world without end. Amen.	World without end	492-7
571	Ephesians 3:21	Unto him be glory in the church by Christ Jesus throughout all ages, world without end. Amen.	"world without end" or worlds without end, are necessary to the expression of Spirit.	493-1
572	Ephesians 4:1-6	I therefore, the prisoner of the Lord, beseech you that ye walk worthy of the vocation wherewith ye are called, With all lowliness and meekness, with longsuffering, forbearing one another in love; Endeavouring to keep the unity of the Spirit in the bond of peace. There is one body, and one Spirit, even as ye are called in one hope of your calling; One Lord, one faith, one baptism, One God and Father of all, who is above all, and through all, and in you all.	There is one body and one Spirit	493-3

Ref. Nr.	Bible Verse	Citation	Ernest Holmes Reference	Page in SOM Text
573	Ephesians 4:1-6	I therefore, the prisoner of the Lord, beseech you that ye walk worthy of the vocation wherewith ye are called, With all lowliness and meekness, with longsuffering, forbearing one another in love; Endeavouring to keep the unity of the Spirit in the bond of peace. There is one body, and one Spirit, even as ye are called in one hope of your calling; One Lord, one faith, one baptism, One God and Father of all, who is above all, and through all, and in you all.	One Lord, one faith, one baptism	493-5
574	Ephesians 4:1-6	I therefore, the prisoner of the Lord, beseech you that ye walk worthy of the vocation wherewith ye are called, With all lowliness and meekness, with longsuffering, forbearing one another in love; Endeavouring to keep the unity of the Spirit in the bond of peace. There is one body, and one Spirit, even as ye are called in one hope of your calling; One Lord, one faith, one baptism, One God and Father of all, who is above all, and through all, and in you all.	One God and Father of all, who is above all, and through all, and in you all.	493-6
575	Ephesians 4:23-24	And be renewed in the spirit of your mind; And that ye put on the new man, which after God is created in righteousness and true holiness.	We are told to be renewed in mind by the Spirit and to put on the new man.	494-1
576	Ephesians 6:10	Finally, my brethren, be strong in the Lord, and in the power of his might.	Be strong in the Lord and in the power of his might	494-3
577	Ephesians 6:12	For we wrestle not against flesh and blood, but against principalities, against powers, against the rulers of the darkness of this world, against spiritual wickedness in high places.	Wickedness in high places means an inverted use of the law of righteousness	494-5
578	Ephesians 6:13	Wherefore take unto you the whole armour of God, that ye may be able to withstand in the evil day, and having done all, to stand.	The armour of God is faith in the good	494-6
579	Galatians 5:23	gentleness, self-control; against such things there is no law.	Against such, there is no law.	494-6
580	Ephesians 6:14	Stand therefore, having your loins girt about with truth, and having on the breastplate of righteousness;	The breastplate of righteousness covers and gives sanctuary to the heart of hearts	495-2
581	Ephesians 6:15	And your feet shod with the preparation of the gospel of peace;	the feet shod with the gospel of peace	495-2
582	Proverbs 3:17	Her ways are ways of pleasantness, and all her paths are peace.	With Solomon are we happy when we find Wisdom, for "Her ways are ways of pleasantness and all her paths are peace."	495-2
583	Ephesians 6:16	Above all, taking the shield of faith, wherewith ye shall be able to quench all the fiery darts of the wicked.	The shield of faith	495-3
584	Ephesians 6:17	And take the helmet of salvation, and the sword of the Spirit, which is the word of God:	And the sword of the Spirit is the word of Truth	495-4
585	Romans 8:31	What shall we then say to these things? If God be for us, who can be against us?	"If God be for us who can be against us?"	495-5

Ref. Nr.	Bible Verse	Citation	Ernest Holmes Reference	Page in SOM Text
586	Philippians 2:5	Let this mind be in you, which was also in Christ Jesus:	We are to let the mind be in us which was in Christ Jesus	495-6
587	Philippians 2:5	Let this mind be in you, which was also in Christ Jesus:	To have the same mind that Jesus used	495-7
588	Philippians 2:5	Let this mind be in you, which was also in Christ Jesus:	not the name of Jesus, but the Mind of Christ	496-3
589	Philippians 4:8	Finally, brethren, whatsoever things are true, whatsoever things are honest, whatsoever things are just, whatsoever things are pure, whatsoever things are lovely, whatsoever things are of good report; if there be any virtue, and if there be any praise, think on these things.	We are to think on those things which are of good report	496-4
590	Philippians 4:19	But my God shall supply all your need according to his riches in glory by Christ Jesus.	And God will supply all our needs.	496-5
591	I Thessalonians 5:16	Rejoice evermore.	We are to rejoice evermore.	496-6
592	I Thessalonians 5:17	Pray without ceasing.	Pray without ceasing	497-1
593	I Thessalonians 5:18	In every thing give thanks: for this is the will of God in Christ Jesus concerning you.	"In everything give thanks"	497-2
594	I Thessalonians 5:19	Quench not the Spirit.	Quench not the Spirit.	497-3
595	I Thessalonians 5:19	Quench not the Spirit.	Quench not the Spirit.	498-1
596	I Thessalonians 5:21	Prove all things; hold fast that which is good.	"Prove all things, hold fast to that which is good."	498-2
597	James 1:5-18	If any of you lack wisdom, let him ask of God, that giveth to all men liberally, and upbraideth not; and it shall be given him. But let him ask in faith, nothing wavering. For he that wavereth is like a wave of the sea driven with the wind and tossed. For let not that man think that he shall receive any thing of the Lord. A double minded man is unstable in all his ways. . . . . Let no man say when he is tempted, I am tempted of God: for God cannot be tempted with evil, neither tempteth he any man: But every man is tempted, when he is drawn away of his own lust, and enticed. . . . Do not err, my beloved brethren. Every good gift and every perfect gift is from above, and cometh down from the Father of lights, with whom is no variableness, neither shadow of turning. Of his own will begat he us with the word of truth, that we should be a kind of firstfruits of his creatures.	Ask in Faith, Believing	498-3
598	James 1:8	A double minded man is unstable in all his ways.	The double-minded man gets nowhere	498-3
599	James 1:6	But let him ask in faith, nothing wavering. For he that wavereth is like a wave of the sea driven with the wind and tossed.	Anything that is not of faith is sin, or a mistake.	498-4

Where'd He Get That? A Biblical Cross-Reference To Ernest Holmes' The Science of Mind

Ref. Nr.	Bible Verse	Citation	Ernest Holmes Reference	Page in SOM Text
600	James 1:5-18	If any of you lack wisdom, let him ask of God, that giveth to all men liberally, and upbraideth not; and it shall be given him.	When we ask for anything, we are to believe that we have it	498-5
601	James 1:13	Let no man say when he is tempted, I am tempted of God: for God cannot be tempted with evil, neither tempteth he any man:	God never tempts	498-6
602	James 1:13	Let no man say when he is tempted, I am tempted of God: for God cannot be tempted with evil, neither tempteth he any man:	God cannot be tempted	498-6
603	Mark 3:25	And if a house be divided against itself, that house cannot stand.	The Universe is not divided against Itself.	499-3
604	James 1:22	But be ye doers of the word, and not hearers only, deceiving your own selves.	"Be ye doers of the word, and not hearers only, deceiving your own selves."	499-5
605	Matthew 7:21	Not every one that saith unto me, Lord, Lord, shall enter into the kingdom of heaven; but he that doeth the will of my Father which is in heaven.	Not everyone who says Lord, Lord, but those who do the will of Truth, enter in.	499-5
606	James 2:9	But if ye have respect to persons, ye commit sin, and are convinced of the law as transgressors.	James speaks of being convinced of the law as transgressors	500-2
607	James 2:1-11	My brethren, have not the faith of our Lord Jesus Christ, the Lord of glory, with respect of persons. For if there come unto your assembly a man with a gold ring, in goodly apparel, and there come in also a poor man in vile raiment; And ye have respect to him that weareth the gay clothing, and say unto him, Sit thou here in a good place; and say to the poor, Stand thou there, or sit here under my footstool: Are ye not then partial in yourselves, and are become judges of evil thoughts? Hearken, my beloved brethren, Hath not God chosen the poor of this world rich in faith, and heirs of the kingdom which he hath promised to them that love him? But ye have despised the poor. Do not rich men oppress you, and draw you before the judgment seats? Do not they blaspheme that worthy name by the which ye are called? If ye fulfil the royal law according to the scripture, Thou shalt love thy neighbour as thyself, ye do well: But if ye have respect to persons, ye commit sin, and are convinced of the law as transgressors. For whosoever shall keep the whole law, and yet offend in one point, he is guilty of all. For he that said, Do not commit adultery, said also, Do not kill. Now if thou commit no adultery, yet if thou kill, thou art become a transgressor of the law.	The Law is No Respecter of Persons	500-2
608	James 5:15	And the prayer of faith shall save the sick, and the Lord shall raise him up; and if he have committed sins, they shall be forgiven him.	The prayer of faith is the unconditional belief in both the ability and desire of Spirit to hear and answer	500-5

Ref. Nr.	Bible Verse	Citation	Ernest Holmes Reference	Page in SOM Text
609	James 5:16	Confess your faults one to another, and pray one for another, that ye may be healed. The effectual fervent prayer of a righteous man availeth much.	James tells us to confess our faults.	501-5
610	Jeremiah 31:34	And they shall teach no more every man his neighbour, and every man his brother, saying, Know the LORD: for they shall all know me, from the least of them unto the greatest of them, saith the LORD: for I will forgive their iniquity, and I will remember their sin no more.	We should learn to let go of our mistakes and remember them no longer against ourselves.	502-2
611	Matthew 5:26	Verily I say unto thee, Thou shalt by no means come out thence, till thou hast paid the uttermost farthing.	BUT THE LAST FARTHING IS PAID WHEN WE LET GO AND TRUST IN THE LAW OF GOOD.	502-3
612	I John 3:2	Beloved, now are we the sons of God, and it doth not yet appear what we shall be: but we know that, when he shall appear, we shall be like him; for we shall see him as he is.	God's love is complete in us, in that we are His sons	502-7
613	I John 3:2	Beloved, now are we the sons of God, and it doth not yet appear what we shall be: but we know that, when he shall appear, we shall be like him; for we shall see him as he is.	Now are we the Sons of God	503-1
614	I John 3:2	Beloved, now are we the sons of God, and it doth not yet appear what we shall be: but we know that, when he shall appear, we shall be like him; for we shall see him as he is.	"We shall see him as he is"	503-3
615	I John 3:7	Little children, let no man deceive you: he that doeth righteousness is righteous, even as he is righteous	Who doeth right, is right, even as He is right.	503-4
616	I John 3:9	Whosoever is born of God doth not commit sin; for his seed remaineth in him: and he cannot sin, because he is born of God.	"Who is born of love is born of God, for God is Love."	503-6
617	I John 4:16	And we have known and believed the love that God hath to us. God is love; and he that dwelleth in love dwelleth in God, and God in him.	"Who is born of love is born of God, for God is Love."	503-6
618	John 14:10	Believest thou not that I am in the Father, and the Father in me? the words that I speak unto you I speak not of myself: but the Father that dwelleth in me, he doeth the works.	It is not I, but the Father Who dwelleth in me, He doeth the works.	507-5
619	Luke 17:19	And he said unto him, Arise, go thy way: thy faith hath made thee whole.	I hear the voice to Truth telling me to arise and walk, for I am healed	506-1
620	Matthew 15:13	But he answered and said, Every plant, which my heavenly Father hath not planted, shall be rooted up.	"Every plant which my Heavenly Father hath not planted, shall be rooted up."	506-4
621	Job 19:26	And though after my skin worms destroy this body, yet in my flesh shall I see God:	"In my flesh I shall see God."	510-3
622	Matthew 3:2	And saying, Repent ye: for the kingdom of heaven is at hand.	Look out and see Thy good. It is not afar off, but is at hand	512-3
623	Ephesians 4:6	One God and Father of all, who is above all, and through all, and in you all.	"In all, over all, and through all."	513-1

Ref. Nr.	Bible Verse	Citation	Ernest Holmes Reference	Page in SOM Text
624	Psalms 46:10	Be still, and know that I am God: I will be exalted among the heathen, I will be exalted in the earth.	"Be still and know that I am god."	514-2
625	Hebrews 12:1	Wherefore seeing we also are compassed about with so great a cloud of witnesses, let us lay aside every weight, and the sin which doth so easily beset us, and let us run with patience the race that is set before us,	Cast aside all doubt	514-3
626	Psalms 23:6	Surely goodness and mercy shall follow me all the days of my life: and I will dwell in the house of the LORD for ever.	And joy shall accompany us through the ages yet to come.	514-3
627	Psalms 102:7	I watch, and am as a sparrow alone upon the house top	"His eye is on the sparrow and I know He watches me."	515-2
628	Psalms 91:1	He that dwelleth in the secret place of the most High shall abide under the shadow of the Almighty.	I have found that the Secret Place of God is within my own Soul	516-2
629	Romans 8:1	There is therefore now no condemnation to them which are in Christ Jesus, who walk not after the flesh, but after the Spirit.	There is no condemnation in me nor operating through me	518-3
630	Matthew 3:2	And saying, Repent ye: for the kingdom of heaven is at hand.	I shall not doubt nor fear, for my salvation is from On High, and the day of its appearing is now at hand.	521-3
631	Psalms 19:7	The law of the LORD is perfect, converting the soul: the testimony of the LORD is sure, making wise the simple.	"The Law of the Lord is perfect."	522-1
632	John 15:7	If ye abide in me, and my words abide in you, ye shall ask what ye will, and it shall be done unto you.	I speak into that Law and it is done unto me.	522-1
633	I John 4:18	There is no fear in love; but perfect love casteth out fear: because fear hath torment. He that feareth is not made perfect in love.	Love dissolves all fear, casts out all doubt and sets the captive free	522-3
634	John 15:7	If ye abide in me, and my words abide in you, ye shall ask what ye will, and it shall be done unto you.	Now it is done unto me.	524-1
635	Acts 9:3	And as he journeyed, he came near Damascus: and suddenly there shined round about him a light from heaven:	The Light of Heaven shines through me and illumines my path	526-2
636	Malachi 1:9	9And now, I pray you, beseech God that he will be gracious unto us: this hath been by your means:	The Seal of Approval is upon me	526-4
637	Psalms 91:1	He that dwelleth in the secret place of the most High shall abide under the shadow of the Almighty.	And I enter into "The Secret Place of The Most High."	527-1
638	I John 4:18	There is no fear in love; but perfect love casteth out fear: because fear hath torment. He that feareth is not made perfect in love.	Perfect Love casteth out all fear.	528-2
639	Psalms 17:5	Uphold my steps in Your paths, That my footsteps may not slip.	My feet shall not falter, for they are kept upon the path of Life through the Power of the Eternal Spirit.	528-4
640	Proverbs 2:9	Then you will understand righteousness and justice, Equity and every good path.	Guide Thou my feet; compel my way; direct my paths and me in Thy Presence.	529-1

Ref. Nr.	Bible Verse	Citation	Ernest Holmes Reference	Page in SOM Text
641	Psalms 23:4	Yea, though I walk through the valley of the shadow of death, I will fear no evil: for thou art with me; thy rod and thy staff they comfort me.	"I will fear no evil, for Thou art with me."	529-4
642	Ephesians 4:6	One God and Father of all, who is above all, and through all, and in you all.	I proclaim the One Life: "In all and through all."	531-3
643	Psalms 23:4	Yea, though I walk through the valley of the shadow of death, I will fear no evil: for thou art with me; thy rod and thy staff they comfort me.	"I will fear no evil, for Thou art with me."	533-2
644	Psalms 103:1	Bless the LORD, O my soul; And all that is within me, bless His holy name!	"Bless the Lord, O my Soul, and all that is within me, bless His holy Name."	534-2
645	Ephesians 3:21	Unto him be glory in the church by Christ Jesus throughout all ages, world without end. Amen.	Life always was and evermore shall be," World without end."	536-2
646	Psalms 91:1	He that dwelleth in the secret place of the most High shall abide under the shadow of the Almighty.	Joy awaits upon me in the "Secret Place of the Most High."	
647	Acts 9:3	And as he journeyed, he came near Damascus: and suddenly there shined round about him a light from heaven:	Let Thy light illumine my path, and let Thy wisdom direct my way.	
648	John 16:20	Most assuredly, I say to you that you will weep and lament, but the world will rejoice; and you will be sorrowful, but your sorrow will be turned into joy.	Despair gives way to joy at the thought of Thee, Indwelling God	537-3
649	Matthew 6:10	Thy kingdom come, Thy will be done in earth, as it is in heaven.	Compel my will to do thy bidding	536-4
650	Psalms 51:6	Behold, You desire truth in the inward parts, And in the hidden part You will make me to know wisdom.	Compel me to follow the course of Truth and Wisdom	537-2
651	Psalms 31:3	For You are my rock and my fortress; Therefore, for Your name's sake, Lead me and guide me.	Command my soul to turn to Thee for guidance and light	537-2
652	Matthew 6:10	Thy kingdom come, Thy will be done in earth, as it is in heaven.	O Spirit of Life, control my every action and thought	537-4
653	Acts 9:3	And as he journeyed, he came near Damascus: and suddenly there shined round about him a light from heaven:	Compel me to follow Thy light that I too may be free and complete	537-4
654	Psalms 85:13	Righteousness will go before Him, And shall make His footsteps our pathway.	I will follow Thy footsteps and learn of Thee all the wondrous secrets of Life	537-4
655	Psalms 121:4	Behold, He who keeps Israel Shall neither slumber nor sleep.	"He who neither slumbers or sleeps"	538-2
656	Revelations 21:5	And he that sat upon the throne said, Behold, I make all things new. And he said unto me, Write: for these words are true and faithful.	Behold, He maketh all things new	540-2
657	Isaiah 40:31	But those who wait on the LORD Shall renew their strength; They shall mount up with wings like eagles, They shall run and not be weary, They shall walk and not faint	In thy Strength do I daily walk and live;	542-2
658	Matthew 28:20	lo, I am with you always, even to the end of the age." Amen	I shall walk no more alone	543-1
659	Isaiah 55:11	So shall my word be that goeth forth out of my mouth: it shall not return unto me void, but it shall accomplish that which I please, and it shall prosper in the thing whereto I sent it.	My word comes back to me laden with the fruits of its own speech	543-3

Where'd He Get That? A Biblical Cross-Reference To Ernest Holmes' The Science of Mind

Ref. Nr.	Bible Verse	Citation	Ernest Holmes Reference	Page in SOM Text
660	Isaiah 55:11	So shall my word be that goeth forth out of my mouth: it shall not return unto me void, but it shall accomplish that which I please, and it shall prosper in the thing whereto I sent it.	The Word of my mouth shall bear fruit. It shall accomplish and prosper, and shall not return unto me void.	544-2
661	Isaiah 55:11	So shall my word be that goeth forth out of my mouth: it shall not return unto me void, but it shall accomplish that which I please, and it shall prosper in the thing whereto I sent it.	My Word is the law unto the thing whereunto it is sent, and it cannot come back empty-handed	544-2
662	Isaiah 55:11	So shall my word be that goeth forth out of my mouth: it shall not return unto me void, but it shall accomplish that which I please, and it shall prosper in the thing whereto I sent it.	My Word is the law unto the thing whereunto it is spoken	544-2
663	Psalms 19:4	Their line is gone out through all the earth, and their words to the end of the world. In them hath he set a tabernacle for the sun,	For his lines have gone out into all places	546-2
664	Ephesians 4:6	One God and Father of all, who is above all, and through all, and in you all.	"For he is all in all, over all and through all."	546-2
665	Matthew 5:48	Be ye therefore perfect, even as your Father which is in heaven is perfect.	Today my body responds to the Divine Behest: "Be perfect."	549-1
666	Psalms 73:24	You will guide me with Your counsel, And afterward receive me to glory.	Compel me to follow Thee and let me not pursue the paths of my own counsel.	550-1
667	Psalms 42:7	Deep calls unto deep at the noise of Your waterfalls; All Your waves and billows have gone over me.	As deep cries unto deep, so my thought cries unto Thee and Thou dost answer	550-1
668	Luke 12:32	Fear not, little flock; for it is your Father's good pleasure to give you the kingdom.	It is the Father's good pleasure to give me the Kingdom of Heaven	556-2
669	Matthew 6:28-29	And why take ye thought for raiment? Consider the lilies of the field, how they grow; they toil not, neither do they spin: And yet I say unto you, That even Solomon in all his glory was not arrayed like one of these.	"Consider the lilies of the field, they toil not neither do they spin, yet...Solomon in all his glory was not arrayed as one of these."	556-6
670	John 15:8	Herein is my Father glorified, that ye bear much fruit; so shall ye be my disciples.	I myself am to blame when these "fruits of the Spirit" fail to appear.	557-1

Where'd He Get That? A Biblical Cross-Reference To Ernest Holmes' The Science of Mind

Ref. Nr.	Bible Verse	Citation	Ernest Holmes Reference	Page in SOM Text
671	II Kings 4:1-4	Now there cried a certain woman of the wives of the sons of the prophets unto Elisha, saying, Thy servant my husband is dead; and thou knowest that thy servant did fear the LORD: and the creditor is come to take unto him my two sons to be bondmen. And Elisha said unto her, What shall I do for thee? tell me, what hast thou in the house? And she said, Thine handmaid hath not any thing in the house, save a pot of oil. Then he said, Go, borrow thee vessels abroad of all thy neighbours, even empty vessels; borrow not a few. And when thou art come in, thou shalt shut the door upon thee and upon thy sons, and shalt pour out into all those vessels, and thou shalt set aside that which is full.	I bring all "the empty vessels" knowing they will be filled	557-3
672	John 14:27	Peace I leave with you, my peace I give unto you: not as the world giveth, give I unto you. Let not your heart be troubled, neither let it be afraid.	"Peace I leave with you, my peace I give unto you, not as the world giveth, give I unto you."	558-2
673	Isaiah 42:16	And I will bring the blind by a way that they knew not; I will lead them in paths that they have not known: I will make darkness light before them, and crooked things straight. These things will I do unto them, and not forsake them.	Therefore, the road is made straight before me	559-3
674	I John 4:18	There is no fear in love; but perfect love casteth out fear: because fear hath torment. He that feareth is not made perfect in love.	We are no longer afraid, for love casts out fear.	560-2
675	John 14:6	Jesus saith unto him, I am the way, the truth, and the life: no man cometh unto the Father, but by me.	When Jesus said," No man cometh unto the Father but by me," of course he meant the I AM.	564-4
676	Philippians 2:5	Let this mind be in you, which was also in Christ Jesus:	Assurance: In reality, assurance is having "the mind which was in Christ Jesus."	576
677	Ephesians 4:23-24	And be renewed in the spirit of your mind; And that ye put on the new man, which after God is created in righteousness and true holiness.	Christ: each one "puts on the Christ"	579
678	Galatians 6:7	Be not deceived; God is not mocked: for whatsoever a man soweth, that shall he also reap.	Compensation: as you sow you reap.	579
679	Luke 20:38	For he is not a God of the dead, but of the living: for all live unto him.	Death:" God is not a God of the dead, but of the living, for in His sight, all are alive."	583
680	I Corinthians 15:40	There are also celestial bodies, and bodies terrestrial: but the glory of the celestial is one, and the glory of the terrestrial is another.	"There are bodies celestial and bodies terrestrial, there is material body and a spiritual body."	583
681	Isaiah 65:24	And it shall come to pass, that before they call, I will answer; and while they are yet speaking, I will hear.	Desire: "Before they call, will I answer."	584

Ref. Nr.	Bible Verse	Citation	Ernest Holmes Reference	Page in SOM Text
682	Matthew 6:22-23	The light of the body is the eye: if therefore thine eye be single, thy whole body shall be full of light. But if thine eye be evil, thy whole body shall be full of darkness. If therefore the light that is in thee be darkness, how great is that darkness!	Duality: "If the eye is "single" to the good, if the vision remains steadfast, we become one with it.	587
683	Hebrews 11:3	Through faith we understand that the worlds were framed by the word of God, so that things which are seen were not made of things which do appear.	Effect: "Things which are seen are not made of things which do appear."	588
684	Luke 6:38	Give, and it shall be given unto you; good measure, pressed down, and shaken together, and running over, shall men give into your bosom. For with the same measure that ye mete withal it shall be measured to you again.	Equivalent: allow the pure spiritual substance to flow through to us, "Pressed down and running over."	
685	Hebrews 11:1	Now faith is the substance of things hoped for, the evidence of things not seen.	Faith: "Faith is the substance of things hoped for, the evidence of things not seen."	591
686	Genesis 3:22	And the LORD God said, Behold, the man is become as one of us, to know good and evil: and now, lest he put forth his hand, and take also of the tree of life, and eat, and live for ever:	Fall: This is the meaning of God saying, "he shall become as one of us and live forever."	592
687	I John 4:18	There is no fear in love; but perfect love casteth out fear: because fear hath torment. He that feareth is not made perfect in love.	Fear: "Perfect love casteth out fear:	593
688	Luke 12:32	Fear not, little flock; for it is your Father's good pleasure to give you the kingdom.	Fear: "Fear not, little flock, it is your Father's good pleasure to give you the kingdom."	593
689	Exodus 3:14	And God said unto Moses, I AM THAT I AM: and he said, Thus shalt thou say unto the children of Israel, I AM hath sent me unto you.	Great Discovery:….The ability to affirm, to say "I AM," to be conscious of one's relationship to the Universe	596
690	Revelation 21:21	And the twelve gates were twelve pearls: every several gate was of one pearl: and the street of the city was pure gold, as it were transparent glass.	Heaven: Heaven is not a place, a locality "with streets of gold and gates of pearl."	598
691	Exodus 14:13	And Moses said unto the people, Fear ye not, stand still, and see the salvation of the LORD, which he will shew to you to day: for the Egyptians whom ye have seen to day, ye shall see them again no more for ever.	Humility: "Stand still and watch the sure salvation of the Lord."	598
692	Ezekiel 3:10	Moreover he said unto me, Son of man, all my words that I shall speak unto thee receive in thine heart, and hear with thine ears.	Illumination: "Speak to Him, thou, for He hears."	599
693	John 7:24	Judge not according to the appearance, but judge righteous judgment.	Illusion: "Judge not according to appearances."	599
694	Matthew 7:1,2	Judge not, that ye be not judged. For with what judgment ye judge, ye shall be judged: and with what measure ye mete, it shall be measured to you again.	Judgment: "Judge not that ye be not judged, for with what judgment ye judge, ye shall be judged."	603

Where'd He Get That? A Biblical Cross-Reference To Ernest Holmes' The Science of Mind

Ref. Nr.	Bible Verse	Citation	Ernest Holmes Reference	Page in SOM Text
695	Matthew 5:45	That ye may be the children of your Father which is in heaven: for he maketh his sun to rise on the evil and on the good, and sendeth rain on the just and on the unjust.	Judgment: "He sendeth rain on the just and on the unjust."	603
696	Luke 17:21	Neither shall they say, Lo here! or, lo there! for, behold, the kingdom of God is within you.	Kingdom: "The Kingdom of Heaven" is not a place; it is "within".	604
697	Matthew 8:13	And Jesus said unto the centurion, Go thy way; and as thou hast believed, so be it done unto thee. And his servant was healed in the selfsame hour.	Knowledge: "It is done unto us as we believe."	604
698	Genesis 1:3	And God said, Let there be light: and there was light.	Light: "Let there be light and there was light."	607
699	John 8:12	Then spake Jesus again unto them, saying, I am the light of the world: he that followeth me shall not walk in darkness, but shall have the light of life.	Light: "I am the light of the world; he that followeth me shall not walk in darkness, but shall have the light of life."	607
700	Acts 13:47	For so hath the Lord commanded us, saying, I have set thee to be a light of the Gentiles, that thou shouldest be for salvation unto the ends of the earth.	Light: I have set thee to be a light	607
701	I John 2:10	He that loveth his brother abideth in the light, and there is none occasion of stumbling in him.	Light: He that loveth his brother abideth in the light	607
702	Philippians 2:15	That ye may be blameless and harmless, the sons of God, without rebuke, in the midst of a crooked and perverse nation, among whom ye shine as lights in the world;	Light: "The sons of God, without rebuke...ye shine as lights in the world."	607
703	John 1:1, 2, 3	In the beginning was the Word, and the Word was with God, and the Word was God. The same was in the beginning with God. All things were made by him; and without him was not any thing made that was made.	Logos: The Word was with God and the Word was God."	608
704	Job 22:28	Thou shalt also decree a thing, and it shall be established unto thee: and the light shall shine upon thy ways.	Logos: Thou shalt also decree a thing, and it shall be established unto thee."	608
705	I John 4:8	He that loveth not knoweth not God; for God is love.	Love: "He that loveth not, knoweth not God; for God is Love."	608
706	Isaiah 58:11	And the LORD shall guide thee continually, and satisfy thy soul in drought, and make fat thy bones: and thou shalt be like a watered garden, and like a spring of water, whose waters fail not.	Lord: "And the Lord shall guide thee continually"	608
707	John 14:27	Peace I leave with you, my peace I give unto you: not as the world giveth, give I unto you. Let not your heart be troubled, neither let it be afraid.	Peace: "Peace I leave with you, my peace I give unto you"	617

Ref. Nr.	Bible Verse	Citation	Ernest Holmes Reference	Page in SOM Text
708	Acts 8:20-21	But Peter said unto him, Thy money perish with thee, because thou hast thought that the gift of God may be purchased with money. Thou hast neither part nor lot in this matter: for thy heart is not right in the sight of God.	Revelation: "But Peter said unto him, Thy money perish with thee, because thou hast thought that the gift of God may be purchased with money. Thou hast neither part nor lot in this matter; for thy heart is not right in the sight of God."	630
709	John 14:12	Verily, verily, I say unto you, He that believeth on me, the works that I do shall he do also; and greater works than these shall he do; because I go unto my Father.	Savior: "The works that I do shall ye do also; and greater works than these shall ye do; because I go unto my father."	631
710	Matthew 6:6	But thou, when thou prayest, enter into thy closet, and when thou hast shut thy door, pray to thy Father which is in secret; and thy Father which seeth in secret shall reward thee openly.	Silence: We enter the inner chamber of our mind and close the door on all discord and confusion	633
711	John 14:10	Believest thou not that I am in the Father, and the Father in me? the words that I speak unto you I speak not of myself: but the Father that dwelleth in me, he doeth the works.	Silence: "the Father within, he doeth the work."	633
712	Luke 15:31	And he said unto him, Son, thou art ever with me, and all that I have is thine.	Supply: "All that the Father hath."	635
713	John 11:41-44	Then they took away the stone from the place where the dead was laid. And Jesus lifted up his eyes, and said, Father, I thank thee that thou hast heard me. And I knew that thou hearest me always: but because of the people which stand by I said it, that they may believe that thou hast sent me. And when he thus had spoken, he cried with a loud voice, Lazarus, come forth. And he that was dead came forth, bound hand and foot with graveclothes: and his face was bound about with a napkin. Jesus saith unto them, Loose him, and let him go.	Thanksgiving: Jesus prayed when he raised Lazarus from the tomb: "Father I thank thee…"	637
714	Isaiah 65:24	And it shall come to pass, that before they call, I will answer; and while they are yet speaking, I will hear.	Thanksgiving: "before they ask will I answer"	637
715	Deuteronomy 6:4	Hear, O Israel: The LORD our God, the LORD is one!	Unity: "The Lord our God is One God…"	640
716	John 17:22	And the glory which You gave Me I have given them, that they may be one just as We are one:	Unity: "That they may all be one, even as Thou, Father, art in me and I in Thee, and they also in us."	641
717	John 15:7	If ye abide in me, and my words abide in you, ye shall ask what ye will, and it shall be done unto you.	Universal Power: "As we believe."	641
718	John 14:10	Believest thou not that I am in the Father, and the Father in me? the words that I speak unto you I speak not of myself: but the Father that dwelleth in me, he doeth the works.	Victory: To the metaphysician, every victory is won in the silence of his own soul; by turning to "the Father within."	643

Ref. Nr.	Bible Verse	Citation	Ernest Holmes Reference	Page in SOM Text
719	John 1:1, 2, 3	In the beginning was the Word, and the Word was with God, and the Word was God. The same was in the beginning with God. All things were made by him; and without him was not any thing made that was made.	Word: The word was with God and the word was God."	646

TABLE III: OTHER THINKERS CITED IN *THE SCIENCE OF MIND* ORGANIZED BY ORDER OF APPEARANCE

CODES TO THIS SECTION:

BLACK NORMAL = sources that could be verified

SHADED = possible sources that could not be verified

ITALICS = miscitations with a suggestion for possible source

Item Nr.	Page in the SOM Text	Phrase Used	Original Author	Primary Source Document	Quotation and commentary
1	026-3	First Cause	Plato (c. 427–c. 347 BCE) Greek philosopher, student of Socrates and teacher to Aristotle	*The Laws* (360 BCE)	To summarize, Plato argued that the motion in the universe must be attributable to a first cause. Plato argues, that the first cause of motion initiated all the motion in the universe. He called this principle, 'soul' or 'life.' Further, any cause that was the ultimate cause must itself be unmoved by anything else–an unmoved mover.
2	026-3	First Cause	Aristotle (384–322 BCE) Greek philosopher, student of Plato and teacher to Alexander the Great	*Metaphysics* (about 340 BCE)	To summarize, Aristotle said that the First Cause is only one because it is the Prime Mover only with pure form without any matter. For there must be only one "Pure Form" because only matter coupled with form can result in the plurality of being. The First Cause as a necessary being has always existed from eternity and cannot be destroyed.
3	026-3	First Cause	St. Thomas Aquinas (1225-1274) Catholic theologian and Scholastic philosopher	*Summa Theologica* (written 1265–1274)	In classic philosophy the "first cause argument" was an attempt by Aquinas to use Aristotelian logic to prove the existence of God. It follows: 1. Everything has a cause. 2. Nothing can cause itself. 3. A causal chain cannot be of infinite length. 4. A First Cause (or something that is not an effect) must exist. 5. That First Cause is God Therefore, God exists.

Item Nr.	Page in the SOM Text	Phrase Used	Original Author	Primary Source Document	Quotation and commentary
4	029-2	[The Subjective Mind is] The Servant of the Eternal Spirit throughout the ages	Exact source unknown for notion "servant of the Spirit." Possibly Josephine A. Jackson and Helen M. Salisbury, where the subconscious is first defined as a "servant." Jackson and Salisbury were two women Freudian psychoanalysts working in southern California. Their book was a best seller as it explained psychoanalysis in lay terms.	*Outwitting Our Nerves: A Primer of Psychotherapy* (1921) NOTE: This text appeared in the footnotes of the 1926 edition of the *Science of Mind*.	(p. 31) The subconscious mind which is not affected by ether, has been exhausting itself in a vain attempt to get the body away from harm. A Tireless Servant. When the conscious mind undertakes a job, it is always more or less subject to fatigue. But the subconscious after its long practice seems never to tire. We say that its activities have become automatic. With all its inherited skill, the subconscious, if left to itself, can be depended upon to run the bodily machinery without effort and without hitch. The only things that can interfere with its work are the wrong kind of emotions and the wrong kind of suggestions from the conscious mind. Barring these, it goes its way like a trusty servant, looking after details and leaving its master's mind free for other things.
5	029-1	Objective Mind	Thomas Troward (1847-1916) British Divisional Judge of the North Indian Punjab whose metaphysical writings had a profound effect on New Thought, in particular The Science of Mind.	*The Edinburgh Lectures on Mental Science* (1909) "Chapter IV: Subjective and Objective Mind" NOTE: This text appeared in the footnotes of the 1926 edition of the Science of Mind.	To summarize, the objective mind reasons inductively and deductively. It impresses the subjective mind with its beliefs and suggestions. It becomes of the highest importance to determine in every case what the nature of the suggestion shall be and from what source it shall proceed.
6	029-1	Subjective Mind	Thomas Troward (1847-1916) British Divisional Judge of the North Indian Punjab whose metaphysical writings had a profound effect on New Thought, in particular The Science of Mind.	*The Edinburgh Lectures on Mental Science* (1909) "Chapter IV: Subjective and Objective Mind" NOTE: This text appeared in the footnotes of the 1926 edition of the Science of Mind.	To summarize, the subjective mind can only reason deductively, will accept any suggestion, however false, but having once accepted any suggestion, it is strictly logical in deducing the proper conclusions from it, and works out every suggestion to the minutest fraction of the results which flow from it. As a consequence of this it follows that the subjective mind is entirely under the control of the objective mind.

Item Nr.	Page in the SOM Text	Phrase Used	Original Author	Primary Source Document	Quotation and commentary
7	029-3	Universal Subjective Mind	Thomas Troward (1847-1916) British Divisional Judge of the North Indian Punjab whose metaphysical writings had a profound effect on New Thought, in particular The Science of Mind.	*The Edinburgh Lectures on Mental Science* (1909) "Chapter V: Further Considerations Regarding Subjective and Objective Mind" NOTE: This text appeared in the footnotes of the 1926 edition of the Science of Mind.	If the student has followed what has been said regarding the presence of intelligent spirit pervading all space and permeating all matter, he will now have little difficulty in recognizing this all-pervading spirit as universal subjective mind.
8	029-3	The one great law of all life	Thomas Troward (1847-1916) British Divisional Judge of the North Indian Punjab whose metaphysical writings had a profound effect on New Thought, in particular The Science of Mind.	*The Edinburgh Lectures on Mental Science* (1909) "Chapter II: Higher Modes of Intelligence Controls the Lower" NOTE: This text appeared in the footnotes of the 1926 edition of the Science of Mind.	Now the business of Mental Science is to ascertain the relation of this individual power of volition to the great cosmic law which provides for the maintenance and advancement of the race;
9	032-2	All men seek some relationship to the Universal Mind, the Over-Soul	Ralph Waldo Emerson (1803-1882) American essayist, philosopher, poet, and leader of the transcendentalist movement in the early 19th century. His teachings directly influenced the growing New Thought movement.	*Essays: First Series* (1841) "Essay IX: The Over-Soul"	...that Unity, that Over-soul, within which every man's particular being is contained and made one with all other; that common heart, of which all sincere conversation is the worship, to which all right action is submission; that overpowering reality which confutes our tricks and talents, and constrains every one to pass for what he is, and to speak from his character, and not from his tongue, and which evermore tends to pass into our thought and hand, and become wisdom, and virtue, and power, and beauty.
10	033-3	The finite alone has wrought and suffered, the infinite lies stretched in smiling repose.	Ralph Waldo Emerson (1803-1882) American essayist, philosopher, poet, and leader of the transcendentalist movement in the early 19th century. His teachings directly influenced the growing New Thought movement.	*Essays: First Series* (1841) "Essay IV: Spiritual Laws"	For it is only the finite that has wrought and suffered; the infinite lies stretched in smiling repose.

Where'd He Get That? A Biblical Cross-Reference To Ernest Holmes' The Science of Mind

Item Nr.	Page in the SOM Text	Phrase Used	Original Author	Primary Source Document	Quotation and commentary
11	036-2	There is Spirit- or this Invisible Cause - and nothing, out of which all things are made. Now, Spirit plus nothing leaves Spirit only.	Thomas Troward (1847-1916) British Divisional Judge of the North Indian Punjab whose metaphysical writings had a profound effect on New Thought, in particular The Science of Mind.	*The Edinburgh Lectures on Mental Science* (1909) "Chapter II: Higher Modes of Intelligence Control the Lower" NOTE: This text appeared in the footnotes of the 1926 edition of the Science of Mind.	We thus find two factors to the making of all things, Spirit and—Nothing; and the addition of Nothing to Spirit leaves only Spirit:
12	036-4	"nestles the seed, perfection"	Walt Whitman (1819–1892) American poet, essayist, journalist, humanist, and part of the Transcendentalist movement.	*Leaves of Grass* (1900) "Song of the Universal"	In this broad earth of ours, Amid the measureless grossness and the slag, Enclosed and safe within its central heart, Nestles the seed perfection.
13	037-3	But if we say with Emerson, "There is no great and no small to the soul that maketh all,"	Ralph Waldo Emerson (1803-1882) American essayist, philosopher, poet, and leader of the transcendentalist movement in the early 19th century. His teachings directly influenced the growing New Thought movement.	*Poems* (1904) "The Informing Spirit" also in his *Essays: First Series* (1841) "Essay I: History"	There is no great and no small To the Soul that maketh all: And where it cometh, all things are; And it cometh everywhere.
14	041-2	Emerson advises we get our *bloated nothingness* out of the way of the divine circuits.	Ralph Waldo Emerson (1803-1882) American essayist, philosopher, poet, and leader of the transcendentalist movement in the early 19th century. His teachings directly influenced the growing New Thought movement.	*Essays: First Series* (1841) "Essay IV: Spiritual Laws"	The lesson which these observations convey is, Be, and not seem. Let us acquiesce. Let us take our bloated nothingness out of the path of the divine circuits.
15	045-4	This is what Emerson meant when he said that Unity passes into variety.	Ralph Waldo Emerson (1803-1882) American essayist, philosopher, poet, and leader of the transcendentalist movement in the early 19th century. His teachings directly influenced the growing New Thought movement.	*Essays: Second Series* (1844) "The Poet"	Here we find ourselves, suddenly, not in a critical speculation, but in a holy place, and should go very warily and reverently. We stand before the secret of the world, there where Being passes into Appearance, and Unity into Variety.

Where'd He Get That? A Biblical Cross-Reference To Ernest Holmes' The Science of Mind

Item Nr.	Page in the SOM Text	Phrase Used	Original Author	Primary Source Document	Quotation and commentary
16	046-2	We already do know. Every man knows right from wrong, in its broadest sense.	*Exact source unknown.* Probably Immanuel Kant (1724-1804) German philosopher from the Prussian city of Königsberg (now Kaliningrad, Russia), regarded as one of the most influential Western thinkers of the late Enlightenment period.	*Fundamental Principles of the Metaphysic of Morals* (1785)	A metaphysic of morals is therefore indispensably necessary, not merely for speculative reasons, in order to investigate the sources of the practical principles which are to be found *a priori* in our reason, but also because morals themselves are liable to all sorts of corruption, as long as we are without that clue and supreme canon by which to estimate them correctly.
17	053-5	its seeming reality is borrowed from illusion, from "chaos and old night"	*Exact source unknown.* Possibly John Milton (1608–1674) English poet, author, and polemicist.	*Paradise Lost,* Book I. Line 540 (1667)	Sonorous metal blowing martial sounds: At which the universal host up sent A shout that tore hell's concave, and beyond Frighted the reign of Chaos and old Night.
18	056-2	"a man convinced against his will is of the same opinion still"	*Exact source unknown.* Perhaps Samuel Butler (1612-1680) British poet and satirist.	in *Hudibras. Part iii. Canto iii. Line 547* (1663)	"He that complies against his will is of his own opinion still."
19	064-2	self-contemplation of God	Thomas Troward (1847-1916) British Divisional Judge of the North Indian Punjab whose metaphysical writings had a profound effect on New Thought, in particular The Science of Mind.	*The Creative Process and the Individual* (1915) - Chapter 2 "The Self-Contemplation of Spirit" NOTE: This text appeared in the footnotes of the 1926 edition of the Science of Mind.	If we ask how the cosmos came into existence we shall find that ultimately we can only attribute it to the Self-Contemplation of Spirit.
20	067-2	Spirit is the power that knows Itself.	Thomas Troward (1847-1916) British Divisional Judge of the North Indian Punjab whose metaphysical writings had a profound effect on New Thought, in particular The Science of Mind.	*Bible Mystery and Bible Meaning* (1913) NOTE: This text appeared in the footnotes of the 1926 edition of the *Science of Mind.*	(p 126) ...he is beginning to understand what is meant by man being the image of God, and to grasp the significance of the old-world saying that "Spirit is the Power that knows Itself."
21	072-4	"Man, know thyself"	Greek devotees of Apollo	Inscription found in the Oracle of Apollo at Delphi, Greece (built 1400 BCE)	*gnōthi seauton,* or σαυτόν (Know Thyself)

Item Nr.	Page in the SOM Text	Phrase Used	Original Author	Primary Source Document	Quotation and commentary
22	075-4	Kant says: We are able to perceive an object because it awakens an intuitive perception within us.	Immanuel Kant (1724-1804) German philosopher from the Prussian city of Königsberg (now Kaliningrad, Russia), regarded as one of the most influential Western thinkers of the late Enlightenment period.	*Critique of Pure Reason,* "Transcendental Aesthetic" (1781)	(p 86-87) It is, therefore, not merely possible or probable, but indubitably certain, that space and time, as the necessary conditions of all outer and inner experience, are merely subjective conditions of all our intuition, and that in relation to these conditions all objects are therefore mere appearances, and not given us as things in themselves which exist in this manner. For this reason also, while such can be said *a priori* as regards the form of appearances, nothing whatsoever can be asserted of the thing in itself, which may underlie these appearances. (p.90) Our mode of intuition is dependent upon the existence of the object, and is therefore possible only if the subject's faculty of representation is affected by that object.
23	076-1	This is what Emerson would have us understand when he says, "There is one mind common to all individual men."	Ralph Waldo Emerson (1803-1882) American essayist, philosopher, poet, and leader of the transcendentalist movement in the early 19th century. His teachings directly influenced the growing New Thought movement.	*Essays: First Series* (1841) "Essay I: History"	There is one mind common to all individual men.
24	076-4	This is the perception that Buddha, Jesus and other great spiritual leaders had. They understood that the Universe has to be One in order to be at all.	Gautama Buddha (563 -483 BCE) Spiritual teacher in the northern region of India who founded Buddhism.	*Buddhist Scriptures, The Tripitaka: Conduct, Discourses, Other Doctrines* (first written 3rd century AD)	The eighth point of the eight fold path:. Right concentration is meditating in such a way as to progressively realize a true understanding of imperfection/suffering, impermanence, and oneness.
25	078-2	Spirit is the power that knows Itself.	Thomas Troward (1847-1916) British Divisional Judge of the North Indian Punjab whose metaphysical writings had a profound effect on New Thought, in particular The Science of Mind.	*Bible Mystery and Bible Meaning* (1913) NOTE: This text appeared in the footnotes of the 1926 edition of the Science of Mind.	(p. 126)...he is beginning to understand what is meant by man being the image of God, and to grasp the significance of the old-world saying that "Spirit is the Power that knows Itself."

Item Nr.	Page in the SOM Text	Phrase Used	Original Author	Primary Source Document	Quotation and commentary
26	078-2	The Karmic Law of Buddha: "the Law than binds the ignorant and frees the wise." as Anna Besant stated it…	Annie Wood Besant, early leader of Theosophy (1847-1933)	*Karma* (1895)	*The Karmic Law that Besant writes about is her quotation and interpretation of Part III "The Secret of Work" from the Bhagavad Gita, a Hindu scripture, not a Buddhist one. In the preface, she remarks that the Buddhist calls it his "Skandha," not Karma.* *(p. 68) Right action is never neglected, but is faithfully performed to the limit of the available powers, renunciation of attachment to the fruit not implying any sloth or carelessness in acting: As the ignorant act from attachment to action, O Bharata, so should the wise act without attachment, desiring the maintenance of mankind. Let no wise man unsettle the mind of ignorant people attached to action; but acting in harmony (with Me) let him render all action attractive.* *…The man who reaches this state of " inaction in action," has learned the secret of the ceasing of Karma.*
27	079-2	Plotinus speaks of it [Universal Subjectivity] as a *doer* but not a *knower*. He called it a blind force, not knowing only doing.	Plotinus, Roman philosopher, founder of neo-Platonic thought (ca. AD 204–270) *Exact text unknown. The notion of "blind force" not found in Plotinus' writings. He describes what Holmes calls "Universal Subjectivity" in detail as a "Phantasm" of undifferentiated substance.*	*The Second Ennead:* Fifth Tractate "On Potentiality and Actuality" (250 AD)	*It [the Phantasm through which Reason-Principle takes form] has never been able to annex for itself even a visible outline from all the forms under which it has sought to creep: it has always pursued something other than itself; it was never more than a Potentiality towards its next: …Grasped, then, as an underlie in each order of Being, it can be no actualization of either: all that is allowed to it is to be a Potentiality, a weak and blurred phantasm, a thing incapable of a Shape of its own.*

Item Nr.	Page in the SOM Text	Phrase Used	Original Author	Primary Source Document	Quotation and commentary
28	080-1	the Law in this sense would be the servant of the Spirit.	Exact source unknown for notion "servant of the Spirit." Possibly Josephine A. Jackson and Helen M. Salisbury, where the subconscious is first defined as a "servant." Jackson and Salisbury were two women Freudian psychoanalysts working in southern California. Their book was a best seller as it explained psychoanalysis in lay terms.	*Outwitting Our Nerves: A Primer of Psychotherapy* (1921) NOTE: This text appeared in the footnotes of the 1926 edition of the *Science of Mind*.	(p. 31) The subconscious mind which is not affected by ether, has been exhausting itself in a vain attempt to get the body away from harm. A Tireless Servant. When the conscious mind undertakes a job, it is always more or less subject to fatigue. But the subconscious after its long practice seems never to tire. We say that its activities have become automatic. With all its inherited skill, the subconscious, if left to itself, can be depended upon to run the bodily machinery without effort and without hitch. The only things that can interfere with its work are the wrong kind of emotions and the wrong kind of suggestions from the conscious mind. Barring these, it goes its way like a trusty servant, looking after details and leaving its master's mind free for other things.
29	083-2	the Soul of the Universe has been called "a blind force, not knowing, only doing."	Exact source unknown for notion of "the Soul of the Universe." Possibly Thomas Troward (1847-1916) British Divisional Judge of the North Indian Punjab whose metaphysical writings had a profound effect on New Thought, in particular The Science of Mind.	*The Creative Process and the Individual* (1915)	The term "soul of the universe" is used once by Troward in this text. However, he uses the term "Soul of Nature" to denote the subjective mind or the Universal Subconscious Mind.
30	083-2	the Soul of the Universe has been called "a blind force, not knowing, only doing."	Anaxagoras (500 BC – 428 BC) Pre-Socratic Greek philosopher famous for introducing the cosmological concept of Nous (mind), the ordering force.	*The Journals of Ralph Waldo Emerson*, Edward Waldo Emerson (1909)	GREEK PHILOSOPHERS: ...the opinions of the first Ionians themselves, had associated the elementary matter of all things to the first cause of all production, and thus conceive the Divinity as the universal soul, the soul of the world, the world itself as an animated whole identical in some sort with its author, Anaxagoras first detached, separated with precision and neatness these two notions until then confounded. The Universe is in his eyes an effect wholly distinct from its Cause.

Item Nr.	Page in the SOM Text	Phrase Used	Original Author	Primary Source Document	Quotation and commentary
31	083-2	the Soul of the Universe has been called "a blind force, not knowing, only doing."	*Exact source unknown for "soul of the Universe."* Possibly referencing Plato (c. 427–c. 347 BCE) Greek philosopher, student of Socrates and teacher to Aristotle	*Phaedrus and the Laws* (360 BCE)	First, there is the immortal nature of which the brain is the seat, Timaeus. and which is akin to the soul of the universe. This alone thinks - and knows and is the ruler of the whole.
32	083-2	the Soul of the Universe has been called "a blind force, not knowing, only doing."	*Exact source unknown for notion of "the Soul of the Universe."* Possibly Gerald Massey (1828-1907) English poet and self-taught Egyptologist	*The Seven Souls of Man and Their Culmination in Christ* (1900)	(p. 232) Hermes describes the one soul of the universe as entering into creeping things, and transforming into the soul of watery things, and this into the soul of things that live on the land; and airy ones are changed into men; and human souls that lay hold of immortality are changed into spirits, and so they ascend up to the region of the fixed stars (or gods), which is the eighth sphere; and this is the most perfect glory of the soul! But this was as the one soul of life, not as the eight, or seven individual souls. The eighth was the immortal blossom on the human branch.
33	083-2	the Soul of the Universe has been called "a blind force, not knowing, only doing."	*Exact source unknown for notion of "the Soul of the Universe."* Possibly Helena Petrovna Blavatsky (1831-1891) Founder of Theosophy and the Theosophical Society.	Article in *Lucifer* (September 15, 1896" "The Mind in Nature"	The ancient Mysteries -- the primitive religions, all without one exception, reflect the most important of the once universal beliefs, such, for instance, as an impersonal and universal divine Principle, absolute in its nature, and unknowable to the "brain" intellect, or the conditioned and limited cognition of man. To imagine any witness to it in the manifested universe, other than as Universal Mind, the Soul of the universe -- is impossible. That which alone stands as an undying and ceaseless evidence and proof of the existence of that One Principle, is the presence of an undeniable design in cosmic mechanism, the birth, growth, death and transformation of everything in the universe, from the silent and unreachable stars down to the humble lichen, from man to the invisible lives now called microbes.

Item Nr.	Page in the SOM Text	Phrase Used	Original Author	Primary Source Document	Quotation and commentary
34	083-2	the Soul of the Universe has been called "a blind force, not knowing, only doing."	*Exact source unknown for notion of "the Soul of the Universe." Possibly Hindu mystic Sri Ramakrishna (1836-1886) and his disciple Swami Vivekananda (1863-1902)*	*Aspects of the Vedanta* (1921)	(p. 40) But the spiritual youth begins when we begin to realize that God is not outside of nature but He is in nature ; He is not outside of us, He is in us; that He is not extra-cosmic but intra-cosmic ; He is immanent and resident in nature ; He is the soul of the universe ; just as the soul of our body is the internal ruler of our body, so the soul of the universe is the internal ruler of the universe. He governs, not from outside, but from inside. He is the Creator, not in the sense that He sits somewhere and commands and creates the world out of the material which dwells outside of His own being, but He creates by pouring His spiritual influx in nature and starting the evolution of that cosmic energy which is called Prakriti, or nature. In fact, the cosmic energy forms the body of the Spiritual Being. God then appears to be both of the efficient and material cause of the universe, and therefore He is not only the Father but the Mother of the universe, Father and Mother, both in one.
35	083-2	the Soul of the Universe has been called "a blind force, not knowing, only doing."	*Exact source unknown for notion of "the Soul of the Universe." Possibly Hermes Treismegistus (circa 64–141 CE)*	*The Divine Pymander,* "Book 4: The Key"	Hast thou not heard in the general Speeches, that from one Soul of the universe are all those Souls which in the world are tossed up and down, as it were, and severally divided?
36	083-2	the Soul of the Universe has been called "a blind force, not knowing, only doing."	*Exact source unknown for notion of "blind force." Idea perhaps borrowed from Arthur Schopenhauer (1788-1860), German pessimistic philosopher who referred to a universal will as am impersonal "blind force".*	*The World as Will and Idea / Representation* (1819), Chapter "The Objectification of the Will"	To summarize, Schopenhauer describes a process of the movement of will from the psychological to the cosmological sphere. This movement is guided by an understanding of willing as an "impersonal, primordial blind force, independent of reason and consciousness." The world is an activity of blind force and "my will permeates the world." While there was only one universal will, it flows through the human mind.

Item Nr.	Page in the SOM Text	Phrase Used	Original Author	Primary Source Document	Quotation and commentary
37	083-2	It [the Soul of the Universe] has been called "The Servant of the Eternal Spirit throughout the ages."	*Exact source unknown.* Possibly Josephine A. Jackson and Helen M. Salisbury, where the subconscious is first defined as a "servant." Jackson and Salisbury were two women Freudian psychoanalysts working in southern California. Their book was a best seller as it explained psychoanalysis in lay terms.	*Outwitting Our Nerves: A Primer of Psychotherapy* (1921) NOTE: This text appeared in the footnotes of the 1926 edition of the *Science of Mind*.	(p. 31) The subconscious mind which is not affected by ether, has been exhausting itself in a vain attempt to get the body away from harm. A Tireless Servant. When the conscious mind undertakes a job, it is always more or less subject to fatigue. But the subconscious after its long practice seems never to tire. We say that its activities have become automatic. With all its inherited skill, the subconscious, if left to itself, can be depended upon to run the bodily machinery without effort and without hitch. The only things that can interfere with its work are the wrong kind of emotions and the wrong kind of suggestions from the conscious mind. Barring these, it goes its way like a trusty servant, looking after details and leaving its master's mind free for other things.
38	084-1	the Law is the servant of the Spirit and is set in motion through Its Word.	*Exact source unknown.* Possibly Josephine A. Jackson and Helen M. Salisbury, where the subconscious is first defined as a "servant." Jackson and Salisbury were two women Freudian psychoanalysts working in southern California. Their book was a best seller as it explained psychoanalysis in lay terms.	*Outwitting Our Nerves: A Primer of Psychotherapy* (1921) NOTE: This text appeared in the footnotes of the 1926 edition of the *Science of Mind*.	(p. 31) The subconscious mind which is not affected by ether, has been exhausting itself in a vain attempt to get the body away from harm. A Tireless Servant. When the conscious mind undertakes a job, it is always more or less subject to fatigue. But the subconscious after its long practice seems never to tire. We say that its activities have become automatic. With all its inherited skill, the subconscious, if left to itself, can be depended upon to run the bodily machinery without effort and without hitch. The only things that can interfere with its work are the wrong kind of emotions and the wrong kind of suggestions from the conscious mind. Barring these, it goes its way like a trusty servant, looking after details and leaving its master's mind free for other things.
39	086-2	"an Infinite Thinker thinking mathematically"	Sir James Jeans (1877-1946) British mathematician and professor at Cambridge	*The Mysterious Universe* (1930)	From the intrinsic evidence of his creation, the Great Architect of the Universe now begins to appear as a pure mathematician.

Where'd He Get That? A Biblical Cross-Reference To Ernest Holmes' The Science of Mind

Item Nr.	Page in the SOM Text	Phrase Used	Original Author	Primary Source Document	Quotation and commentary
40	088-2	The Soul of the Universe is the "Holy Womb of Nature"	*Exact source unknown for notion of a "Holy Womb of Nature."* Perhaps Sir Francis Bacon (1561-1626) English author, statesman, scientist, lawyer, and philosophical advocate and practitioner of the scientific revolution.	*Redargutio Philosophiarum* (1620)	There is therefore much ground for hoping that there are still laid up in the womb of nature many secrets of excellent use, having no affinity or parallelism with any thing that is now known, but lying entirely out of the beat of the imagination, which have not yet been found out.
41	088-2	The Soul of the Universe is the "Holy Womb of Nature"	*Exact source unknown for notion of a "Holy Womb of Nature."* Possibly the *Bhagavad Gita (circa 500 BCE)*	Part XIV: "The Three Gunas or Qualities"	Know thou, *Arjuna,* that Nature is the Great Womb in which I place my seed--from this proceedeth all natural forms, shapes, things, and objects.
42	088-3	the Holy Ghost is "The Servant of the Eternal Spirit throughout the ages"	*Exact source unknown.* Possibly Josephine A. Jackson and Helen M. Salisbury, where the subconscious is first defined as a "servant." Jackson and Salisbury were two women Freudian psychoanalysts working in southern California. Their book was a best seller as it explained psychoanalysis in lay terms.	*Outwitting Our Nerves: A Primer of Psychotherapy* (1921) NOTE: This text appeared in the footnotes of the 1926 edition of the Science of Mind.	(p. 31) The subconscious mind which is not affected by ether, has been exhausting itself in a vain attempt to get the body away from harm. A Tireless Servant. When the conscious mind undertakes a job, it is always more or less subject to fatigue. But the subconscious after its long practice seems never to tire. We say that its activities have become automatic. With all its inherited skill, the subconscious, if left to itself, can be depended upon to run the bodily machinery without effort and without hitch. The only things that can interfere with its work are the wrong kind of emotions and the wrong kind of suggestions from the conscious mind. Barring these, it goes its way like a trusty servant, looking after details and leaving its master's mind free for other things.

Where'd He Get That? A Biblical Cross-Reference To Ernest Holmes' The Science of Mind

Item Nr.	Page in the SOM Text	Phrase Used	Original Author	Primary Source Document	Quotation and commentary
43	091-3	The Soul of the Universe is next in Principle to Spirit and is the servant of Spirit.	*Exact source unknown.* Possibly Josephine A. Jackson and Helen M. Salisbury, where the subconscious is first defined as a "servant." Jackson and Salisbury were two women Freudian psychoanalysts working in southern California. Their book was a best seller as it explained psychoanalysis in lay terms.	*Outwitting Our Nerves: A Primer of Psychotherapy* (1921) NOTE: This text appeared in the footnotes of the 1926 edition of the Science of Mind.	(p. 31) The subconscious mind which is not affected by ether, has been exhausting itself in a vain attempt to get the body away from harm. A Tireless Servant. When the conscious mind undertakes a job, it is always more or less subject to fatigue. But the subconscious after its long practice seems never to tire. We say that its activities have become automatic. With all its inherited skill, the subconscious, if left to itself, can be depended upon to run the bodily machinery without effort and without hitch. The only things that can interfere with its work are the wrong kind of emotions and the wrong kind of suggestions from the conscious mind. Barring these, it goes its way like a trusty servant, looking after details and leaving its master's mind free for other things.
44	093-2	It is a "blind force not knowing, only doing"	*Exact source unknown.* Idea probably borrowed from Arthur Schopenhauer (1788-1860), German pessimistic philosopher who referred to a universal will as am impersonal "blind force".	*The World as Will and Idea / Representation* (1819), Chapter "The Objectification of the Will"	To summarize, Schopenhauer describes a process of the movement of will from the psychological to the cosmological sphere. This movement is guided by an understanding of willing as an "impersonal, primordial blind force, independent of reason and consciousness." The world is an activity of blind force and "my will permeates the world." While there was only one universal will, it flows through the human mind.

Item Nr.	Page in the SOM Text	Phrase Used	Original Author	Primary Source Document	Quotation and commentary
45	093-2	It was called by the ancients "Maya" from which arose the teaching of the illusions of the mind	*Exact source unknown.* Possibly Adi Shankara (788 CE - 820 CE), Hindu philosopher, mystic, and developer the doctrine Advaita Vedanta (literally non-dualism) is often credited with first describing the Maya principle.	*The Vedanta-Sutras with the Commentary by Sankaracarya* Sacred Books of the East, Volume 1, Juliana Horatia Gatty Ewing, (1841-1885) "Introduction"	But if nothing exists but one absolutely simple being, whence the appearance of the world by which we see ourselves surrounded, and, in which we ourselves exist as individual beings?--Brahman, the answer runs, is associated with a certain power called Maya or avidya to which the appearance of this entire world is due. This power cannot be called 'being' (sat), for 'being' is only Brahman; nor can it be called 'non-being' (asat) in the strict sense, for it at any rate produces the appearance of this world. It is in fact a principle of illusion; the indefinable cause owing to which there seems to exist a material world comprehending distinct individual existences.
46	094-2	In an interesting article by Sir Oliver Lodge (in which he writes about ether and the laws of the physical universe)…	Sir Oliver Lodge (1851-1940) British physicist and writer involved in the development of the wireless telegraph.	*The Ether of Space* (1909)	To summarize, this text delineates Oliver Lodge's religio-scientific worldview, beginning with his reticent attraction to metaphysics in the early 1880s to the full formulation of his "ether theology" in the late 1890s. Lodge undertook the study of psychical phenomena such as telepathy, telekinesis, and "ectoplasm" to further his scientific investigations of the ether, speculating that electrical and psychical manifestations were linked phenomena that described the deeper underlying structures of the universe, beneath and beyond matter.

Item Nr.	Page in the SOM Text	Phrase Used	Original Author	Primary Source Document	Quotation and commentary
47	095-2	As Newton said, the fact that we are able to announce the mystery *is* the mystery.	*Exact source unknown.* *No exact quote or paraphrase resembling this idea is found in the writings or familiar quotations of Sir Isaac Newton.*	In the 1726 edition of *Principia*, Newton included a section entitled "Rules of Reasoning in Philosophy." In these four rules, Newton effectively offers a methodology for handling unknown phenomena in nature and reaching towards explanations for them. Isaac Newton's statement of the four rules revolutionized the investigation of phenomena. With these rules, Newton could in principle begin to address all of the world's present unsolved mysteries.	The four Rules of the 1726 edition run as follows : Rule 1: We are to admit no more causes of natural things than such as are both true and sufficient to explain their appearances. Rule 2: Therefore to the same natural effects we must, as far as possible, assign the same causes. Rule 3: The qualities of bodies, which admit neither intensification nor remission of degrees, and which are found to belong to all bodies within the reach of our experiments, are to be esteemed the universal qualities of all bodies whatsoever. Rule 4: In experimental philosophy we are to look upon propositions inferred by general induction from phenomena as accurately or very nearly true, not withstanding any contrary hypothesis that may be imagined, till such time as other phenomena occur, by which they may either be made more accurate, or liable to exceptions.
48	096-3	The Holy Womb of Nature	*Exact source unknown for notion of a "Holy Womb of Nature."* Perhaps Sir Francis Bacon (1561-1626) English author, statesman, scientist, lawyer, and philosophical advocate and practitioner of the scientific revolution.	*Redargutio Philosophiarum* (1620)	There is therefore much ground for hoping that there are still laid up in the womb of nature many secrets of excellent use, having no affinity or parallelism with any thing that is now known, but lying entirely out of the beat of the imagination, which have not yet been found out.
49	096-3	The Holy Womb of Nature	*Exact source unknown for notion of a "Holy Womb of Nature."* Possibly the *Bhagavad Gita* (circa 500 CE)	Part XIV: "The Three Gunas or Qualities"	Know thou, *Arjuna,* that Nature is the Great Womb in which I place my seed--from this proceedeth all natural forms, shapes, things, and objects.

Item Nr.	Page in the SOM Text	Phrase Used	Original Author	Primary Source Document	Quotation and commentary
50	097-2	Plotinus had a clear concept when he said: "Nature is the great No Thing, yet It is not exactly nothing, because it is Its business to receive the impressions of Spirit."	Plotinus, Roman philosopher, founder of neo-Platonic thought (ca. AD 204–270)	*The Six Enneads*: "Ennead One, Eighth Tractate - Nature Contemplation and The One" (250 AD)	For the Vision on which Nature [Non-Beingness] broods, inactive, is a self-intuition, a spectacle laid before it by virtue of its unaccompanied self-concentration and by the fact that in itself it belongs to the order of intuition. It is a Vision silent but somewhat blurred, for there exists another a clearer of which Nature is the image: hence all that Nature produces is weak; the weaker act of intuition produces the weaker object.
51	097-2	He [Plotinus] spoke of that which we call *undifferentiated substance* as an indeterminate thing having no mind of its own.	Plotinus, Roman philosopher, founder of neo-Platonic thought (ca. AD 204–270)	*The Six Enneads*: "Ennead Four, Second Tractate - On the Essence of the Soul" (250 AD)	The Essence, very near to the impartible, which we assert to belong to the kind we are now dealing with, is at once an Essence and an entrant into body; upon embodiment, it experiences a partition unknown before it thus bestowed itself.
52	099-4	Psychology has shown that psychical (or subjective) disturbances produce physical reactions in the body.	*Exact source unknown*. Possibly Wilhelm Wundt (1832-1920), German physiologist, physician, professor and philosopher. Known as the "father of experimental psychology" and the founder of the first psychology laboratory.	*Principles of Physiological Psychology* (1904) "Introduction" NOTE: Around the 1930's a group of behaviorist physicians founded psychophysiology as the branch of physiology that is concerned with the relationship between mental (psyche) and physical (physiological) processes; it is the scientific study of the interaction between mind and body. Dr. Holmes may also be referring to this group of scientists, at that time on the cutting edge of scientific inquiry.	An adequate definition of life, taken in the wider sense, must (as we said just now) cover both the vital processes of the physical organism and the processes of consciousness. Hence, wherever we meet with vital phenomena that present the two aspects, physical and psychical, there naturally arises a question as to the relations in which these aspects stand to each other. So we come face to face with a whole series of special problems, which may be occasionally touched upon by physiology or psychology, but which cannot receive their final solution at the hands of either, just by reason of that division of labour to which both sciences alike stand committed.

Where'd He Get That? A Biblical Cross-Reference To Ernest Holmes' The Science of Mind

Item Nr.	Page in the SOM Text	Phrase Used	Original Author	Primary Source Document	Quotation and commentary
53	100-2	The Soul is the servant of the Spirit and has no purpose other than to execute the purpose given It.	*Exact source unknown.* Possibly Josephine A. Jackson and Helen M. Salisbury, where the subconscious is first defined as a "servant." Jackson and Salisbury were two women Freudian psychoanalysts working in southern California. Their book was a best seller as it explained psychoanalysis in lay terms.	*Outwitting Our Nerves: A Primer of Psychotherapy* (1921) NOTE: This text appeared in the footnotes of the 1926 edition of the Science of Mind.	(p. 31) The subconscious mind which is not affected by ether, has been exhausting itself in a vain attempt to get the body away from harm. A Tireless Servant. When the conscious mind undertakes a job, it is always more or less subject to fatigue. But the subconscious after its long practice seems never to tire. We say that its activities have become automatic. With all its inherited skill, the subconscious, if left to itself, can be depended upon to run the bodily machinery without effort and without hitch. The only things that can interfere with its work are the wrong kind of emotions and the wrong kind of suggestions from the conscious mind. Barring these, it goes its way like a trusty servant, looking after details and leaving its master's mind free for other things.
54	101-2	"Time is a sequence of events in a unitary wholeness;"	Ernest Holmes attributes this quote to Dean Inge, William Ralph Inge (1860 – 1954) English author, Anglican priest, and Dean and Professor of Divinity at Cambridge.	*The Philosophy of Plotinus Volume I* (1918) NOTE: This text appeared in the footnotes of the 1926 edition of the *Science of Mind.*	(p. xiii) Time is the moving image of eternity.
55	102-3	We do not deny the theory of evolution; we affirm its cause to be Intelligence.	Possibly referencing Charles Darwin (1809-1882) English naturalist	*The Origin of Species* (1859)	To summarize, Darwin theorized that humans evolved from a lower order of animals, such as primates. The theory also postulated that species evolved through the survival of the fittest - that is, of the members of the species who best "fitted" their environment survived and the "unfit" died off, thus eliminating weaker elements in the gene pool and promoting the stronger elements.

Where'd He Get That? A Biblical Cross-Reference To Ernest Holmes' The Science of Mind

Item Nr.	Page in the SOM Text	Phrase Used	Original Author	Primary Source Document	Quotation and commentary
56	103-2	we lie in "the lap of an Infinite Intelligence."	Ralph Waldo Emerson (1803-1882) American essayist, philosopher, poet, and leader of the transcendentalist movement in the early 19th century. His teachings directly influenced the growing New Thought movement.	*Essays: First Series* (1841) "Essay II: Self-Reliance"	We lie in the lap of immense intelligence, which makes us receivers of its truth and organs of its activity.
57	103-3	Emerson tells us that *nature* is Spirit reduced to Its greatest thinness	Ralph Waldo Emerson (1803-1882) American essayist, philosopher, poet, and leader of the transcendentalist movement in the early 19th century. His teachings directly influenced the growing New Thought movement.	*Essays: Second Series* (1844) "Essay II: Experience"	Spirit is matter reduced to an extreme thinness: O so thin!
58	103-3	Spinoza says that Mind and matter are the same thing	Benedict Spinoza (1632-1677) Dutch Philosopher	*The Ethics - Part II*, "Of the Nature and Origin of the Mind" (1677)	The order and connection of ideas is the same as the order and connection of things....Thinking substance and extended substance are one and the same thing.
59	103-3	Browning writes of the spark which we may desecrate, but never quite lose, and he further announces at all are gods "though in the germ"	Robert Browning (1812-1889) British poet	The poem "Rabbi Ben Ezra" 1864	Therefore I summon age To grant youth's heritage, Life's struggle having so far reached its term: Thence shall I pass, approved A man, for aye removed From the developed brute; a God tho' in the germ.
60	103-3	Wordsworth sings that Heaven is the native home of all mankind	William Wordsworth (1770-1850) poet and leader of the romantic movement in England.	The Poem "Intimations of Immortality" from *Recollections of Early Childhood* (1806)	Our birth is but a sleep and a forgetting: The soul that rises with us, our life's star, Hath had elsewhere its setting, And cometh from afar. Not in entire forgetfulness, And not in utter nakedness, But trailing clouds of glory, do we come From God, who is our home: Heaven lies about us in our infancy."
61	103-3	Tennyson exclaims that more things are wrought by prayer than this world dreams.	Alfred Lord Tennyson (1809-1892) English poet	From the poem "Morte d'Arthur" (1830)	More things are wrought by prayer Than this world dreams of.

Where'd He Get That? A Biblical Cross-Reference To Ernest Holmes' The Science of Mind

Item Nr.	Page in the SOM Text	Phrase Used	Original Author	Primary Source Document	Quotation and commentary
62	103-3	Shakespeare perceived sermons in stones and good in everything.	William Shakespeare (1564-1616). English poet and playwright wrote the famous 154 Sonnets and numerous oft quoted dramatic works.	*As You Like It,* Act 2 Scene 1	And this our life exempt from public haunt Finds tongues in trees, books in the running brooks, Sermons in stones and good in every thing. I would not change it.
63	104-3	The present hypothesis of science is, that ether is more solid than matter.	Sir Oliver Lodge (1851-1940) physicist and writer; address on the "Ether of Space" given at Bedford College for Women	"Sees Great Future in Study of Ether: Sir Oliver Lodge Believes Our Present Knowledge May Shrink to a "Pinpoint." *New York Times*, February 1, 1914.	"We have reason to believe," said Sir Oliver, "that the density of ether would be the equivalent of 1,000 tons per cubic millimetre of terrestrial matter when compared to it. "
64	110-4	we wish to make clear there is no sin but a mistake	*Exact source unknown. Ernest Holmes attributes this to Emerson, but it is not found in Emerson.* Perhaps *Strong's Exhaustive Concordance of the Bible,* first published in 1890 which contained the etymological meaning of 8674 Hebrew root words used in the Old Testament and 5624 Greek root words used in the New Testament.	*Hebrew word 7686 shagah shaw-gaw':* a primitive root; to stray (causatively, mislead), usually (figuratively) to mistake, especially (morally) to transgress; by extension (through the idea of intoxication) to reel, (figuratively) be enraptured:--(cause to) go astray, deceive, err, be ravished, sin through ignorance, (let, make to) wander. *Greek word 264. hamartano ham-ar-tan'-o:* properly, to miss the mark (and so not share in the prize), i.e. (figuratively) to err;	NOTE: Rocco Ericco, Modern scholar of the Aramaic sources of the Bible writes that the Aramaic word *hataya* used in these contexts, means "to miss" or "to miss the mark," thus a "mistake." See *Setting a Trap for God*, Unity House Publishing (1997) p. 89.
65	112-4	Emerson said that we animate what we see and see what we animate.	Ralph Waldo Emerson (1803-1882) American essayist, philosopher, poet, and leader of the transcendentalist movement in the early 19th century. His teachings directly influenced the growing New Thought movement.	*Essays: Second Series* (1844) "Essay I: Experience"	We animate what we can, and we see only what we animate. Nature and books belong to the eyes that see them. It depends on the mood of the man, whether he shall see the sunset or the fine poem.

Where'd He Get That? A Biblical Cross-Reference To Ernest Holmes' The Science of Mind

Item Nr.	Page in the SOM Text	Phrase Used	Original Author	Primary Source Document	Quotation and commentary
66	113-2	Plotinus tells us that there are three way by which we gather knowledge: through science, through opinion, and through intuition or illumination.	Plotinus, Roman philosopher, founder of neo-Platonic thought (ca. AD 204–270)	*Letter to Flaccus* (his student), 260 AD	Knowledge has three degrees: opinion, science, illumination. The means or instrument of the first is sense; of the second dialectic; of the third, intuition.
67	115-2	the collective subjectivity of all humanity - called by some the "collective unconscious."	*Exact source unknown.* Perhaps Carl Jung, Swiss psychologist (1875-1961)	*The Collected Works of Carl Jung Volume 9.1: The Archetypes of the Collective Unconscious* (1934)	To summarize, the Collective Unconscious, sometimes known as Collective Subconscious, is a term of analytical psychology, coined by Carl Jung. This collective unconscious is considered to consist of preexistent thought forms, called archetypes, which give form to certain psychic material which then enters the conscious.
68	116-1	Plotinus, perhaps the greatest of the Neo-Platonic philosophers, in personifying Nature said: "I do not argue, I contemplate; and as I contemplate, I let fall the forms of my thought"	Plotinus, Roman philosopher, founder of neo-Platonic thought (ca. AD 204–270)	*Third Ennead "Fate"* Eighth Tractate (250 AD)	Whatsoever comes into being is my is my vision, seen in my silence, the vision that belongs to my character who, sprung from vision, am vision-loving and create vision by the vision-seeing faculty within me. The mathematicians from their vision draw their figures: but I draw nothing: I gaze and the figures of the material world take being as if they fell from my contemplation.
69	116-3	We are told that matter is not a solid, stationary thing; but a constantly flowing formless substance, which is forever coming and going - "an etheric whirl of energy" it has been called.	*Exact source unknown.* Perhaps Anna Besant, early leader of Theosophy (1847-1933) who also wrote of "etheric whirls" of energy.	"Cosmic Consciousness in Man", *Theosophist Magazine*, February 1910	Each physical material, such as hydrogen, gold, etc. has a different etheric whirl in its physical atom.
70	117-1	cabbages and kings	Lewis Carroll (1832-1898), British children's writer and mathematician.	"The Walrus and the Carpenter" from *Through the Looking-Glass and What Alice Found There* (1872)	"The time has come," the Walrus said, "To talk of many things: Of shoes--and ships--and sealing-wax-- Of cabbages--and kings-- And why the sea is boiling hot-- And whether pigs have wings."

Item Nr.	Page in the SOM Text	Phrase Used	Original Author	Primary Source Document	Quotation and commentary
71	118-4	This is what decides how the Law of Attraction Works	*Exact source unknown.*	Earliest reference to a "Law of Attraction" is in the Vedas (ancient Hindu scriptures) dating back to 4000 BCE.	See attached history of "The Law of Attraction" up until Ernest Holmes. He could have received this idea from any number of sources
72	120-3	The meaning of the Flood or Deluge (which is recorded in every sacred scripture we have ever heard of or read)	The story of a Great Flood sent by a deity or deities to destroy civilization as an act of divine retribution is a widespread theme among many cultural myths and scriptures. The claim that it is in "every" recorded scripture is difficult to verify.	http://en.wikipedia.org/wiki/Deluge_(mythology) Mark Isaak, "Flood Stories from Around the World" http://home.earthlink.net/~misaak/floods.htm	For example, though it is best known to westerners by the story of Noah found in the Bible (Genesis 6,7,8) or the Torah (Beshit 6-9), a similar version of Noah is also found in the Koran (Surah 11:Section 4). Researcher Mark Isaak references 87 such accounts on his website.
73	121-2	We recognize Subconscious Mind as the Great Servant of our thought	*Exact source unknown.* Possibly Josephine A. Jackson and Helen M. Salisbury, where the subconscious is first defined as a "servant." Jackson and Salisbury were two women Freudian psychoanalysts working in southern California. Their book was a best seller as it explained psychoanalysis in lay terms.	*Outwitting Our Nerves: A Primer of Psychotherapy* (1921) NOTE: This text appeared in the footnotes of the 1926 edition of the Science of Mind.	(p. 31) The subconscious mind which is not affected by ether, has been exhausting itself in a vain attempt to get the body away from harm. A Tireless Servant. When the conscious mind undertakes a job, it is always more or less subject to fatigue. But the subconscious after its long practice seems never to tire. We say that its activities have become automatic. With all its inherited skill, the subconscious, if left to itself, can be depended upon to run the bodily machinery without effort and without hitch. The only things that can interfere with its work are the wrong kind of emotions and the wrong kind of suggestions from the conscious mind. Barring these, it goes its way like a trusty servant, looking after details and leaving its master's mind free for other things.

Where'd He Get That? A Biblical Cross-Reference To Ernest Holmes' The Science of Mind

Item Nr.	Page in the SOM Text	Phrase Used	Original Author	Primary Source Document	Quotation and commentary
74	123-2	what we call sin is nothing more than a mistake.	*Exact source unknown. Ernest Holmes attributes this to Emerson, but it is not found in Emerson.* Perhaps *Strong's Exhaustive Concordance of the Bible,* first published in 1890 which contained the etymological meaning of 8674 Hebrew root words used in the Old Testament and 5624 Greek root words used in the New Testament.	*Hebrew word 7686 shagah shaw-gaw':* a primitive root; to stray (causatively, mislead), usually (figuratively) to mistake, especially (morally) to transgress; by extension (through the idea of intoxication) to reel, (figuratively) be enraptured:--(cause to) go astray, deceive, err, be ravished, sin through ignorance, (let, make to) wander. *Greek word 264. hamartano ham-ar-tan'-o:* properly, to miss the mark (and so not share in the prize), i.e. (figuratively) to err;	NOTE: Rocco Ericco, Modern scholar of the Aramaic sources of the Bible writes that the Aramaic word *hataya* used in these contexts, means "to miss" or "to miss the mark," thus a "mistake." See *Setting a Trap for God*, Unity House Publishing (1997) p. 89.
75	130-2	"Alls Love, yet all is Law," mused Robert Browning	Robert Browning (1812-1889) British poet	from "Saul" (1855)	His creation's approval or censure: I spoke as I saw: `I report, as a man may of God's work---all's love, yet all's law.'
76	132-7	"Spirit is the power that knows Itself"	Thomas Troward (1847-1916) British Divisional Judge of the North Indian Punjab whose metaphysical writings had a profound effect on New Thought, in particular The Science of Mind.	*Bible Mystery and Bible Meaning* (1913) NOTE: This text appeared in the footnotes of the 1926 edition of the Science of Mind.	(p.126) He is beginning to understand what is meant by man being the image of God, and to grasp the significance of the old-world saying that "Spirit is the Power that knows Itself."
77	137-1	*What we expect, said Aristotle, that we find*	*Exact source unknown. This quotation or a paraphrase thereof was not found in the collected writings of Aristotle.* Perhaps referring to Elbert Hubbard, American editor, publisher and writer (1856-1915).	*Old John Burroughs* (1901)	(p. 13) This habit of expectancy always marks the strong man. It is a form of attraction — our own comes to us because we desire it; we find what we expect to find, and we receive what we ask for. All life is a prayer — strong natures pray most — and every earnest, sincere prayer is answered.

Where'd He Get That? A Biblical Cross-Reference To Ernest Holmes' The Science of Mind

Item Nr.	Page in the SOM Text	Phrase Used	Original Author	Primary Source Document	Quotation and commentary
78	137-1	*What we wish,* said Demosthenes, *that we believe.*	Demosthenes (384–322 BC), a prominent Greek statesman and orator of ancient Athens.	*The Olynthiacs and the Phillippics of Demosthenes* (351–349 BC)	The wishes of men are indeed a great help to such arguments, and therefore the easiest thing in the world is self-deceit; for every man believes what he wishes, though the reality is often different.
79	137-1	Shakespeare is accredited with the saying: "There is nothing either good or bad but thinking makes it so."	William Shakespeare (1564-1616). English poet and playwright wrote the famous 154 Sonnets and numerous highly successful oft quoted dramatic works	*Hamlet* Act 2, Scene 2 (1601)	HAMLET Why, then, 'tis none to you; for there is nothing either good or bad, but thinking makes it so: to me it is a prison.
80	137-2	"He can who *thinks* he can."	*Exact source unknown.* Perhaps Orison Swett Marden (1850 - 1924) American New Thought writer	*He Can Who Thinks He Can* (1908)	Also possibly from *Your Forces and How to Use Them*, by Christian D. Larson (1912), "Chapter IX: He Can Who Thinks He Can"
81	139-2	We believe in the unity of all life, and that the highest God and the innermost God is One God.	Ernest Holmes, Religious Science Declaration of Principles	from "What I Believe," published in the first issue of *Science of Mind Magazine*, (October 1927)	We believe in the unity of all life, and that the highest God and the innermost God is One God.
82	144-4	Modern psychology affirms that all the thoughts and emotions we have experienced since we came into conscious existence are still present in Mind.	*Exact source unknown.* Perhaps Carl Jung, Swiss psychologist (1875-1961) who first coined the term "collective unconscious."	*The Collected Works of Carl Jung Volume 9.1: The Archetypes of the Collective Unconscious* (1934)	To summarize, the Collective Unconscious, sometimes known as Collective Subconscious, is considered to consist of preexistent thought forms, called archetypes, which give form to certain psychic material which then enters the conscious.
83	147-3	"Act as though I am and I will be"	*Exact source unknown.* Perhaps Blaise Pascal (1623-1662). French mathematician, physicist, and religious philosopher.	*Thoughts (Pensees)* (1670)	In his book *The Power of Your Subconscious Mind* - chapter 6 (1961) Joseph Murphy credited this exact quote to William James. A search of James's essay *"The Will to Believe"* (1896) stated, "The whole defense of religious faith hinges upon action." To support his claim, James references a quote in French by Blaise Pascal, "cela vous fera croire et vous abetira." Translated to English, this means "That [acting as if] will make you believe and will stupefy your proudly critical intellect."

Where'd He Get That? A Biblical Cross-Reference To Ernest Holmes' The Science of Mind

Item Nr.	Page in the SOM Text	Phrase Used	Original Author	Primary Source Document	Quotation and commentary
84	147-3	"Act as though I am and I will be"	*Exact source unknown.* Perhaps German philosopher Hans Vaihinger (1852-1933) a contemporary of Holmes, who devoted the last years of his life to developing his as-if philosophy, based upon Kant's notion of 'heuristic fictions'.	*The Philosophy of 'As-If'* (1911)	To summarize, Vaihinger postulated that believing in an idea that was "false" at the moment, has great practical importance, which now made them useful and therefore "true." An example would be a sick person affirming "I am well." as a beneficial hypothesis about life. Hypotheses can be then proven true, therefore transforming the ideation of the individual.
85	152-2	Emerson said: "Is not prayer a study of truth, a sally of the Soul into the unfound Infinite?"	Ralph Waldo Emerson (1803-1882) American essayist, philosopher, poet, and leader of the transcendentalist movement in the early 19th century. His teachings directly influenced the growing New Thought movement.	*Nature: Addresses and Lectures* (1849) "Chapter VIII: Prospects"	Is not prayer also a study of truth, — a sally of the soul into the unfound infinite?
86	160-1	that God Himself goes forth anew into creation through each one of us	Ralph Waldo Emerson (1803-1882) American essayist, philosopher, poet, and leader of the transcendentalist movement in the early 19th century. His teachings directly influenced the growing New Thought movement.	*Nature: Addresses and Lectures* (1849) "Chapter VIII: Prospects"	But when a faithful thinker, resolute to detach every object from personal relations, and see it in the light of thought, shall, at the same time, kindle science with the fire of the holiest affections, then will God go forth anew into the creation.
87	160-3	All human misery is a result of ignorance	*Bhagavad Gita*, (circa 500 BCE)	Chapter 14 "The Three Gunas or Qualities"	As far as the mode of ignorance is concerned, the performer is without knowledge, and therefore all his activities result in present misery.
88	169-1	Browning called this "the spark which we may desecrate, but never quite lose,"	*Exact source unknown. Not found in Robert Browning's writings.* Possibly George Washington (1732-1799) first president of the United States.	*Book of Etiquette* (1747)	Unity author and teacher Eric Butterworth uses this quote in his radio speech "The Truth in a Nutshell": Every person contains within himself or herself a Spark of Divinity, "that little Spark of Celestial Fire that a man may desecrate but never quite lose." Butterworth credits its origin to George Washington who wrote it as the last of 110 rules of etiquette: "Labor to keep alive in your breast the little spark of celestial fire called conscience."

Where'd He Get That? A Biblical Cross-Reference To Ernest Holmes' The Science of Mind

Item Nr.	Page in the SOM Text	Phrase Used	Original Author	Primary Source Document	Quotation and commentary
89	185-3	"Behold thou my face forevermore."	*Exact source unknown.* Perhaps from Rev. Charles H. Spurgeon, famous English clergyman from the late 19th century.	"The Beatific Vision", sermon given in 1856, published in *The New Park Street Pulpit*, based around Spurgeon's interpretation of I John 3:1-7.	"We have I believe, all of us who love his name, a most insatiable wish to behold his person. The thing for which I would pray above all others, would be for ever to behold his face, for ever to lay my head upon his breast, for ever to know that I am his, for ever to dwell with him."
90	207-4	"What is true on one plane is true on all."	Thomas Troward (1847-1916) British Divisional Judge of the North Indian Punjab whose metaphysical writings had a profound effect on New Thought, in particular The Science of Mind.	*The Hidden Power* (1921) NOTE: This text appeared in the footnotes of the 1926 edition of the Science of Mind.	(p. 17) "We must never lose sight of the old-world saying that "a truth on one plane is a truth on all." If a principle exists at all it exists universally. NOTE: Troward does not specify the source of this 'old world saying.'
91	217-2	"Arise, O Son and take."	*Exact source unknown.* The only other place those words "Arise, O Son" appear in the English language is found in *The English and Scottish Popular Ballads*, by Francis James Child (1882-1898)	Ballad 211: "Bewick and Graham" (from the end of the Middle Ages)	'Arise, arise, O son!' he said, 'For I see thou's won the victory. 'Arise, arise, O son!' he said, 'For I see thou's won the victory:'
92	218-3	We must relight the torch of our imagination by "fire caught from heaven."	*Exact source unknown.* Possibly Charles Robert Maturin (1782-1824), Anglo-Irish Protestant clergyman and writer of gothic plays and novels.	*Melmoth the Wanderer* (1820)	(p. 418) Is all the energy of intellect, and all the enthusiasm of feeling, to be expended in contrivances how to meet or shift off the petty but torturing pangs of hourly necessity? Is the fire caught from heaven to be employed in lighting a faggot to keep the cold from the numbed and wasted fingers of poverty?
93	218-3	We must relight the torch of our imagination by "fire caught from heaven."	*Exact source unknown.* Possibly Margaret Fuller (1810-1850) Transcendentalist writer and early feminist	As recorded by Elizabeth Palmer Peabody, a participant in Fuller's "Conversations for Women" 1839 later republished in *The Dial, A Transcendentalist Magazine* edited by Fuller.	"Is it not so," said Miss Fuller, "Is not man's intellect the fire caught from heaven--woman's the flower called forth from the earth by the ray?"
94	222-3	A habit is a desire objectified - "the continuous character of one's thoughts and feelings"	*Exact source unknown.* Perhaps Marcus Aurelius (121-180 AD), Roman Emperor and Stoic philosopher	*Meditations - Book 5* (180 AD)	"Your mind will be like its habitual thoughts; for the soul becomes dyed with the color of its thoughts. Soak it then in such trains of thoughts as, for example: Where life is possible at all, a right life is possible."

Where'd He Get That? A Biblical Cross-Reference To Ernest Holmes' The Science of Mind

Item Nr.	Page in the SOM Text	Phrase Used	Original Author	Primary Source Document	Quotation and commentary
95	222-3	A habit is a desire objectified - "the continuous character of one's thoughts and feelings"	*Exact source unknown.* Perhaps Wallace Wattles (1860 – 1911) American New Thought writer.	*How To Be a Genius of The Science of Being Great* (1911)	(p. 80) Whatever you habitually think yourself to be, that you are. You must form, now, a greater and better habit; you must form a conception of yourself as a being of limitless power, and habitually think that you are that being. It is the habitual, not the periodical thought that decides your destiny.
96	222-4	"For each, for the joy of working and each in his separate star, Shall paint the thing as he see It, for the God of things as they are."	Rudyard Kipling (1865-1936) English author and poet	*Collected Verse of Rudyard Kipling* "When Earth's Last Picture Is Painted" (1907)	And only the Master shall praise us, and only the Master shall blame; And no one shall work for money, and no one shall work for fame; But each for the joy of the working, and each, in his separate star, Shall draw the Thing as he sees It, for the God of Things as They Are!
97	230-2	The eyes can truly be called "the windows of the soul."	*Exact source unknown.* Idea of eyes being the window to the soul is credited to William Blake, English poet, mystic and painter (1757-1827)	*The Oxford Book of English Mystical Verse* (1917) Poem "The Everlasting Gospel"	This life's dim windows of the soul Distorts the heavens from pole to pole And leads you to believe a lie When you see with, not through, the eye.
98	237-2	It has been said: "Life is a comedy to him who *thinks*, a tragedy to him who *feels*."	Horace Walpole (1717-1797) English writer, connoisseur, and collector	Letter to Anne, Countess of Ossory (1776)	"Life is a tragedy for those who feel, but a comedy to those who think."
99	268-3	All nature conspires to produce and manifest the freedom of the individual	Ralph Waldo Emerson (1803-1882) American essayist, philosopher, poet, and leader of the transcendentalist movement in the early 19th century. His teachings directly influenced the growing New Thought movement.	"Goethe; or, the Writer" from *Representative Men* (1850)	"Nature conspires. Whatever can be thought can be spoken, and still rises for utterance, though to rude and stammering organs. If they can not compass it, it waits and works, until at last it moulds them to its perfect will and is articulated." NOTE: A common quote attributed to Emerson that "Once you make a decision, the universe conspires to make it happen." This quotation could not be located in Emerson's writings.

Where'd He Get That? A Biblical Cross-Reference To Ernest Holmes' The Science of Mind

Item Nr.	Page in the SOM Text	Phrase Used	Original Author	Primary Source Document	Quotation and commentary
100	268-3	All nature conspires to produce and manifest the freedom of the individual	*Exact source unknown.* Perhaps Friedrich Wilhelm Joseph von Schelling (1775-1854) German philosopher	*System der gesammten Philosophie und der Naturphilosophie insbesondere* (1804) and *Freedom Essay* (1809)	As paraphrased by Jason Wirth in his analysis of Schelling, *The Conspiracy of Life* (2003) pp 88-89: "Nature is not simply *there* for us to use and abuse. We are not in nature, nor do we belong to nature if by that one means that we are things among things in some kind of conglomeration of things under the heading of the natural. We are no more *in* nature than we are *in* time. Our life belongs to the conspiracy of nature, to the conspiracy of life itself.... ...We are nature and it has us We belong to the demiurgic circulation. It does not belong to us. ...This circulation produces itself freely from out of itself as a "divine imagination."...
101	269-1	It has to be beauty, truth and harmony, as Troward said as this is the true relationship of the Whole to its parts and the parts to the Whole.	Thomas Troward (1847-1916) British Divisional Judge of the North Indian Punjab whose metaphysical writings had a profound effect on New Thought, in particular The Science of Mind.	*The Creative Process and the Individual* (1915)	(p. 22) In this threefold Law of Truth, Life, and Beauty, we find the whole underlying nature of the Spirit, and no action on the part of the individual can be at variance with the Originating Unity which does not controvert these fundamental principles.
102	273-3	"the flight of the Alone to the Alone"	Plotinus, Roman philosopher, founder of neo-Platonic thought (ca. AD 204–270)	*The Six Enneads:* Ennead Six, Ninth Tractate "On the Good, or the One"	This is the life of the Gods and the godlike and happy men, liberation from the alien which besets us here, a life taking no pleasure in things on earth, a flight of the alone into the Alone."
103	273-3	"the One to Itself"	Plato (c. 427–c. 347 BCE) Greek philosopher, student of Socrates and teacher to Aristotle	*The Dialogues of Plato : Parmenides. Theaetetus. Sophist. Statesman.* circa 387 BCE	And this will be true also of the relation of the one to itself; having neither greatness nor smallness in itself, it will neither exceed nor be exceeded by itself, but will be on an equality with and equal to itself.
104	274-4	Troward says that we enter the Absolute in such degree as we withdraw from the relative; and that we withdraw from the relative in such degree as we enter the Absolute"	Thomas Troward (1847-1916) British Divisional Judge of the North Indian Punjab whose metaphysical writings had a profound effect on New Thought, in particular The Science of Mind.	*The Edinburgh Lectures on Mental Science* (1909) "Chapter XIII. In Touch with Sub-conscious Mind" NOTE: This text appeared in the footnotes of the 1926 edition of the Science of Mind.	We come into touch with the absolute exactly in proportion as we withdraw ourselves from the relative: they vary inversely to each other.

Where'd He Get That? A Biblical Cross-Reference To Ernest Holmes' The Science of Mind

Item Nr.	Page in the SOM Text	Phrase Used	Original Author	Primary Source Document	Quotation and commentary
105	276-1	We fail to recognize with Browning that "All's love, yet all's law."	Robert Browning (1812-1889) British poet	from "Saul" (1855)	His creation's approval or censure: I spoke as I saw: ``I report, as a man may of God's work---all's love, yet all's law.
106	279-1	Mental Equivalent	Emmet Fox (1886-1951) New Thought writer and lecturer associated with Unity	*The Mental Equivalent: The Secret of Demonstration* (1943), based on lectures given at Unity in the 1930's	"Supply yourself with a mental equivalent, and the thing must come to you."
107	280-3	Lowell said, "The gift without the giver is bare"	James Russell Lowell (1819 – 1891) American Romantic poet, critic, editor, and diplomat.	From the poem "The Vision of Sir Launfal" (1848)	The Holy Supper is kept, indeed, In whatso we share with another's need; Not what we give, but what we share, For the gift without the giver is bare;
108	286-1	The Bhagavad-Gita says that we shall never arrive at peace while we deal with the Pairs of Opposites.	*Bhagavad Gita*, (circa 500 BCE)	Chapter XII: "The Book of Religion by Discernment."	By passion for the "pairs of opposites," By those twain snares of Like and Dislike, Prince! All creatures live bewildered, save some few Who, quit of sins, holy in act, informed, Freed from the "opposites," and fixed in faith, Cleave unto Me.
109	287-1	It is just the old law that we can expand the finite but we cannot contract the Infinite.	Thomas Troward (1847-1916) British Divisional Judge of the North Indian Punjab whose metaphysical writings had a profound effect on New Thought, in particular The Science of Mind.	*The Edinburgh Lectures on Mental Science* (1909) "Chapter VII: Receptivity" NOTE: This text appeared in the footnotes of the 1926 edition of the Science of Mind.	It is a mathematical truism that you cannot contract the infinite, and that you can expand the individual; and it is precisely on these lines that evolution works.
110	289-3	"To him who can perfectly practice inaction, all things are possible."	*Exact source unknown.* Possibly Lao Tzu (circa 600 BCE), father of Taoism.	*The Sayings of Lao-Tzu*, Lionel Giles translation (1905) "The Doctrine of Inaction"	(p. 31) Practice inaction, and there is nothing which cannot be done.
111	294-1	Law of Attraction	*Exact source unknown.*	Earliest reference to a "Law of Attraction" is in the Vedas (ancient Hindu scriptures) dating back to 4000 BCE.	See attached history of "The Law of Attraction" up until Ernest Holmes. He could have received this idea from any number of sources

Item Nr.	Page in the SOM Text	Phrase Used	Original Author	Primary Source Document	Quotation and commentary
112	295-3	this is called, in mysticism, High Invocation; invoking the Divine Mind.	*Exact source unknown.* Perhaps George Stanton and Charles Kingold founders of an English magical order The Aurum Solis (Gold of the Sun) in 1897. Stanton and Kingold claimed descent of the order's rituals from the ancient esoteric traditions of early Western civilization.	The Aurum Solis (1897). Reprinted in Melita Denning and Osborne Phillilps, *Mysteria Magica: Fundamental Techniques of High Magick*, Chapter on "Basic Magical Practices of the Aurum Solis" (1981)	"High invocation" defined as "an exalted celebration, rich in allusion and potent in utterance of the mystic HA, asking the divine aid for the perfect accomplishment of the operation [ritual]." "followed by aspiration to be a worthy vehicle for the operation of that Divine Influence in the rite about to be performed."
113	295-3	the teachers of olden times used to instruct their pupils to cross their hands over their chests and say: "Wonderful, wonderful, wonderful me!"	*Exact source unknown.* Perhaps referring to "The Kabalistic Cross" ritual was written by Samuel Mathers, a freemason and founding member of the Order of the Golden Dawn, a secret order founded in England in 1888.	Mathers "Kabalistic Cross" ritual format was similar to that described in Eliphas Levi's book *Transcendental Magic, its Doctrine and Ritual* (1855)	To summarize, "The Kabalistic Cross" is a basic ritual used as a tool to become conscious of the own divine self and to come into contact with the cosmic sources of power and creation. Participants cross their hands over their chests as Dr. Holmes describes. However, the chant used as one crosses the arms is "thou art the power and the glory forever, so be it!"
114	295-3	"Act as though I am and I will be"	*Exact source unknown.* Perhaps Blaise Pascal (1623-1662). French mathematician, physicist, and religious philosopher.	Thoughts (Pensees) (1670)	In his book *The Power of Your Subconscious Mind* - chapter 6 (1961) Joseph Murphy credited this exact quote to William James. A search of James's essay *"The Will to Believe"* (1896) stated, "The whole defense of religious faith hinges upon action." To support his claim, James references a quote in French by Blaise Pascal, "cela vous fera croire et vous abetira." Translated to English, this means "That [acting as if] will make you believe and will stupefy your proudly critical intellect."

Where'd He Get That? A Biblical Cross-Reference To Ernest Holmes' The Science of Mind

Item Nr.	Page in the SOM Text	Phrase Used	Original Author	Primary Source Document	Quotation and commentary
115		"Act as though I am and I will be"	*Exact source unknown.* Perhaps German philosopher Hans Vaihinger (1852-1933) a contemporary of Holmes, who devoted the last years of his life to developing his as-if philosophy, based upon Kant's notion of 'heuristic fictions'.	*The Philosophy of 'As-If'* (1911)	To summarize, Vaihinger postulated that believing in an idea that was "false" at the moment, has great practical importance, which now made them useful and therefore "true." An example would be a sick person affirming "I am well." as a beneficial hypothesis about life. Hypotheses can be then proven true, therefore transforming the ideation of the individual.
116	295-4	One of the ancient sayings is that "To the man who can perfectly practice inaction, all things are possible."	*Exact source unknown.* Possibly Lao Tzu (circa 600 BCE), father of Taoism.	*The Sayings of Lao-Tzu*, Lionel Giles translation (1905) "The Doctrine of Inaction"	(p. 31) Practice inaction, and there is nothing which cannot be done.
117	297-2	"Life is the mirror of king and slave."	Madeline Bridges, American Poet (1840-1920)	Poem "Life's Mirror" published in *World's Best Loved Poems* (1927)	"For life is the mirror of king and slave, 'Tis just what we are and do. Then give to the world the best you have, And the best will come back to you."
118	297-2	Emerson said: "If you want a friend, be a friend."	Ralph Waldo Emerson (1803-1882) American essayist, philosopher, poet, and leader of the transcendentalist movement in the early 19th century. His teachings directly influenced the growing New Thought movement.	"Friendship" from *Essays: First Series* (1841) p.230	The only reward of virtue is virtue; the only way to have a friend is to be one.
119	306-2	The limit of our ability to demonstrate depends upon our ability to provide a mental equivalent of our desires, for the law of correspondence works from the belief to the thing.	*Exact source unknown* for notion of The Law of Correspondence. Often credited to Hermes Treismegistus, who also is credited with the Law of Correspondents. NOTE: Dr. Holmes references both laws in the text.	*The Kybalion, A Study of The Hermetic Philosophy of Ancient Egypt and Greece*, by Three Initiates (1912), "Chapter 8: The Planes of Correspondence"	"As above, so below; as below, so above." The great Second Hermetic Principle embodies the truth that there is a harmony, agreement, and correspondence between the several planes of Manifestation, Life and Being. This truth is a truth because all that is included in the Universe emanates from the same source, and the same laws, principles, and characteristics apply to each unit, or combination of unit, of activity, as each manifests its own phenomena upon its own plane.

Item Nr.	Page in the SOM Text	Phrase Used	Original Author	Primary Source Document	Quotation and commentary
120	306-2	The limit of our ability to demonstrate depends upon our ability to provide a mental equivalent of our desires, for the law of correspondence works from the belief to the thing.	*Exact source unknown for notion of The Law of Correspondence. Perhaps Unity Founder Charles Filmore (1854 – 1948)*	*The Twelve Powers of Man* (1936)	Charles Filmore was famous for creating own tables of correspondences in his writings. In *The Twelve Powers of Man*, this is especially apparent, where each spiritual power corresponds to a disciple of Jesus, a color, a specific body part, and a subconscious center of action. This process was later expanded upon by Louise Hay in her book *Heal Your Body A-Z: The Mental Causes for Physical Illness and the Way to Overcome Them* (1984) presents a table of hundreds of correspondences of diseases and health conditions and the erroneous thoughts that create them. Likewise she presents the thoughts that will heal these conditions.
121	306-2	The limit of our ability to demonstrate depends upon our ability to provide a mental equivalent of our desires, for the law of correspondence works from the belief to the thing.	*Exact source unknown for notion of The Law of Correspondence*	Glossary to *The Science of Mind*	The Law of Correspondence works from the belief to the thing. If we believe we shall have only a little good, only a little good will come into our experience. The
122	307-3	"Act as though I am and I will be"	*Exact source unknown. Perhaps Blaise Pascal (1623-1662). French mathematician, physicist, and religious philosopher.*	*Thoughts (Pensees)* (1670)	In his book *The Power of Your Subconscious Mind* - chapter 6 (1961) Joseph Murphy credited this exact quote to William James. A search of James's essay *"The Will to Believe"* (1896) stated, "The whole defense of religious faith hinges upon action." To support his claim, James references a quote in French by Blaise Pascal, "cela vous fera croire et vous abetira." Translated to English, this means "That [acting as if] will make you believe and will stupefy your proudly critical intellect."

Where'd He Get That? A Biblical Cross-Reference To Ernest Holmes' The Science of Mind

Item Nr.	Page in the SOM Text	Phrase Used	Original Author	Primary Source Document	Quotation and commentary
123		"Act as though I am and I will be"	*Exact source unknown.* Perhaps German philosopher Hans Vaihinger (1852-1933) a contemporary of Holmes, who devoted the last years of his life to developing his as-if philosophy, based upon Kant's notion of 'heuristic fictions'.	*The Philosophy of 'As-If'* (1911)	To summarize, Vaihinger postulated that believing in an idea that was "false" at the moment, has great practical importance, which now made them useful and therefore "true." An example would be a sick person affirming "I am well." as a beneficial hypothesis about life. Hypotheses can be then proven true, therefore transforming the ideation of the individual.
124	307-3	"Onlook thou the Deity and the Deity will onlook thee."	*Exact source unknown.* Possibly a paraphrase from the writings of Professor and religion editor Charles Horne, PhD	*The Sacred Books and Early Literature of the East, Volume 2 Egypt* (1917) Chapter "Of Making the Transformation into a Divine Hawk"	(p. 217) I shall see Osiris, I shall pay homage to him on the right hand and on the left, I shall pay homage unto Nut, and she shall look upon me, and the gods shall look upon me, together with the Eye of Horus who is without sight. They (i.e., the gods) shall make their arms to come forth unto me. I rise up as a divine Power...
125	309-5	Recent research in the field of physics has revealed that this metaphysical abstraction is the thing that physics begins with-- energy and intelligence.	*Exact source unknown.* Perhaps referring to the early ideas of astronomer and theoretical physicist Sir Fred Hoyle (1915 - 2001), author of *The Intelligent Universe* (1983) and proponent of Astro Genesis (life has its origins in space, not in terrestrial compounds).	Hoyle began publishing in 1937	To summarize, Hoyle proposed that due to the complex organic coating on interstellar dust, he concluded energy must have intelligence.
126	310-2	As stated above, physics has chased this form, as it were, back into a primordial unity of energy and intelligence.	*Exact source unknown.* Perhaps referring to the early ideas of astronomer and theoretical physicist Sir Fred Hoyle (1915 - 2001), author of *The Intelligent Universe* (1983) and proponent of Astro Genesis (life has its origins in space, not in terrestrial compounds).	Hoyle began publishing in 1937	To summarize, Hoyle proposed that due to the complex organic coating on interstellar dust, he concluded energy must have intelligence.

Item Nr.	Page in the SOM Text	Phrase Used	Original Author	Primary Source Document	Quotation and commentary
127	310-2	Perhaps this is what Emerson had in mind when he said that every fact is fluid	Ralph Waldo Emerson (1803-1882) American essayist, philosopher, poet, and leader of the transcendentalist movement in the early 19th century. His teachings directly influenced the growing New Thought movement.	"Circles" from *Essays: First Series* (1841)	The universe is fluid and volatile. Permanence is but a word of degrees. Our globe seen by God is a transparent law, not a mass of facts. The law dissolves the fact and holds it fluid.
128	310-2	or what Spinoza had in mind when he said: "I do not say that mind is one thing and matter another; I say they are the same thing."	Benedict Spinoza (1632-1677) Dutch Philosopher	*The Ethics - Part II* "Of the Nature and Origin of the Mind" (1677)	The order and connection of ideas is the same as the order and connection of things. ..Thinking substance and extended substance are one and the same thing.
129	311-2	Science tells us that all form comes from One Substance, made manifest through vibration.	*Exact source unknown.* Perhaps Dr. Holmes was referring to the findings of the emerging field of quantum physics which received much public attention in the 1920s and 30s. Many of these scientists received Nobel Prizes.	Douglas C. Giancoli, *Physics Principles with Applications* (2008) Chapter 27: "Early Quantum Theory and Models of the Atom" See also www.nobelprize.org for a more detailed description of the early quantum pioneers' contributions to the field.	For example, Dutch physicist Pieter Zeeman discovered the electron in 1896, was able to measure the axis of its vibration, and won the Nobel Prize in 1902 for his discovery that light was composed of vibrating electrons. The ground breaking work of Max Planck's discovering the quanta, for which he was awarded a Nobel Prize in 1918, led the field of physics that studied energy density as a function of wavelength and the movement or vibration of waves through all substance. Neils Bohr and Erwin Schroedinger, both Nobel prize winners, were studying wave functions at the atomic level and the radiation emanating from them. Prince Louis-Victor Pierre Raymond de Broglie was awarded the Nobel Prize in 1930 for his discovery of the wave nature of electrons. Although shadowed by his experiments in relativity, Einstein was also at work at the atomic vibration of light waves and behavior of particles.

Where'd He Get That? A Biblical Cross-Reference To Ernest Holmes' The Science of Mind

Item Nr.	Page in the SOM Text	Phrase Used	Original Author	Primary Source Document	Quotation and commentary
130	311-3	but that substance, indefinable and indivisible, when men like Socrates announced	Plato (c. 427–c. 347 BCE) Greek philosopher, student of Socrates and teacher to Aristotle	"Timaeus" *Dialogues* Written 360 B.C.E Persons of the Dialogue SOCRATES CRITIAS TIMAEUS HERMOCRATES	Out of the indivisible and unchangeable, and also out of that which is divisible and has to do with material bodies, he compounded a third and intermediate kind of essence, partaking of the nature of the same and of the other, and this compound he placed accordingly in a mean between the indivisible, and the divisible and material.
131	311-4	As Emerson said "There is no great and no small, to the Soul that maketh all; and whence It cometh all things are, and It cometh everywhere."	Ralph Waldo Emerson (1803-1882) American essayist, philosopher, poet, and leader of the transcendentalist movement in the early 19th century. His teachings directly influenced the growing New Thought movement.	"History" from *Essays: First Series* (1841)	There is no great and no small To the Soul that maketh all: And where it cometh, all things are; And it cometh everywhere.
132	314-1	That is what Plato meant when he gave us the story of the slaves in the cave.	Plato (c. 427–c. 347 BCE) Greek philosopher, student of Socrates and teacher to Aristotle	*The Republic* Book VII: "The Allegory of the Cave" (360 BCE)	Read entire selection at http://classics.mit.edu/Plato/republic.8.vii.html
133	315-1	Emerson says to cast them upon every wind of heaven, do not hold them. "Beware of holding too much good in your hand."	Ralph Waldo Emerson (1803-1882) American essayist, philosopher, poet, and leader of the transcendentalist movement in the early 19th century. His teachings directly influenced the growing New Thought movement.	"Compensation" from *Essays: First Series* (1841)	Beware of too much good staying in your hand. It will fast corrupt and worm worms. Pay it away quickly in some sort.
134	322-1	The manifest universe is a result of the Self-Contemplation of God	Thomas Troward (1847-1916) British Divisional Judge of the North Indian Punjab whose metaphysical writings had a profound effect on New Thought, in particular The Science of Mind.	*The Creative Process and the Individual*, Chapter II: "The Self-Contemplation of Spirit" (1915) NOTE: This text appeared in the footnotes of the 1926 edition of the Science of Mind.	If we ask how the cosmos came into existence we shall find that ultimately we can only attribute it to the Self-Contemplation of Spirit.

Item Nr.	Page in the SOM Text	Phrase Used	Original Author	Primary Source Document	Quotation and commentary
135	323-2	"Act as though I am and I will be"	*Exact source unknown.* Perhaps Blaise Pascal (1623-1662). French mathematician, physicist, and religious philosopher.	*Thoughts (Pensees)* (1670)	In his book *The Power of Your Subconscious Mind* - chapter 6 (1961) Joseph Murphy credited this exact quote to William James. A search of James's essay *"The Will to Believe"* (1896) stated, "The whole defense of religious faith hinges upon action." To support his claim, James references a quote in French by Blaise Pascal, "cela vous fera croire et vous abetira." Translated to English, this means "That [acting as if] will make you believe and will stupefy your proudly critical intellect."
136	323-2	"Act as though I am and I will be"	*Exact source unknown.* Perhaps German philosopher Hans Vaihinger (1852-1933) a contemporary of Holmes, who devoted the last years of his life to developing his as-if philosophy, based upon Kant's notion of 'heuristic fictions'.	*The Philosophy of 'As-If'* (1911)	To summarize, Vaihinger postulated that believing in an idea that was "false" at the moment, has great practical importance, which now made them useful and therefore "true." An example would be a sick person affirming "I am well." as a beneficial hypothesis about life. Hypotheses can be then proven true, therefore transforming the ideation of the individual.
137	330-2	It is also "that Whose Center is everywhere and Whose Circumference is nowhere."	Empedocles (ca. 490–430 BC) was a Greek pre-Socratic philosopher	This quote was first reference to Empedocles in the 14th century text *Liber Hermetis,* on the teachings of Hermes Treismegistus	God is a circle whose center is everywhere and circumference nowhere. "Deus est circulus cuius centrum est ubique, circumferentia vero nusquam." In the form "Deus est sphaera infinita" (God is an infinite sphere) also comes from the *Liber Hermetis, Liber Termegisti*, Cod. Paris. 6319 (14th cent.); Cod. Vat. 3060 (1315). The quotation is also attributed to Pascal, Voltaire, St. Augustine, Hermes Treismegistus, Nicholas Cusanus, Meister Eckhart and Carl Jung.
138	330-3	It is "That thread of the All-sustaining beauty which runs through all and doth all unite."	James Russell Lowell (1819 – 1891) American Romantic poet, critic, editor, and diplomat.	From the poem "The Vision of Sir Launfal" (1848), Prelude to Part First, Section VI	That thread of the All-sustaining beauty which runs through all and doth all unite.

Where'd He Get That? A Biblical Cross-Reference To Ernest Holmes' The Science of Mind

Item Nr.	Page in the SOM Text	Phrase Used	Original Author	Primary Source Document	Quotation and commentary
139	330-3	"There is no place where God is not."	John Greenleaf Whittier 1807-1892	Poem "The Hermit Of The Thebaid" 1884	"O child!" he said, "thou teachest me There is no place where God is not; That love will make, where'er it be, A holy spot."
140	330-3	"There is no place where God is not."	Mary Baker Eddy, founder of Christian Science	*Science and Health with Key to the Scriptures* (1917)	(p. 480) Where the spirit of God is, and there is no place where God is not, evil becomes nothing, - the opposite of the something of Spirit.
141	332-1	for the Law is "the servant of the Eternal Spirit throughout all the ages."	*Exact source unknown.* Possibly Josephine A. Jackson and Helen M. Salisbury, where the subconscious is first defined as a "servant." Jackson and Salisbury were two women Freudian psychoanalysts working in southern California. Their book was a best seller as it explained psychoanalysis in lay terms.	*Outwitting Our Nerves: A Primer of Psychotherapy* (1921) NOTE: This text appeared in the footnotes of the 1926 edition of the *Science of Mind*.	(p. 31) The subconscious mind which is not affected by ether, has been exhausting itself in a vain attempt to get the body away from harm. A Tireless Servant. When the conscious mind undertakes a job, it is always more or less subject to fatigue. But the subconscious after its long practice seems never to tire. We say that its activities have become automatic. With all its inherited skill, the subconscious, if left to itself, can be depended upon to run the bodily machinery without effort and without hitch. The only things that can interfere with its work are the wrong kind of emotions and the wrong kind of suggestions from the conscious mind. Barring these, it goes its way like a trusty servant, looking after details and leaving its master's mind free for other things.
142	334-4	Man will never be satisfied until his whole being responds to this thought, and then, indeed, will "God go forth again into Creation."	Ralph Waldo Emerson (1803-1882) American essayist, philosopher, poet, and leader of the transcendentalist movement in the early 19th century. His teachings directly influenced the growing New Thought movement.	"Prospects" Chapter VIII from *Nature*, published as part of *Nature; Addresses and Lectures* (1849)	But when a faithful thinker, resolute to detach every object from personal relations, and see it in the light of thought, shall, at the same time, kindle science with the fire of the holiest affections, then will God go forth anew into the creation.
143	335-4	Man would have no burdens if he kept this "High Watch toward The One."	*Exact source unknown.* Probably Emma Curtis Hopkins (1853-1925) New Thought teacher and writer who also named her ministry The High Watch.	*High Mysticism* (1888)	(p. 48) "I will give power unto My two watchers," was the promise John heard from above, meant for any two of us who now begin the high watch that wooeth the God power."

Item Nr.	Page in the SOM Text	Phrase Used	Original Author	Primary Source Document	Quotation and commentary
144	336-2	Emerson said he was often conscious of Jove nodding to Jove from behind our backs.	Ralph Waldo Emerson (1803-1882) American essayist, philosopher, poet, and leader of the transcendentalist movement in the early 19th century. His teachings directly influenced the growing New Thought movement.	Essays: First Series *(1841)*: "The Over-Soul"	We do not yet possess ourselves, and we know at the same time that we are much more. I feel the same truth how often in my trivial conversation with my neighbours, that somewhat higher in each of us overlooks this by-play, and Jove nods to Jove from behind each of us.
145	339-1	Man being an individual, may do as he wills with himself - as Browning said, he may desecrate but he can never lose his life.	*Exact source unknown. Not found in Robert Browning's writings.* Possibly George Washington (1732-1799) first president of the United States.	*Book of Etiquette* (1747)	Unity author and teacher Eric Butterworth uses this quote in his radio speech "The Truth in a Nutshell": Every person contains within himself or herself a Spark of Divinity, "that little Spark of Celestial Fire that a man may desecrate but never quite lose." Butterworth credits its origin to George Washington who wrote it as the last of 110 rules of etiquette: "Labor to keep alive in your breast the little spark of celestial fire called conscience."
146	341-2	Dr. Bucke defines Cosmic Consciousness as :"One's consciousness of his unity with the Whole."	Dr. Richard Maurice Bucke (1837-1902) Canadian progressive psychiatrist.	*Cosmic Consciousness* (1901) NOTE: This text appeared in the footnotes of the 1926 edition of the Science of Mind.	(p. 61) Especially does he [who experiences cosmic consciousness] obtain such a conception of THE WHOLE, or at least of an immense WHOLE, as dwarfs all conceptions, imagination, or speculation, springing from and belonging to ordinary self consciousness.
147	341-2	The mystic intuitively perceives Truth, and often without any process of reasoning - immediately is aware, with what Swedenborg called a sort of "interior awareness," a spiritual sense.	Emanuel Swedenborg (1688-1772) Swedish scientist, inventor, philosopher, and Christian mystic. The Church of the New Jerusalem is founded on his writings.	*Arcana Celestia* (1749-1756),	(p 1807) "Truth from good is the power by which the interior arranges all things into order in the exterior" "Interius amare Dominum" Latin for "Love the Lord interiorly" To love the Lord interiorly is interiorly to love His precepts; that is, from the delight of love to perceive, to will and to do them. *(from Glossary of Terms Used by Swedenborg by John Bogg, 1915).*

Item Nr.	Page in the SOM Text	Phrase Used	Original Author	Primary Source Document	Quotation and commentary
148	341-3	Dean Inge, perhaps the best thinker in the Anglican Church of today, tells us that Plotinus had seven distinct periods of *cosmic consciousness*, in which state he was so completely unified with the Universe that he became One with It.	William Ralph Inge (1860 – 1954) English author, Anglican priest, and Dean and Professor of Divinity at Cambridge.	*The Philosophy of Plotinus Volume II* (1918) NOTE: This text appeared in the footnotes of the 1926 edition of the Science of Mind. NOTE: There are no seven periods or distinct visions described in either volume, but Plotinus does describe in great detail the nature of a mystic vision.	(p. 132) The best answer to these questions is to consider what Plotinus has to tell us about the vision of the One. For it is unquestionably a genuine experience of his own—this ecstatic love of the Absolute. Moreover, the great army of mystics, Christian, Pagan, Mohammedan, corroborate all that the great Neo-Platonist describes to us. The ' Spirit in love ' is the culmination of personal religion; and the object of this adoration is not the limited half-human God of popular religion, but the ineffable mysterious Power to whom we shrink from ascribing any human attributes whatever.
149	341-4	Dr. Bucke, the author of that most rational book, "Cosmic Consciousness," cites many instances of known and authentic records of people who have had definite Cosmic experiences.	Dr. Richard Maurice Bucke (1837-1902) Canadian progressive psychiatrist.	*Cosmic Consciousness* (1901) NOTE: This text appeared in the footnotes of the 1926 edition of the *Science of Mind*.	To summarize, Bucke described his own experience of cosmic consciousness e, that of contemporaries (most notably Walt Whitman, but also unknown figures like "C.P."), and the experiences and outlook of historical figures including Buddha, Jesus, Paul, Plotinus, Muhammad, Dante, Francis Bacon, and William Blake.
150	342-1	Therefore, we may read Buddha, Jesus, Plato, Socrates, Aristotle, Swedenborg, Emerson, Whitman, Browning or any of the other great mystics, no matter in what age they have lived, and we shall find the same Ultimate [First Cause].	Gautama Buddha (563 -483 BCE) Spiritual teacher in the northern region of India who founded Buddhism NOTE: Buddha emphatically taught against a notion of a First Cause in his discourses.	*Samyutta Nikaya, II, Anamatagga Samyutta* ["Connected Discourses" or "Kindred Sayings"] Buddhist scripture (p.179)	To paraphrase, the Buddha declared that the first beginning of existence is something inconceivable, and that such notions and speculations of a first beginning may lead to mental derangement. If one posits a 'First Cause' one is justified in asking for the cause of that 'First Cause'; for nothing can escape the law of condition and cause which is patent in the world to all but those who will not see. According to the Buddha, it is inconceivable to find a first cause for life or anything else. For in common experience, the cause becomes the effect and the effect becomes the cause. In the circle of cause and effect, a first cause is incomprehensible.

Item Nr.	Page in the SOM Text	Phrase Used	Original Author	Primary Source Document	Quotation and commentary
151	342-1	Therefore, we may read Buddha, Jesus, Plato, Socrates, Aristotle, Swedenborg, Emerson, Whitman, Browning or any of the other great mystics, no matter in what age they have lived, and we shall find the same Ultimate [First Cause].	Plato (c. 427–c. 347 BCE) Greek philosopher, student of Socrates and teacher to Aristotle	*The Laws* (360 BCE)	To summarize, Plato argued that the motion in the universe must be attributable to a first cause. Plato argues, that the first cause of motion initiated all the motion in the universe. He called this principle, 'soul' or 'life.' Further, any cause that was the ultimate cause must itself be unmoved by anything else—an unmoved mover. Since the world was good and orderly, The First Cause itself was created by a *demiurge*, a good and orderly force. Plato's ideas on First Cause were later adopted by Thomas Aquinas who concluded the First Cause is God.
152	342-1	Therefore, we may read Buddha, Jesus, Plato, Socrates, Aristotle, Swedenborg, Emerson, Whitman, Browning or any of the other great mystics, no matter in what age they have lived, and we shall find the same Ultimate [First Cause].	Socrates (469-399 BCE) Greek philosopher	*Plato's Dialogue Phaedo: or, A Dialogue of the Immortality of the Soul*	Socrates never penned anything himself, but his ideas were written down by his students, Plato in particular. Socrates appears in several of Plato's dialogues and presents his idea of First Cause. To summarize, Socrates raises his thoughts to immaterial qualities, and eternal ideas: that is, he affirms that there is something that is in itself, good, fine, just, and great, which is the First Cause; and that all things in this world that are good, fine, just, or great, are only such by the communication of that first cause: since there is no other cause of the existence of things, but the participation of the essence proper to each subject.
153		Therefore, we may read Buddha, Jesus, Plato, Socrates, Aristotle, Swedenborg, Emerson, Whitman, Browning or any of the other great mystics, no matter in what age they have lived, and we shall find the same Ultimate [First Cause].	Aristotle (384–322 BCE) Greek philosopher, student of Plato and teacher to Alexander the Great	*Metaphysics* (about 340 BCE)	To summarize, Aristotle said that the First Cause is only one because it is the Prime Mover only with pure form without any matter. For there must be only one "Pure Form" because only matter coupled with form can result in the plurality of being. The First Cause as a necessary being has always existed from eternity and cannot be destroyed.

Where'd He Get That? A Biblical Cross-Reference To Ernest Holmes' The Science of Mind

Item Nr.	Page in the SOM Text	Phrase Used	Original Author	Primary Source Document	Quotation and commentary
154	342-1	Therefore, we may read Buddha, Jesus, Plato, Socrates, Aristotle, Swedenborg, Emerson, Whitman, Browning or any of the other great mystics, no matter in what age they have lived, and we shall find the same Ultimate [First Cause].	Emanuel Swedenborg (1688-1772) Swedish scientist, inventor, philosopher, and Christian mystic. The Church of the New Jerusalem is founded on his writings.	*Emanuel Swedenborg: His Life and Writings,* Ed: William White (1867) Essay "The Infinite and the Final Cause of Creation, and the Mechanism of the Intercourse between the Soul and the Body"	If we admit then that the Universe, Nature, or Creation is finite, we must next inquire, By whom was the Universe created, caused, or finited? If it be answered, that Nature created or originated itself, a reply is made which is flatly repugnant to Reason; for that is saying that it existed before it did exist; that it created itself. If it be said that God created Nature, and God be thought of as finite, the question is not answered, but evaded or deferred; for, if God be finite, we renew our inquiry, and ask, By whom was God finited, created, or caused? We have here the child's question, following his instruction that God made him—Then, who made God? Thus driven inwards from Finite to Finite, from Cause to Cause, we are at last compelled to stop and own a first and original Cause, un-caused and un-finite, and therefore Infinite.

Item Nr.	Page in the SOM Text	Phrase Used	Original Author	Primary Source Document	Quotation and commentary
155	342-1	Therefore, we may read Buddha, Jesus, Plato, Socrates, Aristotle, Swedenborg, Emerson, Whitman, Browning or any of the other great mystics, no matter in what age they have lived, and we shall find the same Ultimate [First Cause].	Ralph Waldo Emerson (1803-1882) American essayist, philosopher, poet, and leader of the transcendentalist movement in the early 19th century. His teachings directly influenced the growing New Thought movement.	*The Journals of Ralph Waldo Emerson,* Edward Waldo Emerson (1909)	GREEK PHILOSOPHERS: ...the opinions of the first Ionians themselves, had associated the elementary matter of all things to the first cause of all production, and thus conceive the Divinity as the universal soul, the soul of the world, the world itself as an animated whole identical in some sort with its author, Anaxagoras first detached, separated with precision and neatness these two notions until then confounded. The Universe is in his eyes an effect wholly distinct from its Cause.

This Cause has nothing common with the rest of beings. It hath its peculiar nature, one, eternal, acts on the world as workman on materials. So the idea of the first Cause, which until then was essentially defined by the attribute of Power, was determined by Anaxagoras to receive chiefly the attribute of intelligence.. . .Anaxagoras said, one single soul ran through all being, ordering matter, but intimately present to man. |
| 156 | 342-1 | Therefore, we may read Buddha, Jesus, Plato, Socrates, Aristotle, Swedenborg, Emerson, Whitman, Browning or any of the other great mystics, no matter in what age they have lived, and we shall find the same Ultimate [First Cause]. | Walt Whitman (1819–1892) American poet, essayist, journalist, humanist, and part of the Transcendentalist movement. | From *November Boughs* (1892) | Found considerable satisfaction in his [Paul's] first epistle to the Corinthians in which he shows the danger of some in setting too high a value on those who were instrumental in bringing to them the knowledge of the truth, without looking through and beyond to the great First Cause, and Author of every blessing, to whom all the praise and honor are due. |

Where'd He Get That? A Biblical Cross-Reference To Ernest Holmes' The Science of Mind

Item Nr.	Page in the SOM Text	Phrase Used	Original Author	Primary Source Document	Quotation and commentary
157	342-1	Therefore, we may read Buddha, Jesus, Plato, Socrates, Aristotle, Swedenborg, Emerson, Whitman, Browning or any of the other great mystics, no matter in what age they have lived, and we shall find the same Ultimate [First Cause].	Robert Browning (1812-1889) British poet	*Parleyings with Certain People of Importance in Their Day: Francis Furini*, Section X. (1886)	Want was the promise of supply, defect Ensured completion, — where and when and how? Leave that to the First Cause! Enough that now, Here where I stand, this moment's me and mine. Shows me what is, permits me to divine What shall be. Wherefore? Nay, how otherwise?
158	343-2	"Speak to Him, thou, for He hears."	Alfred Lord Tennyson (1809-1892) English poet	Poem "The Higher Pantheism" from *The Holy Grail and Other Poems* (1870).	"Speak to Him, thou, for He hears, and Spirit with Spirit can meet - Closer is He than breathing, and nearer than hands and feet."
159	343-5	They have taught the "Mystical Marriage"	*Exact source unknown.* Probably Florence Scovel Shinn (1871-1940) American illustrator and author of prosperity books in the early 20th century	*The Game of Life and How to Play It* (1925), Chapter 3 "The Power of the Word"	The "mystical marriage" is the marriage of the soul and the spirit, or the subconscious and superconscious mind. They must be one. When the subconscious is flooded with the perfect ideas of the superconscious, God and man are one, "I and the Father are one." That is, he is one with the realm of perfect ideas; he is the man made in God's likeness and image (imagination) and is given power and dominion over all created things, his mind, body and affairs.
160	344-1	Tagore, in seeking to explain this, says that the individual is immersed in, but not lost in, Mirana, and he uses the illustration . . ."as an arrow is lost in its mark," still remaining an arrow.	Rabindranath Tagore, (1861-1941) Indian poet and author	*Sadhana: The Realisation of Life*, Chapter VIII: "The Realisation of the Infinite" (1916)	The Upanishads say: "Be lost altogether in Brahma like an arrow that has completely penetrated its target." Thus to be conscious of being absolutely enveloped by Brahma is not an act of mere concentration of mind. It must be the aim of the whole of our life. In all our thoughts and deeds we must be conscious of the infinite.

Where'd He Get That? A Biblical Cross-Reference To Ernest Holmes' The Science of Mind

Item Nr.	Page in the SOM Text	Phrase Used	Original Author	Primary Source Document	Quotation and commentary
161	344-1	The mysticism of Buddha did not teach the annihilation of the soul, but the eternality of an ever-expanding principle of the soul.	*Exact source unknown.* Perhaps Buddhist scholar C.L. Whittimore (dates and title unknown)	*The Gospel of Buddha According to Old Records* Chapter "What is Buddhism?" (1894)	Buddhism does not propose the doctrine of the annihilation of the soul at the moment of death, but teaches the continuance of the soul according to the deeds done during life, which is called the law of Karma. It does address the annihilation of the false doctrines of the ego and craving.
162	344-3	All mystics have seen this Cosmic Light. This is why it is said there were illumined. They have all had the same experience, whether it was . . . . Emerson walking across the Common in Concord--where suddenly he became conscious of this light.	Ralph Waldo Emerson (1803-1882) American essayist, philosopher, poet, and leader of the transcendentalist movement in the early 19th century. His teachings directly influenced the growing New Thought movement. Emerson lived most of his years as a writer in Concord, MA and is buried there. *Exact story of such a sudden illumination is not in the biographical material about Emerson but he describes it in his poem.*	Poems (1839) *"Each and All"*	Around me stood the oaks and firs; Pine cones and acorns lay on the ground; Above me soared the eternal sky, Full of light and deity; Again I saw, again I heard, The rolling river, the morning bird;— Beauty through my senses stole, I yielded myself to the perfect whole.

Where'd He Get That? A Biblical Cross-Reference To Ernest Holmes' The Science of Mind

Item Nr.	Page in the SOM Text	Phrase Used	Original Author	Primary Source Document	Quotation and commentary
163	345-1	Whitman refers to it [Cosmic Light] as that which "stuck its forked tongue" into his being as he lay on the grass	Walt Whitman (1819–1892) American poet, essayist, journalist, humanist, and part of the Transcendentalist movement.	From *Song of Myself* (1855), Stanza V	I believe in you my soul, the other I am must not abase itself to you, And you must not be abased to the other. Loafe with me on the grass, loose the stop from your throat, Not words, not music or rhyme I want, not custom or lecture, not even the best, Only the lull I like, the hum of your valved voice. I mind how once we lay such a transparent summer morning, How you settled your head athwart my hips and gently turn'd over upon me, And parted the shirt from my bosom-bone, and plunged your tongue to my bare-stript heart, And reach'd till you felt my beard, and reach'd till you held my feet. Swiftly arose and spread around me the peace and knowledge that pass all the argument of the earth, And I know that the hand of God is the promise of my own,
164	345-1	or whether it was Edward Carpenter who, after leaving Whitman and looking up, thought all of New York City was in flames.	Edward Carpenter (1844 – 1929) was an English socialist poet, anthologist, early gay activist and socialist philosopher. Close friend (and thought lover) of Walt Whitman. *The chronology seems a few years off as Carpenter wrote this poem in 1873, first visited Whitman in Camden New Jersey in 1877 and again in 1884. Carpenter wrote about Whitman's sudden illumination in his Days with Walt Whitman (1906) but not his own.*	From "Earth's Voices" (1873)	And past me, with a shriek from East and West, And feet of thunder up the sloping ways, The great town drew in fiery grim unrest Her steaming traffic through its iron maze ; And all the roads a flickering dust did raise, Like white flames o'er the country far and wide, Because of those who in the wheeling chaise Or huge deliberate wain on every side About her to and fro their busy errands plied.

Item Nr.	Page in the SOM Text	Phrase Used	Original Author	Primary Source Document	Quotation and commentary
165	345-2	Bucke points out that the illumination of all mystics has been accompanied by a great light	Dr. Richard Maurice Bucke (1837-1902) Canadian progressive psychiatrist.	*Cosmic Consciousness* (1901) NOTE: This text appeared in the footnotes of the 1926 edition of the Science of Mind.	(p. 62) The instantaneousness of the illumination is one of its most striking features. It can be compared with nothing so well as a dazzling flash of lightning on a dark night, bringing the landscape which had been hidden into clear view.
166	345-2	He [Bucke] feels that Emerson walked on the verge of this light for many years	Dr. Richard Maurice Bucke (1837-1902) Canadian progressive psychiatrist.	*Cosmic Consciousness* (1901) NOTE: This text appeared in the footnotes of the 1926 edition of the Science of Mind.	
167	352-5	anyone tuning into our thought, will enter into our stream of consciousness	*Exact source unknown.* Probably William James (1842-1910), pioneering American psychologist and philosopher, often called the father of modern psychology, first coined the term "stream of consciousness"	*Principles of Psychology* 1892, Chapter XI	"Consciousness, then, does not appear to itself chopped up in bits. Such words as 'chain' or 'train' do not describe it fitly as it presents itself in the first instance. It is nothing jointed; it flows. A 'river' or a 'stream' are the metaphors by which it is most naturally described. In talking of it hereafter, let us call it the stream of thought, of consciousness, or of subjective life."
168	357-2	Eckhart, one of the great mystics of the Middle Ages, said: "God never begot but *one* Son, but the Eternal is forever begetting the only begotten."	Meister Eckhart (c. 1260-1327), Dominican philosopher and Catholic mystic.	*The Commentaries on Genesis* (circa 1275).	To summarize, Eckhart in turn quotes St. Augustine's (354-430) *Homilies on John 14:7* [A.D. 416]. St. Augustine was a Christian philosopher and theologian, and author of 113 works. St. Augustine writes: "The Father eternally conceives and begets the perfect expression [of] it himself which is the Word."

Where'd He Get That? A Biblical Cross-Reference To Ernest Holmes' The Science of Mind

Item Nr.	Page in the SOM Text	Phrase Used	Original Author	Primary Source Document	Quotation and commentary
169	358-1	We should speak the word with belief in its power, because the Law is the servant of the Spirit	*Exact source unknown.* Possibly Josephine A. Jackson and Helen M. Salisbury, where the subconscious is first defined as a "servant." Jackson and Salisbury were two women Freudian psychoanalysts working in southern California. Their book was a best seller as it explained psychoanalysis in lay terms.	*Outwitting Our Nerves: A Primer of Psychotherapy* (1921) NOTE: This text appeared in the footnotes of the 1926 edition of the Science of Mind.	(p. 31) The subconscious mind which is not affected by ether, has been exhausting itself in a vain attempt to get the body away from harm. A Tireless Servant. When the conscious mind undertakes a job, it is always more or less subject to fatigue. But the subconscious after its long practice seems never to tire. We say that its activities have become automatic. With all its inherited skill, the subconscious, if left to itself, can be depended upon to run the bodily machinery without effort and without hitch. The only things that can interfere with its work are the wrong kind of emotions and the wrong kind of suggestions from the conscious mind. Barring these, it goes its way like a trusty servant, looking after details and leaving its master's mind free for other things.
170	360-2	Poem beginning with "Asleep in the heart of Cosmic Love, Unborn...Universal...Potential, The Christ Child lay." continuing for 7 verses ending on p 361 with: "And in my right, peace forevermore, All that I am--all that I have-- I give."	Ernest Holmes original poetry 1938		
171	365-5	Poem beginning with "HOLY, HOLY, HOLY, Inner Presence, Great and Mighty," continuing for two verses and ending on page 366-1 with: HOLY, HOLY, HOLY-- Lord God within me."	Ernest Holmes original poetry 1938		

Where'd He Get That? A Biblical Cross-Reference To Ernest Holmes' The Science of Mind

Item Nr.	Page in the SOM Text	Phrase Used	Original Author	Primary Source Document	Quotation and commentary
172	366-3	Poem beginning with "Thou art the center and circumference of my life, The beginningless and endless part of me," and ending with "O Lord, God, Eternal and forever Blessed, Though art my whole being?"	Ernest Holmes original poetry 1938		
173	367-2	Poem beginning with "Sweet song of the Silence, forever singing in my heart!" and ending with "I am lost in the mighty depths of Thy inner calm and peace."	Ernest Holmes original poetry 1938		
174	368-2	Poem beginning with "I AM, what more can I say? I am, it is enough!" and ending with "Birthless and Changeless and Deathless, I AM! I AM! and evermore shall be."	Ernest Holmes original poetry 1938		
175	369-2	Poem beginning with "Be still, O Soul, and *know*. Look unto the One and be illumined." and ending with Be sill in His presence and rejoice in HI Love forevermore."	Ernest Holmes original poetry 1938		

Item Nr.	Page in the SOM Text	Phrase Used	Original Author	Primary Source Document	Quotation and commentary
176	370-2	Poem beginning with "Through the long night watches, His hand clasps mine." and ends with "And Space and Worlds shall be swallowed up in everlasting blessedness. his hand will clasp mine!"	Ernest Holmes original poetry 1938		
177	374-2	factors that constitute human personality and an individualized stream of consciousness have departed.	*Exact source unknown*. Probably William James (1842-1910), pioneering American psychologist and philosopher, often called the father of modern psychology, first coined the term "stream of. consciousness"	*Principles of Psychology* 1892, Chapter XI	"Consciousness, then, does not appear to itself chopped up in bits. Such words as 'chain' or 'train' do not describe it fitly as it presents itself in the first instance. It is nothing jointed; it flows. A 'river' or a 'stream' are the metaphors by which it is most naturally described. In talking of it hereafter, let us call it the stream of thought, of consciousness, or of subjective life."
178	375-2	ether is more solid than matter	Sir Oliver Lodge (1851-1940) physicist and writer; address on the "Ether of Space" given at Bedford College for Women	"Sees Great Future in Study of Ether: Sir Oliver Lodge Believes Our Present Knowledge May Shrink to a "Pinpoint." *New York Times*, February 1, 1914	"We have reason to believe," said Sir Oliver, "that the density of ether would be the equivalent of 1,000 tons per cubic millimetre of terrestrial matter when compared to it."
179	376-1	The "resurrection body" then, will not be snatched from some cosmic Shelf, as the soul soars aloft.	*Exact source unknown*. Perhaps referring to notion of the " resurrection body" which believers (both alive and the buried dead) will receive at the time of "The Rapture", a notion presented by the American theologian Cyrus I. Scofield (1843 - 1921) in his *Scofield Reference Bible* (1909, 1917), famous for its propagation of the teaching known as premillennialism.	See footnote (5) after I Corinthians 15 "The mortal body will be related to the resurrection body as grain sown is related to the harvest; that body will be incorruptible glorious powerful and spiritual."	Note that The words "rapture" and "resurrection body" do not appear in the Bible. The Premillennialsits coined the word "Rapture" from the Latin "rapio or rapere which means to "catch up or snatch away."

Item Nr.	Page in the SOM Text	Phrase Used	Original Author	Primary Source Document	Quotation and commentary
180	377-4	More than forty years ago. . . Hudson, in his "Law of Psychic Phenomena," carefully goes through an elaborate process of reasoning	Thomson Jay Hudson (1834-1903) Chief Examiner of the US Patent Office and Psychical researcher.	*Law of Psychic Phenomena* (1893) NOTE: This text appeared in the footnotes of the 1926 edition of the Science of Mind.	(p 398) I have now summarized enough of the leading points in the history of Jesus of Nazareth and of his doctrines, and compared them with known phenomena with sufficient particularity to show that the inductions of modern science demonstrate the essential truth of the history of his physical manifestations, and to prove, as far as inductive reasoning from known phenomena can prove anything not physically demonstrable, the truth of every essential doctrine of his spiritual philosophy.
181	380-3	"The Return of Peter Grimm"	David Belasco (1853 - 1931) American playwright, impresario, director and theatrical producer.	Broadway play (1911) later made into a movie (1935) starring Lionel Barrymore	In the story, the ghost of a recently deceased family patriarch tries to help his surviving relatives, in part by preventing a marriage that he knows will go wrong.
182	382-3	"What is true on one plane, is true on all."	Thomas Troward (1847-1916) British Divisional Judge of the North Indian Punjab whose metaphysical writings had a profound effect on New Thought, in particular The Science of Mind.	*The Hidden Power* (1921) NOTE: This text appeared in the footnotes of the 1926 edition of the Science of Mind.	(p. 17) "We must never lose sight of the old-world saying that "a truth on one plane is a truth on all." If a principle exists at all it exists universally. NOTE: Troward does not specify the source of this 'old world saying.'
183	383-1	Can we think of reward and punishment from any other viewpoint than that sin is a mistake and punishment a consequence,	*Exact source unknown. Ernest Holmes attributes this to Emerson, but it is not found in Emerson.* Perhaps *Strong's Exhaustive Concordance of the Bible,* first published in 1890 which contained the etymological meaning of 8674 Hebrew root words used in the Old Testament and 5624 Greek root words used in the New Testament.	*Hebrew word 7686 shagah shaw-gaw':* a primitive root; to stray (causatively, mislead), usually (figuratively) to mistake, especially (morally) to transgress; by extension (through the idea of intoxication) to reel, (figuratively) be enraptured:--(cause to) go astray, deceive, err, be ravished, sin through ignorance, (let, make to) wander. *Greek word 264. hamartano ham-ar-tan'-o:* properly, to miss the mark (and so not share in the prize), i.e. (figuratively) to err;	NOTE: Rocco Ericco, Modern scholar of the Aramaic sources of the Bible writes that the Aramaic word *hataya* used in these contexts, means "to miss" or "to miss the mark," thus a "mistake." See *Setting a Trap for God*, Unity House Publishing (1997) p. 89.

Where'd He Get That? A Biblical Cross-Reference To Ernest Holmes' The Science of Mind

Item Nr.	Page in the SOM Text	Phrase Used	Original Author	Primary Source Document	Quotation and commentary
184	388-1	Every man is an incarnation of eternity, a manifestation in the finite, of that Infinite which, Emerson tells us, "lies stretched in smiling repose."	Ralph Waldo Emerson (1803-1882) American essayist, philosopher, poet, and leader of the transcendentalist movement in the early 19th century. His teachings directly influenced the growing New Thought movement.	*Essays: First Series* (1841) "Essay IV: Spiritual Laws"	For it is only the finite that has wrought and suffered; the infinite lies stretched in smiling repose.
185	389-1	Poem beginning "When death shall com And the spirit, free, shall mount the air" and ends with "For the spirit, freed now from clod, Shall go alone to meet its God."	Ernest Holmes original poetry 1938		
186	394-4	"The Highest God and the innermost God is One God."	Ernest Holmes, *Religious Science Declaration of Principles*	from "What I Believe," published in the first issue of *Science of Mind Magazine* (October 1927)	We believe in the unity of all life, and that the highest God and the innermost God is One God.
187	409-5	Troward tells us that the Divine Spirit is the limitless potential of human life.	Thomas Troward (1847-1916) British Divisional Judge of the North Indian Punjab whose metaphysical writings had a profound effect on New Thought, in particular The Science of Mind.	*The Creative Process and the Individual* (1915)	(p. 38) We now know ourselves to be Reciprocals of the Divine Spirit, centers in which It finds a fresh standpoint for Self-contemplation; and so the way to rise to the heights of this Great Pattern is by contemplating it as the Normal Standard of our own Personality.
188	410--4	"God if thou seest God, Dust if thou seest dust."	*Exact source unknown.* Probably Saint Brother Angelus (1185 - 1220) a Hebrew-Catholic saint and martyr from the Holy Land.	*Biography of Angelus of Sicily* by Henoch, a Sicilian Carmelite, dating from the early 15th century	"That thou seest, man, become too thou must; God, if thou seest God, dust, if thou seest dust."
189	418-5	"With right glance and with right speech man superintendeth the animate and the inanimate."	Emma Curtis Hopkins (1853-1925) New Thought teacher and writer	*High Mysticism*, 1888 Chapter 8 "Sight - The Spiritual Mind is Never Deceived"	With right glance and with right speech we may superintend the universe, animate and inanimate.

Item Nr.	Page in the SOM Text	Phrase Used	Original Author	Primary Source Document	Quotation and commentary
190	422-2	Each maintains a stream of consciousness in the One Mind	*Exact source unknown.* Probably William James (1842-1910), pioneering American psychologist and philosopher, often called the father of modern psychology, first coined the term "stream of consciousness"	*Principles of Psychology* (1892) Chapter XI	Consciousness, then, does not appear to itself chopped up in bits. Such words as 'chain' or 'train' do not describe it fitly as it presents itself in the first instance. It is nothing jointed; it flows. A 'river' or a 'stream' are the metaphors by which it is most naturally described. In talking of it hereafter, let us call it the stream of thought, of consciousness, or of subjective life.
191	423-2	"I am that which thou art; thou art that which I am."	*Exact source unknown.* Probably excerpts from *The Upanishads,* a collection of over Hindu scriptures that constitute the core teachings of Vedanta the Upanishads were started circa 500 BCE and the last one was written in the 1670s.)	"I am that" is a refrain from the *Amritbindu Upanishad* (date unknown - a Yoga Upanishad) Tat Tvam Asi, a Sanskrit sentence, translating variously to "Thou art that," "That thou art," or "You are that," is one of the Mahavakyas (Grand Pronouncements) in Vedantic Hinduism. *Chandogya Upanishad 6.8.7,* (circa 500 BCE).	That in whom reside all beings and who resides in all beings, who is the giver of grace to all, the Supreme Soul of the universe, the limitless being -- I am that. Tat Tvam Asi appears in the dialogue between Uddalaka and his son Svetaketu; it appears at the end of a section, and is repeated at the end of the subsequent sections as a refrain.
192	433-2	This Law [of Cause and Effect] Emerson called the "High Chancellor of God."	*No such notion of the law being a "High Chancellor of God" is found in the writings of Emerson.* Perhaps James Porter Mills, MD (1847-??) New York doctor, New Thought author and instructor of meditation.	*Mind's Silent Partner: The High Counselor Within,* 1922. NOTE: This text appeared in the footnotes of the 1926 edition of the Science of Mind.	To summarize, to Mills, "the high counselor within" is the embodiment of the Christ consciousness, not the Law of Cause and Effect.
193	440-2	Emerson tells us to beware of holding too much good in our hands.	Ralph Waldo Emerson (1803-1882) American essayist, philosopher, poet, and leader of the transcendentalist movement in the early 19th century. His teachings directly influenced the growing New Thought movement.	"Compensation" from *Essays: First Series* (1841)	Beware of too much good staying in your hand. It will fast corrupt and worm worms. Pay it away quickly in some sort.

Where'd He Get That? A Biblical Cross-Reference To Ernest Holmes' The Science of Mind

Item Nr.	Page in the SOM Text	Phrase Used	Original Author	Primary Source Document	Quotation and commentary
194	457-5	Virtue does not know that it is virtuous	*Exact source unknown.* Holmes credits Emerson for this quote, but Emerson said quite the opposite: "More striking examples are his moral conclusions. Plato affirms the coincidence of science and virtue; for vice can never know itself and virtue, but virtue knows both itself and vice." from "Plato: New Readings" from *Representative Men (1850).* Perhaps from Taoist texts.	*The Babylonian and Oriental Record: Monthly Magazine of the Antiquities of the East,* Volume Six (July 1892-June 1893).	In the 8th Century AD Taoist text, *Shang-fsing-talng-king (The Book of Constant Purity)* by Si-wang-mu she writes: "True virtue is ignorant of itself: he who possesses Tao does not know it." In the *Tao Te Ching*, Lao Tzu (4th Century AD) writes similarly, " Superior virtue is unvirtue." from the "Canon of Reason and Virtue."
195	464-3	"There are no gods to say us nay, for we are the life we live."	Original poetry by Ernest Holmes	*Immortality* (1927) Epilogue	The life we give is the life we take, And we are the life we give; There are no Gods to say us nay, For we are the life we live.
196	466-3	"Act as though I am and I will be"	*Exact source unknown.* Perhaps Blaise Pascal (1623-1662). French mathematician, physicist, and religious philosopher.	*Thoughts (Pensees)* (1670)	In his book *The Power of Your Subconscious Mind* - chapter 6 (1961) Joseph Murphy credited this exact quote to William James. A search of James's essay *"The Will to Believe"* (1896) stated, "The whole defense of religious faith hinges upon action." To support his claim, James references a quote in French by Blaise Pascal, "cela vous fera croire et vous abetira." Translated to English, this means "That [acting as if] will make you believe and will stupefy your proudly critical intellect."
197		"Act as though I am and I will be"	*Exact source unknown.* Perhaps German philosopher Hans Vaihinger (1852-1933) a contemporary of Holmes, who devoted the last years of his life to developing his as-if philosophy, based upon Kant's notion of 'heuristic fictions'.	*The Philosophy of 'As-If'* (1911)	To summarize, Vaihinger postulated that believing in an idea that was "false" at the moment, has great practical importance, which now made them useful and therefore "true." An example would be a sick person affirming "I am well." as a beneficial hypothesis about life. Hypotheses can be then proven true, therefore transforming the ideation of the individual.

Item Nr.	Page in the SOM Text	Phrase Used	Original Author	Primary Source Document	Quotation and commentary
198	474-2	Emerson tells us that virtue does not know it is virtuous."	*Exact source unknown. Holmes credits Emerson for this quote, but Emerson said quite the opposite: "More striking examples are his moral conclusions. Plato affirms the coincidence of science and virtue; for vice can never know itself and virtue, but virtue knows both itself and vice." from "Plato: New Readings" from Representative Men (1850).* *Perhaps from Taoist texts.*	*The Babylonian and Oriental Record: Monthly Magazine of the Antiquities of the East,* Volume Six (July 1892-June 1893).	In the 8th Century AD Taoist text, *Shang-fsing-talng-king (The Book of Constant Purity)* by Si-wang-mu she writes: "True virtue is ignorant of itself: he who possesses Tao does not know it." In the *Tao Te Ching*, Lao Tzu (4th Century AD) writes similarly, " Superior virtue is unvirtue." from the "Canon of Reason and Virtue."
199	482-2	God goes forth anew into creation whenever anyone discovers a new truth	Ralph Waldo Emerson (1803-1882) American essayist, philosopher, poet, and leader of the transcendentalist movement in the early 19th century. His teachings directly influenced the growing New Thought movement.	"Prospects" Chapter VIII from *Nature*, published as part of *Nature; Addresses and Lectures* (1849).	But when a faithful thinker, resolute to detach every object from personal relations, and see it in the light of thought, shall, at the same time, kindle science with the fire of the holiest affections, then will God go forth anew into the creation.
200	483-1	This teaching incorporates the great law of correspondents.	*Exact source unknown.* Probably Egyptian astrologer and priest Hermes Treismegistus (circa 64–141 CE).	"The Law of Correspondents" is the inscription on the Emerald Tablets, a short cryptic text thought to be authored by Hermes. Later these words were repeated in Aristotle's correspondence to Alexander the Great, with the earliest translations to Latin dating from 650AD. Many manuscripts of this copy of the Emerald Tablet still survive, dating at least as far back as the 15th century.	The inscription reads: "That which is below is as that which is above, and that which is above is as that which is below, to perform the miracles of the one thing." Note: there is no glossary definition for the "Law of Correspondents" in *The Science of Mind,* but Dr. Holmes defines this in his book *The Bible in Light of Religious Science.* He writes, "This teaching incorporates the great law of correspondents. The spiritual world contains an image of the physical; the physical is a counterpart of the spiritual. A true estimate of the outward symbol points to the spiritual reality behind it." (p. 145)

Item Nr.	Page in the SOM Text	Phrase Used	Original Author	Primary Source Document	Quotation and commentary
201	486-1	Emerson tells us that there is no sin but ignorance.	*Exact source unknown. Not found in the writings of Ralph Waldo Emerson.* Perhaps Ralph Waldo Trine (1866-1958), American Philosopher, mystic, teacher and author of many books, and was one of the early mentors of the New Thought Movement.	*In Tune with the Infinite* (1897)	(p. 89) And then when we fully realize the fact that selfishness is at the root of all error, sin, and crime, and that ignorance is the basis of all selfishness, with what charity we come to look upon the acts of all. It is the ignorant man who seeks his own ends at the expense of the greater whole. It is the ignorant man, therefore, who is the selfish man. The truly wise man is never selfish.
202	489-7	Emerson tells us that we are inlets and might become outlets to the Divine Nature.	Ralph Waldo Emerson (1803-1882) American essayist, philosopher, poet, and leader of the transcendentalist movement in the early 19th century. His teachings directly influenced the growing New Thought movement.	*First Essays* (1841): Essay XII "Art"	What is that abridgment and selection we observe in all spiritual activity, but itself the creative impulse? for it is the inlet of that higher illumination which teaches to convey a larger sense by simpler symbols. What is a man but nature's finer success in self-explication? ... Nothing less than the creation of man and nature is its end. A man should find in it an outlet for his whole energy. He may paint and carve only as long as he can do that. Art should exhilarate, and throw down the walls of circumstance on every side, awakening in the beholder the same sense of universal relation and power which the work evinced in the artist, and its highest effect is to make new artists.
203	489-7	A great mystic tells us that the upper part of the soul is merged with God and the lower part with time and condition.	Plotinus, Roman philosopher, founder of neo-Platonic thought (ca. AD 204–270)	*The First Ennead*, First Tractate: "The Animate and the Man"	To summarize, the entire first ennead elucidates this theory of the Upper Soul and Lower Soul and how they interact as a unity in man.

Item Nr.	Page in the SOM Text	Phrase Used	Original Author	Primary Source Document	Quotation and commentary
204	489-7	Plotinus says that when the soul looks to God alone for its inspiration, its work is done better	Plotinus, Roman philosopher, founder of neo-Platonic thought (ca. AD 204–270)	*The Third Ennead*, Second Tractate "On Providence"	As things are, the Divine, of course, exists, but has reached forth to something other- not to reduce that to nothingness but to preside over it; thus in the case of Man, for instance, the Divine presides as the Providence, preserving the character of human nature, that is the character of a being under the providential law, which, again, implies subjection to what that law may enjoin. And that law enjoins that those who have made themselves good shall know the best of life, here and later, the bad the reverse.
205	496-5	Lowell tells us that "Heaven alone is given away"	James Russell Lowell (1819 – 1891) American Romantic poet, critic, editor, and diplomat.	From the Poem "The Vision of Sir Launfal" (1848) Prelude	Tis heaven alone is given away, 'Tis only God may be had for asking, There is no price set on the lavish summer, And June may be had by the poorest comer.
206	497-4	What is true on one plane is true on all.	Thomas Troward (1847-1916) British Divisional Judge of the North Indian Punjab whose metaphysical writings had a profound effect on New Thought, in particular The Science of Mind.	*The Hidden Power* (1921)	(p. 17) "We must never lose sight of the old-world saying that "a truth on one plane is a truth on all." If a principle exists at all it exists universally. NOTE: Troward does not specify the source of this 'old world saying.'

Item Nr.	Page in the SOM Text	Phrase Used	Original Author	Primary Source Document	Quotation and commentary
207	500-3	"There is no sin but a mistake and no punishment but a consequence."	*Exact source unknown. Ernest Holmes attributes this to Emerson, but it is not found in Emerson.* Perhaps *Strong's Exhaustive Concordance of the Bible,* first published in 1890 which contained the etymological meaning of 8674 Hebrew root words used in the Old Testament and 5624 Greek root words used in the New Testament.	*Hebrew word 7686 shagah shaw-gaw':* a primitive root; to stray (causatively, mislead), usually (figuratively) to mistake, especially (morally) to transgress; by extension (through the idea of intoxication) to reel, (figuratively) be enraptured:--(cause to) go astray, deceive, err, be ravished, sin through ignorance, (let, make to) wander. *Greek word 264. hamartano ham-ar-tan'-o:* properly, to miss the mark (and so not share in the prize), i.e. (figuratively) to err;	NOTE: Rocco Ericco, Modern scholar of the Aramaic sources of the Bible writes that the Aramaic word *hataya* used in these contexts, means "to miss" or "to miss the mark," thus a "mistake." See *Setting a Trap for God*, Unity House Publishing (1997) p. 89.
208	500-3	In like manner, Emerson tells us "there is no sin but ignorance"	*Exact source unknown. Not found in the writings of Ralph Waldo Emerson.* Perhaps Ralph Waldo Trine (1866-1958), American Philosopher, mystic, teacher and author of many books, and was one of the early mentors of the New Thought Movement.	*In Tune with the Infinite* (1897)	(p. 89) And then when we fully realize the fact that selfishness is at the root of all error, sin, and crime, and that ignorance is the basis of all selfishness, with what charity we come to look upon the acts of all. It is the ignorant man who seeks his own ends at the expense of the greater whole. It is the ignorant man, therefore, who is the selfish man. The truly wise man is never selfish.

Where'd He Get That? A Biblical Cross-Reference To Ernest Holmes' The Science of Mind

Item Nr.	Page in the SOM Text	Phrase Used	Original Author	Primary Source Document	Quotation and commentary
209	502-1	Sin means making mistakes, and while we continue to make them, we continue to perpetuate their dire results.	Exact source unknown. Ernest Holmes attributes this to Emerson, but it is not found in the writings of Ralph Waldo Emerson. Perhaps *Strong's Exhaustive Concordance of the Bible,* first published in 1890 which contained the etymological meaning of 8674 Hebrew root words used in the Old Testament and 5624 Greek root words used in the New Testament.	Hebrew word 7686 shagah shaw-gaw': a primitive root; to stray (causatively, mislead), usually (figuratively) to mistake, especially (morally) to transgress; by extension (through the idea of intoxication) to reel, (figuratively) be enraptured:--(cause to) go astray, deceive, err, be ravished, sin through ignorance, (let, make to) wander. Greek word 264. hamartano ham-ar-tan'-o: properly, to miss the mark (and so not share in the prize), i.e. (figuratively) to err;	NOTE: Rocco Ericco, Modern scholar of the Aramaic sources of the Bible writes that the Aramaic word *hataya* used in these contexts, means "to miss" or "to miss the mark," thus a "mistake." See *Setting a Trap for God*, Unity House Publishing (1997) p. 89.
210	531-3	I arise and go forth into the Dawn of the New Day	Exact source unknown. Perhaps Shoghi Effendi (1897-1957), Guardian and appointed head of the Bahá'í Faith from 1921 until his death.	*Dawn of a New Day - Handbook of the Bahá'í Faith* (1923) "Guardian's Letter"	"...the dawn of a New Day shall break upon that land and the Rays of this Divine Revelation shall make of India a spiritually-quickened, peaceful and united country."
211	535-2	Behold thou His Face forevermore	Exact source unknown. Perhaps from Rev. Charles H. Spurgeon, famous English clergyman from the late 19th century	"The Beatific Vision", sermon given in 1856, published in *The New Park Street Pulpit*, based around Spurgeon's interpretation of I John 3:1-7.	"We have I believe, all of us who love his name, a most insatiable wish to behold his person. The thing for which I would pray above all others, would be for ever to behold his face, for ever to lay my head upon his breast, for ever to know that I am his, for ever to dwell with him."

Item Nr.	Page in the SOM Text	Phrase Used	Original Author	Primary Source Document	Quotation and commentary
212	561-1	"All in all, we know Thee, God, omnipresent, full and free; on with every pathway trod, our immortal destiny."	*Exact source unknown.* Perhaps inspired by the writings of the potato salesman and self acclaimed British poet laureate, Joseph Gwyer (1835-?) whose earlier poetry collections were considered so bad that people needed to buy it just for the novelty. His 1895 collection was acclaimed by England's royalty and his reputation was exonerated.	*Sketches and Poems by the Penge Poet with Anecdotes of and Personal Interviews with the Late Rev. CH Spurgeon*, 1895 Poem, "Tunbridge Wells and Its Environs" p 216	"In nature's every pathway trod, Her realm shows forth the hand of God ; No single thing His power doth lack, To cheer us on our Heavenward track"
213	566-1	Divine Influx	*Exact source unknown.* Term liberally used by Swedish scientist, philosopher, Christian mystic Emanuel Swedenborg (1688–1772) to signify abilities, words, wisdom that appear at the moment they are needed, which are imparted in man by the Divine Principle.	*Swedenborg's Heaven and its Wonders and Hell* (describes in detail the intricacies of the various degrees of Divine Influx with references to his seminal work *Arcana Celestia*.	(p. 217-218) "The Lord's influx is into good and through good into truth, and not the reverse; thus into the will and through that into the understanding, and not the reverse." "Influx from the Lord is direct from Himself and also mediate through on heaven into another, and in like manner into man's interiors." "Without influx from heaven man cannot even move a step."
214	576	Androgynous: Coleridge conveyed the idea as "The truth is, a great mind must be androgynous."	Samuel Taylor Coleridge (1772 – 1834) English poet, critic and philosopher who was, along with his friend William Wordsworth, one of the founders of the Romantic Movement in England	From *Specimens of the Table Talk of S.T. Coleridge* (1835) by Henry N. Coleridge	"The truth is, a great mind must be androgynous." (1832)
215	576	Attribute (of God): "That which the mind perceives as constituting the essence of substance."	Benedict Spinoza (1632-1677) Dutch Philosopher	*The Ethics Part II*, "Of the Nature and Origin of the Mind: Proposition 7" (1677)	Before going any further, I wish to recall to mind what has been pointed out above-- attribute is that which the intellect perceives as constituting the essence of substance.
216	577	Belief: "Belief admits of all degrees, from the slightest suspicion to the fullest assurance."	Thomas Reid (1710 – 1796), Scottish philosopher, and a contemporary of David Hume, was the founder of the Scottish School of Common Sense.	*Essays on the powers of the human mind* (1827)	Reid's words: "Belief admits of all degrees, from the slightest suspicion to the fullest assurance." is also frequently used to illustrate the word 'belief' in dictionaries.

Where'd He Get That? A Biblical Cross-Reference To Ernest Holmes' The Science of Mind

Item Nr.	Page in the SOM Text	Phrase Used	Original Author	Primary Source Document	Quotation and commentary
217	580	Conscious Mind: "the One Mind common to all individual men."	Ralph Waldo Emerson (1803-1882) American essayist, philosopher, poet, and leader of the transcendentalist movement in the early 19th century. His teachings directly influenced the growing New Thought movement.	"History" from *Essays: First Series* (1841)	"There is one mind common to all individual men. Every man is an inlet to the same and to all of the same."
218	583	Demand: "We do not have to struggle, we do not have to strive. We only have to know."	Fenwicke L. Holmes (1883-1973) Brother to Ernest Holmes and New Thought author and lecturer in his own right.	*Being and Becoming - A Book of Lessons in the Science of Mind Showing How to Find the Personal Spirit* (1920) NOTE: This text appeared in the footnotes of the 1926 edition of the Science of Mind.	(p. 16) We do not have to struggle, we only have to know. The poet truly said [Orison Sweet Marden (1850 - 1924) in *How to Get What You Want* (1917):] "I am not fighting my fight I am singing my song."
219	584	"Desire for anything is the thing itself in incipiency."	Warren Felt Evans (1817-1889) Swedenborgian minister, mental healer, and early New Thought author	*The Primitive Mind-Cure* (1886)	(p. 135) For desire is the incipiency of the thing or state desired, and faith its full fruition.
220	588	Emotion: "Emotion is consciousness attendant upon other forms of consciousness (as perception or ideation) to which it gives their feeling tone."	*Exact source unknown.* Perhaps inspired by the writings of Peter Deminaovich Ouspensky (1878–1947). Russian philosopher who invoked Euclidean and non-Euclidean geometry in his discussions of psychology and higher dimensions of existence. Gained international fame with his book *Tertium Organum.*	*Tertium Organum: The Fourth Dimension as the Esoteric Nature of Reality* (1922)	(p. 345) Cosmic consciousness may develop in purely emotional soil, I.e. in the given case of religious emotion. Cosmic consciousness is also possible of attainment through the emotion attendant upon creation-in painters, musicians, and poets.
221	591	Faculty: "any mode of bodily or mental behavior regarded as implying a natural endowment or acquired power; the faculties of seeing, hearing, feeling, etc."	William Mack, William Benjamin Hale, Donald J. Kiser, Harvard University Law Professors	*Corpus Juris: Being a Complete and Systematic Statement of the Whole Body of the Law as Embodied in and Developed by All Reported Decisions* (1921)	FACULTIES. The term includes any mode of bodily or mental behavior regarded as implying a natural endowment or acquired power.

Item Nr.	Page in the SOM Text	Phrase Used	Original Author	Primary Source Document	Quotation and commentary
222	593	Force: Some of the early philosophers referred to the Soul, or Creative Medium, as "Blind force, not knowing, only doing."	Exact source unknown for notion of "blind force." Idea perhaps borrowed from Arthur Schopenhauer (1788-1860), German pessimistic philosopher who referred to a universal will as am impersonal "blind force".	*The World as Will and Idea / Representation* (1819), Chapter "The Objectification of the Will"	To summarize, Schopenhauer describes a process of the movement of will from the psychological to the cosmological sphere. This movement is guided by an understanding of willing as an "impersonal, primordial blind force, independent of reason and consciousness." The world is an activity of blind force and "my will permeates the world." While there was only one universal will, it flows through the human mind.
223	597	Harmony: "In tune with the Infinite"	Ralph Waldo Trine (1866-1958) American Philosopher, mystic, teacher and author of many books, and was one of the early mentors of the New Thought Movement.	*In Tune with the Infinite* (1897)	Phrase taken from the title of Trine's seminal book on metaphysics which sold over 2 million copies in its day and was praised by Henry Ford and Queen Victoria. The book ends: "As one comes into and lives continually in the full, conscious realization of his oneness with the Infinite Life and Power, then all else follows. This it is that brings the realization of such splendors, and beauties, and joys as a life that is thus related with the Infinite Power alone can know. This it is to come into the realization of heaven's richest treasures while walking the earth. This it is to bring heaven down to earth, or rather to bring earth up to heaven. This it is to exchange weakness and impotence for strength; sorrows and sighing for joy; fears and forebodings for faith; longings for realizations This it is to come into fullness of peace, power, and plenty. This it is to be in tune with the Infinite."
224	598	Humility: Emerson tells us to get our "bloated nothingness out of the way of the Divine Circuits."	Ralph Waldo Emerson (1803-1882) American essayist, philosopher, poet, and leader of the transcendentalist movement in the early 19th century. His teachings directly influenced the growing New Thought movement.	*Essays: First Series* (1841) Essay IV: "Spiritual Laws"	The lesson which these observations convey is, Be, and not seem. Let us acquiesce. Let us take our bloated nothingness out of the path of the divine circuits.

Item Nr.	Page in the SOM Text	Phrase Used	Original Author	Primary Source Document	Quotation and commentary
225	599	Illusion: Plotinus said, "Nature is the great no-thing, yet it is not exactly nothing."	Plotinus, Roman philosopher, founder of neo-Platonic thought (ca. AD 204–270)	*The First Ennead*, Eighth Tractate, "On the Nature and Source of Evil"	By this Non-Being, of course, we are not to understand something that simply does not exist, but only something of an utterly different order from Authentic-Being: there is no question here of movement or position with regard to Being; the Non-Being we are thinking of is, rather, an image of Being or perhaps something still further removed than even an image. Now this [the required faint image of Being] might be the sensible universe with all the impressions it engenders, or it might be something of even later derivation, accidental to the realm of sense, or again, it might be the source of the sense-world or something of the same order entering into it to complete it.
226	599	Imagination and Will: Coue announced a great truth when he said that the imagination is superior to the will; but he did not explain the philosophy behind this truth.	Émile Coué de Châtaigneraie (1857 – 1926) French psychologist and pharmacist who introduced a method of psychotherapy and self-improvement based on optimistic autosuggestion (or self-hypnosis). He is also known for encouraging his patients to say to themselves 20-30 times each night before going to sleep, "Everyday in every way, I am getting better and better".	*Self Mastery Through Conscious Autosuggestion* (1922) Chapter 3: "Will and Imagination"	(p. 9) This will that we claim so proudly, always yields to the imagination. It is an absolute rule that admits of no exception.

Where'd He Get That? A Biblical Cross-Reference To Ernest Holmes' The Science of Mind

Item Nr.	Page in the SOM Text	Phrase Used	Original Author	Primary Source Document	Quotation and commentary
227	608	Logos: "It has been called "the universal source of light and reason."	*Exact source unknown.* Possibly Samuel Taylor Coleridge (1772 – 1834) British poet, critic and philosopher who was, along with his friend William Wordsworth, one of the founders of the Romantic Movement in England.	*The Complete Works of Samuel Taylor Coleridge (1854)* "Essay on Faith"	(p. 565) " Faith subsists in the synthesis of the reason and the individual will. By virtue of the latter therefore it must be an energy, and inasmuch as it relates to the whole moral man, it must be exerted in each and all of his constituents or incidents, faculties and tendencies ;—it must be a total, not a partial; a continuous, not a desultory or occasional energy. And by virtue of the former, that is, reason, faith must be a light, a form of knowing, a beholding of truth. In the incomparable words of the Evangelist, therefore—-faith must be a light originating in the Logos, or the substantial reason, which is co-eternal and one with the Holy Will, and which light is at the same time the life of men.
228	612	Mistakes: "There is no sin, but a mistake, and no punishment but a consequence."	*Exact source unknown. Ernest Holmes attributes this to Emerson, but it is not found in Emerson.* Perhaps *Strong's Exhaustive Concordance of the Bible,* first published in 1890 which contained the etymological meaning of 8674 Hebrew root words used in the Old Testament and 5624 Greek root words used in the New Testament.	*Hebrew word 7686 shagah shaw-gaw':* a primitive root; to stray (causatively, mislead), usually (figuratively) to mistake, especially (morally) to transgress; by extension (through the idea of intoxication) to reel, (figuratively) be enraptured:--(cause to) go astray, deceive, err, be ravished, sin through ignorance, (let, make to) wander. *Greek word 264. hamartano ham-ar-tan'-o:* properly, to miss the mark (and so not share in the prize), i.e. (figuratively) to err;	NOTE: Rocco Ericco, Modern scholar of the Aramaic sources of the Bible writes that the Aramaic word *hataya* used in these contexts, means "to miss" or "to miss the mark," thus a "mistake." See *Setting a Trap for God*, Unity House Publishing (1997) p. 89.
229	616	Opportunity: "Desire for anything is the thing itself in incipiency"	Warren Felt Evans (1817-1889) Swedenborgian minister, mental healer, and early New Thought author	*The Primitive Mind-Cure* (1886)	(p. 135) For desire is the incipiency of the thing or state desired, and faith its full fruition.

Item Nr.	Page in the SOM Text	Phrase Used	Original Author	Primary Source Document	Quotation and commentary
230	617	Passive Activity: Emerson must have meant this when he said: "I see action to be good, when the need is, and sitting still to be also good."	Ralph Waldo Emerson (1803-1882) American essayist, philosopher, poet, and leader of the transcendentalist movement in the early 19th century. His teachings directly influenced the growing New Thought movement.	"Spiritual Laws" from *Essays: First Series* (1841)	I see action to be good, when the need is, and sitting still to be also good.
231	621	Problem: "the problem of evil" will be a problem as long as we believe in it.	*Exact source unknown.* It is unclear if Dr. Holmes is referring to "the problem of evil" in philosophy and theology, which is a classic argument for God's nonexistence and is expressed in the following syllogism: If God existed, there would be no unnecessary suffering in the world. There is unnecessary suffering in the world. Therefore, God does not exist.	*The Stanford Encyclopedia of Philosophy (2002)*	Epicurus, Greek philosopher (circa 341 BCE– 270 BCE, is generally credited with first expounding the problem of evil, and it is sometimes called "the Epicurean paradox" or "the riddle of Epicurus." In the philosophy of religion and theology, the problem of evil is the problem of reconciling the existence of evil or suffering in the world with the existence of God. The problem follows with the belief that God is omnipotent, omniscient and omnibenevolent whilst at the same time evil exists. God either cannot stop evil or he will not. If he cannot then he is argued to not be omnipotent. If he will not then he is argued to not be omnibenevolent.

Item Nr.	Page in the SOM Text	Phrase Used	Original Author	Primary Source Document	Quotation and commentary
232	632	"Servant of the Spirit Throughout the Ages"	Exact source unknown. Possibly Josephine A. Jackson and Helen M. Salisbury, where the subconscious is first defined as a "servant." Jackson and Salisbury were two women Freudian psychoanalysts working in southern California. Their book was a best seller as it explained psychoanalysis in lay terms.	*Outwitting Our Nerves: A Primer of Psychotherapy* (1921) NOTE: This text appeared in the footnotes of the 1926 edition of the *Science of Mind*.	(p. 31) The subconscious mind which is not affected by ether, has been exhausting itself in a vain attempt to get the body away from harm. A Tireless Servant. When the conscious mind undertakes a job, it is always more or less subject to fatigue. But the subconscious after its long practice seems never to tire. We say that its activities have become automatic. With all its inherited skill, the subconscious, if left to itself, can be depended upon to run the bodily machinery without effort and without hitch. The only things that can interfere with its work are the wrong kind of emotions and the wrong kind of suggestions from the conscious mind. Barring these, it goes its way like a trusty servant, looking after details and leaving its master's mind free for other things.
233	636	Thanksgiving: It has been said that "the prayer of thanksgiving is the prayer of appropriation."	*Exact source unknown.* Perhaps Rav (Rabbi) Se'adyah Gaon (882-942 AD) Written from oral Hebrew tradition, the Prayer of Appropriation was included in the 10th century manuscript *Siddur* (Daily Prayers) This prayer is called the *birkat ha-mazon* and is thought to be closest to the one Jesus actually spoke at the Last Supper.	*Siddur,* Rav Se'adyah Gaon - in English (1941)	The Birkat Ha-Mazon is now spoken after meals: *Blessing of Him who nourishes* Blessed are you, Lord our God, King of the universe, for you nourish us and the whole world with goodness, grace, kindness and mercy. Blessed are you Lord, for you nourish the universe. *Blessing for the land* We will give thanks to you Lord our God, because you have given us for our inheritance a desirable land, good and wide, the covennatn and the law, life and food... ...And for all these things we give you thanks and bless your name forever and beyond. Blessed are you, Lord, for the land and for food....

Item Nr.	Page in the SOM Text	Phrase Used	Original Author	Primary Source Document	Quotation and commentary
234	636	Thanksgiving: It has been said that "the prayer of thanksgiving is the prayer of appropriation."	*Exact source unknown.* Conventionally, "the prayer of appropriation" is the table prayer Jesus spoke at the last supper. Quite possibly Dr. Holmes could have retrieved this from any church hymnal of his day.	Geoffry Wainwright and Karn Beth Westerfield-Tucker, The Oxford History of Christian Worship, (2006) "The Apostolic Tradition"	"The prayer of appropriation" is referenced in the Gospels, but not offered in its entirety. The orthodox Christians call this prayer the Eucharista or The Anaphora which is recited over holy communion. The Anaphora of Hippolytus is arguably the oldest known complete anaphora or communion liturgy, having been written in the early to mid 3rd century by Hippolytus of Rome and is still used by among others, the United Methodists.
235	638	Time: "Sequence of events in a Unitary Whole"	Ernest Holmes attributes this quote to Dean Inge, William Ralph Inge (1860 – 1954) English author, Anglican priest, and Dean and Professor of Divinity at Cambridge.	*The Philosophy of Plotinus Volume I* (1918) NOTE: This text appeared in the footnotes of the 1926 edition of the Science of Mind.	(p. xiii) "Time is the moving image of eternity.
236	645	since we know that desire is the thing itself in incipiency	Warren Felt Evans (1817-1889) Swedenborgian minister, mental healer, and early New Thought author	*The Primitive Mind-Cure* (1886)	(p. 135) For desire is the incipiency of the thing or state desired, and faith its full fruition.
237	646	Word: The Word of God means the Self-Contemplation of Spirit	Thomas Troward (1847-1916) British Divisional Judge of the North Indian Punjab whose metaphysical writings had a profound effect on New Thought, in particular The Science of Mind.	*The Creative Process and the Individual* (1915) - Chapter 2 "The Self-Contemplation of Spirit" NOTE: This text appeared in the footnotes of the 1926 edition of the Science of Mind.	If we ask how the cosmos came into existence we shall find that ultimately we can only attribute it to the Self-Contemplation of Spirit.

APPENDIX A: NEW THOUGHT FAMILY TREE
(USED WITH PERMISSION)

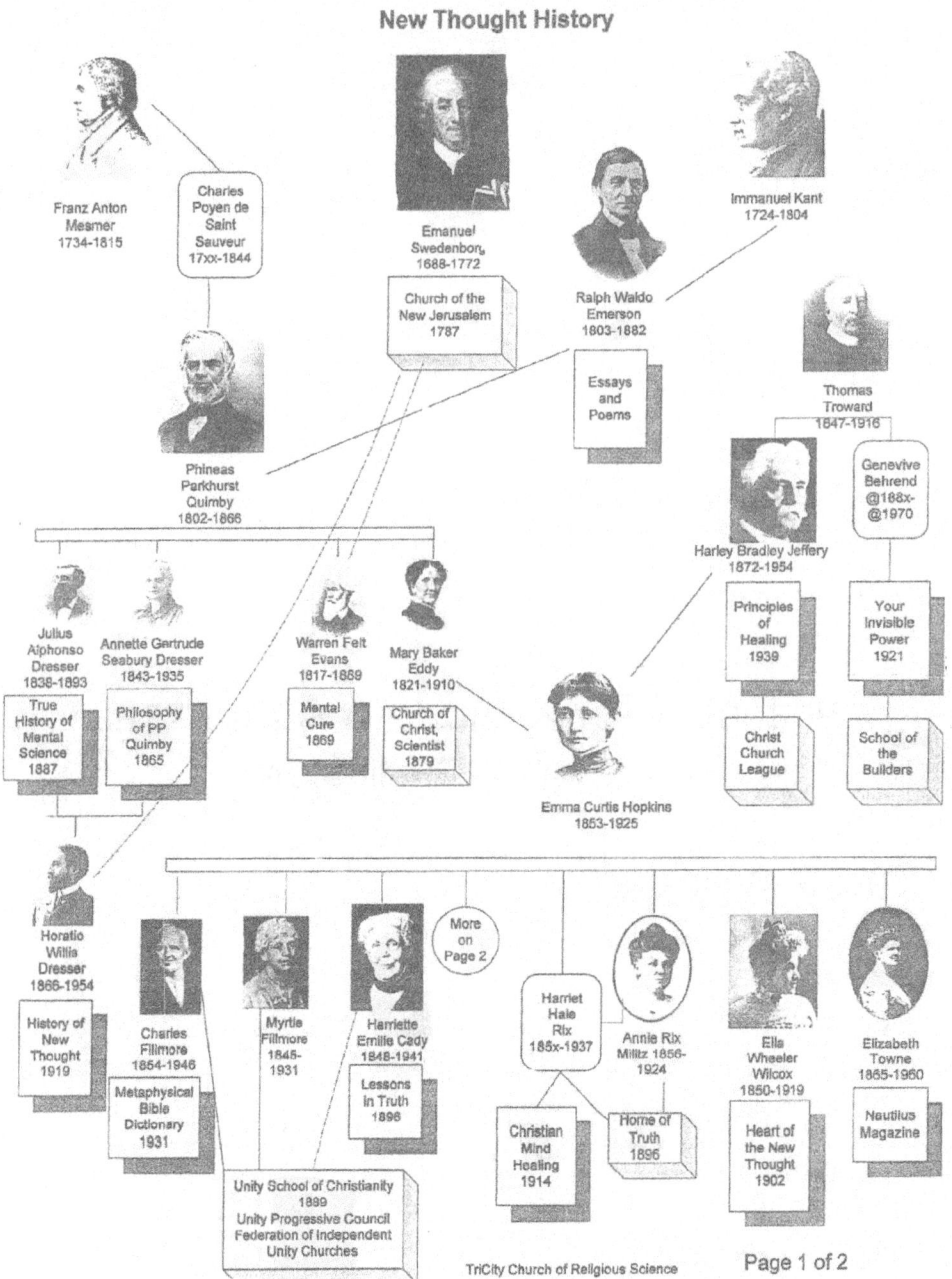

Where'd He Get That? A Biblical Cross-Reference To Ernest Holmes' The Science of Mind

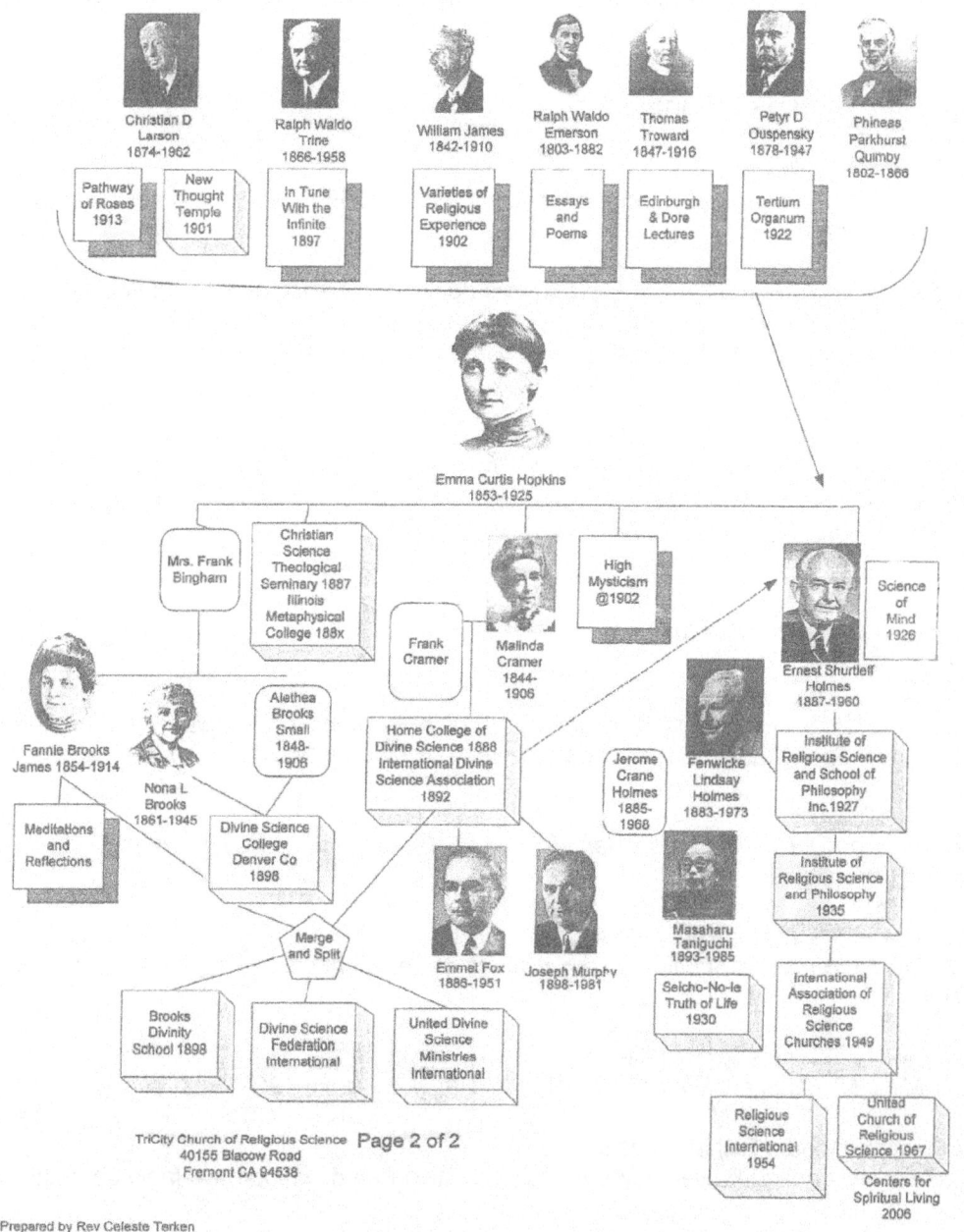

APPENDIX B: FULL BIBLIOGRAPHY FROM THE 1926 EDITION OF *THE SCIENCE OF MIND*

As cited in Part II: The Lessons as endnotes (Corrected citations in italics)

Lesson One: The Nature of Being

Edinburgh Lectures – T. Troward
Thomas Troward, The Edinburgh Lectures on Mental Science, 1909. Full text free download at www.newthoughtlibrary.com

Creative Mind – Ernest S. Holmes 1917. *Full text free download at www.newthoughtlibrary.com*

The Axioms of Truth – Burnell *George Edwin Burnell, Axioms: The Book of Health and Science of Truth, 1902.*

Philosophy of Plotinus – Dean Inge
William Ralph Inge (he was an academic dean) The Philosophy of Plotinus was published in two volumes 1917 and 1918.
Full text free download of both volumes on Google Books

Lesson Two: The Nature of Man

Being and Becoming – F.L. Holmes
Fenwicke Lindsay Holmes, Being and Becoming - A Book of Lessons in the Science of Mind Showing How to Find the Personal Spirit 1920. Full text free download on Google Books

Doré Lectures- T. Troward
Thomas Troward, The Doré Lectures on Mental Science, 1909. Full text free download at www.newthoughtlibrary.com

From Existence to Life – James Porter Mills
James Porter Mills, From Existence to Life: the Science of Self-Consciousness, 1916. Free download on Google Books

Mind's Silent Partner – James Porter Mills
James Porter Mills, Mind's Silent Partner: The High Counselor Within, 1922.

History and Power of Mind – Richard Ingalese
Richard Ingalese, History and Power of Mind, 1902. Full text free download available on archive.org

Lesson Three: Mental Healing

Teachings and Addresses – Edward S. Kimball
Edward A. Kimball, Lectures and Articles on Christian Science, Privately printed, 1921.

The Law of Mind in Action – F.L. Holmes
Fenwicke Lindsay Holmes, The Law of Mind in Action - Daily Lessons and Treatments in Mental and Spiritual Science 1919.
Full text free download on Google Books

The Faith That Heals – F.L. Holmes
Fenwicke Lindsay Holmes, How to Develop the Faith That Heals, 1921. Full text free download on Google Books

Christian Healing – Fillmore
Charles Fillmore, Christian Healing: the science of being, 1917. Full text free download at www.newthoughtlibrary.com

Lessons in Truth – Cady
H. Emilie Cady, *Lessons In Truth, 1896.* Full text free download at www.newthoughtlibrary.com

Primary Lessons – Militz
Annie Rix Militz, Primary Lessons in Christian Living and Healing, 1914. Full text download at www.newthoughtlibrary.com

Outwitting our Nerves – Jackson
Josephine A. Jackson, M.D. and Helen M. Salisbury, Outwitting our Nerves – A Primer of Psychotherapy, 1921
Full text free download at www.gutenberg.org

Lesson Four: Control of Conditions

That Something, The Edinburgh Lectures – T. Troward
Thomas Troward, *The Edinburgh Lectures on Mental Science, 1909*
Full text free download at www.newthoughtlibrary.com

NOTE: Thomas Troward did not write That Something as it is inferred in the text. Rather, it was penned by William W. Woodbridge in 1914, a popular book on success, read and commended by Thomas Edison among others.

The Law and The Word – T. Troward
Thomas Troward, *The Law and The Word, 1917.*
Full text free download at www.newthoughtlibrary.com

Creative Mind and Success – E.S. Holmes 1919.
Full text free download at www.newthoughtlibrary.com

How to Visualize – Behrend
NOTE: No such writing by Behrend.
Genevieve Behrend, Attaining Your Desires by Letting Your Subconscious Mind Work for You, "Lesson V: Making Your Subjective Mind Work for You", section "How to Visualize and Objectify the Mental Image" 1929.
Free full text download of Attaining Your Desires at http://www.mrfire.com/desiresbonus/bonus.pdf

Financial Success Through Creative Thought – Wattles
Financial Success Through Creative Thought or The Science of Getting Rich 1915
NOTE: Financial Success Through Creative Thought was a posthumously published update to Wattles' original classic text, The Science of Getting Rich, 1910. Full text free download of 1910 version at www.newthoughtlibrary.com

Lesson Five: The Perfect Whole

Cosmic Consciousness – Bucke
Richard Maurice Bucke (1837-1902), ed.: Cosmic Consciousness: A Study in the Evolution of the Human Mind, 1901.
Free full text download at http://onlinebooks.library.upenn.edu

Twelve Lessons in Mysticism – Hopkins
NOTE: No book by Hopkins with that title.
Emma Curtis Hopkins, Resume: Practice Book for The Twelve Lessons in High Mysticism 1892.
Emma Curtis Hopkins, High Mysticism: A Series of Twelve Studies in the Wisdom of the Sages of the Ages (12-book set) 1888.

The Impersonal Life and Creative Process in the Individual – T. Troward
Thomas Troward, The Creative Process in the Individual, 1915
Full text free download at www.newthoughtlibrary.com

NOTE: *The Impersonal Life* was not written by Troward as inferred in the text, but was written by Joseph Benner around 1916 under his pen name Anonymous.
Free full text version downloadable from http://pure-research.net/healing/bestill/

Bible Mystery and Meaning – T. Troward
Thomas Troward, *Bible Mystery and Meaning*, 1922
Full text free download at www.newthoughtlibrary.com

Sayings of Jesus – Red Letter Testament
It became popular around the turn of the 20th century for Bible publishers to highlight the words of Jesus in red in The New Testament. Ernest Holmes used the Scofield Reference Edition of the King James Bible.

Lesson Six: Psychic Phenomenon and Immortality

The Law of Psychic Phenomena – Hudson
Thomson Jay Hudson, *The Law of Psychic Phenomena: A Working Hypothesis for the Systematic Study of Hypnotism, Spiritism, Mental Therapeutics, Etc. 1916.* Full text free download on Google Books

Life After Death – Hyslop
James Hervey Hyslop, Life After Death: Problems of the Future Life and Its Nature, 1918
Full text free download on Google Books

The Unknown Guest – Maeterlinck
Maurice Maeterlinck, The Unknown Guest, 1914. Free full text download at www.gutenberg.org

Science and Immortality – Lodge
Sir Oliver Lodge, *Science and Immortality, 1908.* Full text free download on Google Books

The Hidden Power – Troward
Thomas Troward, The Hidden Power, 1921. Full text free download at www.newthoughtlibrary.com

From the Unconscious to the Conscious – Geley
Geley, Gustave. *From the Unconscious to the Conscious***,** 1920. Full text free download on Google Books

APPENDIX C: CHRONOLOGICAL HISTORY OF REFERENCES TO "THE LAW OF ATTRACTION" IN RELIGIOUS AND METAPHYSICAL LITERATURE

4000 BCE	The first mention of the Law of Attraction originated in early 4000 BC by Hindu practitioners in their use of the word Karma. Some people think that the Law of Attraction's roots go all the way back to the Hindu concept of karma and dharma described in the Vedas, the Sanskrit scriptures of the Vedic cultures. Karma understood as that which causes the entire cycle of cause and effect originating in ancient India and treated in Hindu, Jain, Sikh and Buddhist philosophies. Sanskrit word "karma" literally means "action, activity, work", and because other languages again lack any synonym exactly explaining its meaning, it is not recommended to translate it.
900 BCE – 180 AD	In Judeo-Christian tradition it has an analogy in God's judgment (Greek *krima* 'krima' in New Testament 'krino' in New Testament). The idea of 'as you sow, you shall reap' (Job 4:8, Galatians 6:7) is a common sense. Jesus was referring to the law of attraction when he said, "It is done unto you as you believe."
563-483 BCE	Gautama Buddha, said, "What you have become is the result of what you have thought". (not found in search of the Buddhist Scriptures; but there are many references to Buddha having said this in the popular literature)
500 BCE	In the *Bhagavad Gita*, Krishna says to Arjuna: BG 6.5: One must deliver himself with the help of his mind, and not degrade himself. The mind is the friend of the conditioned soul, and his enemy as well. BG 6.6: For him who has conquered the mind, the mind is the best of friends; but for one who has failed to do so, his mind will remain the greatest enemy.
384–322 BCE	Aristotle writes in *Metaphysics* of the attraction, sometimes of an impulsion exercised by the Prime Mover (God) on the whole of the world. The movement of the universe is an aspiration of things toward the divine perfection, and consequently an ascent toward God. Attraction of the Prime Mover is also the effect of God descending into creation.
Hermes Treismegistus (circa 64–141 AD)	The Law of Attraction Is the fourth of Seven Ancient Hermetic Laws which were passed down orally for centuries by secret sects and made public in America in a writing called *The Kybalion*, written by an anonymous "Three Initiates" in 1909. The Three Initiates dedicated *The Kybalion* to Hermes Trismegistus whom they credit for this information. The book purports to be based upon ancient Hermeticism, though many of its ideas are relatively modern concepts arising from the New Thought movement. The most common proposal is that *The Kybalion* was authored by William Walker Atkinson, either alone or with others. Atkinson was known to use many pseudonyms, and to self-publish his works. He was also the owner of the "Yogi Publication Society of Chicago", the publisher of *The Kybalion.*
1855	Victorian biologist and early social philosopher Herbert Spencer wrote a book, *The Principles of Psychology* in which he dedicates an entire chapter to "The Law of Intelligence" where the reference to a Law of Attraction and how it applies to consciousness is explained.
1877	In West this term was also used by Russian theosophist Helena P. Blavatsky (1831-1891) in her book on esoteric mysteries. The phrase "Law of Attraction" also appeared in the writings of other Theosophical writers William Quan Judge in 1915, and Annie Besant in 1919.
1902	One of the most important early books on this subject in the English language is *As a Man Thinketh* by James Allen (1864 – 1912).. Allen took this ambiguous idea of a correspondence between "a man's heart" and his existence to a logical extreme, stating that, *"The soul attracts that which is secretly harbors, that which it loves, and also that which it fears. It reaches the height of its cherished aspirations. It falls to the level of its unchastened desires -- and circumstances are the means by which the soul receives its own."* The title derives from the ancient Book of Proverbs, chapter 23, verse 7: "As a man thinketh in his heart, so he is."
1902	Richard Ingalese writes in *History and Power of Mind* about a Law of Vibration in the universe and that the source of man's vibration is his thought. This writer is referenced in Ernest Holmes 1926 edition of the Science of Mind pertaining to his discussion of the Law of Attraction.
1902	Physicists discover an "energy of attraction." John Ambrose Fleming an electrical engineer and turn of the century physicist described "every completed manifestation, of whatever kind and on whatever scale," as "an unquenchable energy of attraction" that causes objects to "steadily increase in power and definiteness of purpose, until the process of growth is completed and the matured form stands out as an accomplished fact."

Where'd He Get That? A Biblical Cross-Reference To Ernest Holmes' The Science of Mind

1906	The law of attraction began to gain popularity in the western hemisphere in the 19th century, as people began to appreciate the power of positive thinking and apply it to their life. This new concept was first introduced to the general public by William Walker Atkinson, the editor of New Thought magazine, who published a book called Thought Vibration or the Law of Attraction in the Thought World in 1906. The principle that he talked about was summarized as "You are what you think, not what you think you are".
1909	Judge Thomas Troward published his *Edinburgh and Dore Lectures* where he included the first mentions of "The Law of Attraction" in his treatise on mental science.
1913	The first mention of the phrase "Law of Attraction" not merely the concept, which is probably known for millennia, I found in Charles F. Haanel's (1866-1949) book *The Master Key System*. He wrote, "Abundance, therefore, depends upon recognition of the laws of Abundance, and the fact that Mind is not only the creator, but the only creator of all there is." Haanel was a noted American author and businessman, often noted as the "godfather" of personal development.
1914	James Porter Mills publishes *From Existence to Life* and describes the power to attract positive conditions into our lives is a sign of our Divine nature.
1920	Fenwicke Holmes describes the Law of Attraction in his book *Being and Becoming – A Book of Lessons in the Science of Mind Showing How to Find the Personal Spirit*. He speaks of vibration of thought as its mechanism and cites Troward.
1922	James Porter Mills publishes *Mind's Silent Partner: the High Counselor Within* which the law of attraction was called "the law of incarnation" and was contingent upon the cultivation of "Divine Expectancy" in the individual to transform the individual life.
1926	Ernest Holmes first writes about the Law of Attraction in *The Science of Mind* Part II: Lesson II. His references include: Note: Read carefully "Being and Becoming," F.L. Holmes; "Doré Lectures," T. Troward; "From Existence to Life," James Porter Mills; "Mind's Silent Partner," James Porter Mills; "History and Power of Mind," Richard Ingalese.
1936	*Prosperity*, Charles Fillmore 1854- 1948. Refers to it as the law of manifestation, the law of increase, the law of supply.